A MEMOIR ABOUT RAPTUROUS LOVE, LOSING LOVE, FINDING SELF AND DISCOVERING MAGIC

FLYING
where
ICARUS FELL

CYNTHIA LEIER

Flying Where Icarus Fell

Copyright © 2024 by Cynthia Leier

All rights reserved.

Published by Red Penguin Books

Bellerose Village, New York

Library of Congress Control Number: 2024905003

ISBN:

Print 978-1-63777-568-4

Digital 978-1-63777-567-7

No part of this book may be reproduced in any form or by any electronic or mechanical means, including information storage and retrieval systems, without written permission from the author, except for the use of brief quotations in a book review.

Contents

The Myth of Icarus — vii

Part I: Flight Into Love — ix

1. Venice: An Ordinary Señora Alone — 1
2. Italy: Potential for Love — 7
3. Calgary: Falling Apart — 17
4. Italy: Falling Under a Spell — 25
5. Il Lago: Breathed You In — 35
6. Il Lago: Falling Star — 43
7. Florence: Not a Lily at All — 51
8. Il Lago: Falling from Heaven — 59

Part II: A Hard Landing — 65

9. Calgary: Clipped Wings — 67
10. Ravenna: Putting Pieces Together — 75
11. Calgary: This is Not-Love — 87
12. Calgary: This is Love — 93
13. Calgary: Fall From Grace — 103
14. Calgary: Fallen Angel — 109
15. Waskesiu: La Vie en Rose — 115
16. Calgary: Falling Ill — 121
17. Calgary: After the Storm — 129
18. California: An Uncommon Retreat — 135
19. Springbank: A Healing Refuge — 141
20. Springbank: An Extraordinary Encounter — 147

Part III Updraft — 155

21. Discovery: Frankincense & Roses — 157
22. Kosovo: Small Miracles — 165
23. Calgary: A Little Bit of Magic — 177
24. Saskatoon: The Family Fishbowl — 185
25. Calgary: Choices — 195
26. Calgary: A Perfect Storm — 205
27. Saskatoon: A Game of Chess — 209
28. Saskatoon: Nice Day for a Drive — 213
29. Rome: Committing — 225
30. Croatia: Traveling Writer — 233
31. Calgary: Isabella Rossellini — 237
32. Greece: Where Icarus Fell — 241

Acknowledgments — 247
About the Author — 249

The Myth of Icarus

Laughing with excitement, Icarus ran barefoot, ahead of his father, Dedalus, up the cliff on the stony path lined by fragrant rosemary and wild Greek greens growing in the dry, powdery soil. Following his young son, Dedalus came at a slower pace as he carried the two sets of enormous wings that he and his son had fashioned from bird feathers and wax. As Dedalus arrived breathless at the top, he went to stand beside Icarus, where together they viewed the expanse of the blue Aegean sea shimmering below them from the dizzying height of the cliff.

Icarus quivered with anticipation as Dedalus strapped one pair of wings on the back of his son, then the other on himself. They stood together, smiled widely at each other, and extended their wing-encased arms to catch the summer breeze rising over the sea. On an intake of breath, they leaped.

A playful current of air caught their wings before they could fall. It carried them upward and outward to soar over the sea sparkling below. Father and son swooped and soared together with the feathers on their wings fluttering and buffeted by the current that carried them. Dedalus smiled as he caught sight of the joy-filled face of his beloved son caught in the rapture of flying until Dedalus noticed Icarus soaring higher and higher, farther and farther away and beyond his reach. With the tempered wisdom of age, Dedalus sensed some folly within his son's naïve joy. He called out to him, but Icarus was too far away now, heedless of his father's desperate calls and oblivious to any dangers as he flew closer and closer to the blazing summer sun. He was heedless and oblivious until he noticed the liquid warmth of melting wax wetting his shoulders and trickling down his back. Suddenly, he realized his mistake. Too late.

One by one, the feathers of Icarus' wings began to fall free of the wax that held them. One by one, they twirled and floated down toward the sea below. Crying in alarm, Icarus flailed and grasped for the feathers, only to grasp the air that passed through his fingers like an illusion. He began to tumble downward, passing the feathers loosened from his wings, faster and faster as he fell from the sky until, with barely a sound or a splash, Icarus hit the salty sea, and the Aegean swallowed him, broken wings and all.

Forevermore, the story of Icarus is found in Greek myth, a tale and a warning. It's an old teaching fable of a boy who, in his naive enthusiasm and lust to fly to the greatest of heights, died by flying too close to the sun.

PART I

Flight into Love

Chapter 1

Venice: An Ordinary Señora Alone

I was standing on a wooden dock outside Venice's Marco Polo airport after having thumped and scraped my suitcase down the dusty earthen path that meandered from the terminal to a pier on the lagoon where I was to catch a water taxi into the city. The dock was a small wooden structure of four beams and a simple roof. It seemed to float on the lagoon, which filled the air with the smell of salty sea, a sea that swelled and lapped soft kisses at the legs of the dock in the brisk air. From the pier and over a shimmering watery expanse that stretched out in sun-tipped waves before me, I had an indistinct view of Venice, which formed a horizontal line pressed between the vast sea and towering sky in the distance.

I had stepped inside the little dock, breathed in the revitalizing salt sea scent, and drawn the melting warmth of the sun into my body. The sparkling lagoon seemed to respond to my pleasure by setting prism rays of light and color dancing around me. It was a delicious sensation of standing in a crystal glinting in the sun. Lightness of spirit filled me. Laughter bubbled up. I was on the doorstep of Venice. Beautiful, magical Venice.

In the excitement of the moment, I made a phone call to my 20-year-old daughter at home in Canada.

"Well, I'm here! I can hardly believe it. Right now, I'm standing on a dock filled with sunshine reflecting off the sea. It's beautiful! My plane arrived at the airport after popping through towering white cumulus clouds, one after another, from massive clouds to golden sunshine, again and again as the plane dropped down toward the ground. It was incredible. Every now and then, the view to the land below would clear, and I could see the red roofs of Venice. I could see the curving contour of the island. It's a city floating on a blue sea. I felt like I was waking up to find that I was in a dream."

My daughter said, "I can see exactly what it's like."

"The trip from home was alright, except for being frisked going through Frankfurt airport security." I grinned. "A big frau in a white uniform took me behind a curtained partition and actually groped my breasts to make sure I wasn't hiding something."

She laughed. "That's why I like having little boobs. No need for them to be frisked."

We both laughed, me more exuberantly than she. There was an older couple standing in the dock near me. They turned when I laughed and gave me a disapproving glance. Too loud. Too happy. It only made me laugh more.

My daughter and I ended our call. It was wonderful to hear her voice and share my excitement. Her enthusiasm for my adventure warmed me. I had been planning this painting trip to Italy for months. The trip was a departure from anything I had ever done before. It was a trip to a foreign country alone.

I sensed I had my daughter's unspoken support from the beginning of my planning. It was unspoken until two weeks prior to my departure when I suddenly got cold feet.

"I can't go on this trip!" I shouted. "I can't go off alone to someplace in the world I've never been. Alone? What was I thinking?"

"Of course, you can go. You're going!" she asserted. Her young woman's self-assurance bolstered me.

* * *

My September trip to paint in Italy was the beginning of a life change. It was a transition from being a reader and a dreamer of foreign lands and adventures that I only lived through books to a woman who ventured out on her own. I went from being a teacher and lover of music that swept me away to other places and times to a woman romancing herself by being in the world. I was 49 years old. I had been a good mother and wife who worked at home and took pleasure in making that home beautiful for my family. This coming change was the start of becoming uniquely and completely me.

I made the choice to take this trip, and the choice created a whole new trajectory in my life. The change happened as fast as the snap of my fingers. It was a shock. It was as if I had been traveling on a pokey train for 25 years and suddenly found myself on an express train on a completely different track going somewhere of which I had no clue. An unknown destination seemed to stretch far, far into the distance, into my future, carrying me inexorably, mysteriously, as if there was some Future Me beckoning and waiting for me.

I could never have foreseen the change I got. It was completely unexpected. In some ways, my life became greater and more exhilarating, like I was learning to fly. In other ways, the change brought about events and circumstances that were staggering and broke me wide open.

It began with just one choice to go.

* * *

The water taxi arrived, and I got in. The craft rose and fell as it bumped over the waves created by oncoming passing boats as my driver steered the taxi in the water lane toward the city. Wooden pilings marked the route and offered respite to calling seabirds who perched on them. The air was fresh with the spray of sea mist. A breeze ruffled my blonde bobbed hair, hair which I had always taken great care to style to perfection. Did I care? Resoundingly, No! I let the moist breeze stroke my eager, uplifted face. I breathed in the sense of adventure. Was there anywhere to be that was more blissful than where I was at that moment? I relaxed back in my seat and let myself be carried away.

As we entered the city, the driver pointed the prow of the boat through the watery thoroughfare of the Grand Canal. A streaming flow of water vessels filled the route. There were barges unloading their catch at the famous Rialto fish market, and gondoliers perched precariously but confidently as they rowed their boats through the teeming canal. Large *Alilaguna* buses churned the water as they sped past with tourist faces framed in the windows. All along the course of the waterway, people were embarking or disembarking from docks, some marked with red and white barbershop poles that jutted festively up from the water. With a taxi to myself, I had a luxurious, wide-open view to take in the white-trimmed, pastel-colored buildings gliding by me, still standing above the sea since the days Venice had been at the height of its wealth, power, and romance. Venice. *La Serenissima*.

We landed at the dock at Piazza San Marco, with its rows of gondolas waiting for passengers. I stepped out onto the platform and turned to view the expanse of the lagoon. I gazed out to where the endless blue sea met the limitless blue sky, broken by islands of floating city and magnificent cathedrals. My heart flew open.

Once again dragging my suitcase behind me, I made my way past the Byzantine Basilica of San Marco, through its famous square surrounded by arched walkways and buildings. I wound through the maze of narrow streets called *"calle"* and yanked my bag up stone bridges over canals. With only a tourist map and my inner compass as my guides, I somehow found the hotel I had booked. Hotel La Fenice et Des Artistes. It was across from the Teatro La Fenice, Venice's grand opera house. I could imagine the glorious music that had been performed there. I had been a musician much of my life, sitting at my piano in my house. Now, here I was, bringing music to life.

I only had two days in Venice before I was scheduled to meet the group of painters I would be joining in Tuscany for a week-long painting course. Two days and three nights to explore and savor Venice. I dropped my bag in my room, made a quick change of clothes, and hurried out. My itinerary for the next two days was chockful and very carefully planned. There were churches and museums to see. There was shopping to do. Historic quarters to explore. From the moment I arrived, I went non-stop.

On my first night in Venice, I dined at a small restaurant with an outdoor patio near my hotel. After my evening meal that first night, the tuxedoed waiters, standing daily four in a row outside the café, recognized me and greeted me with a slow, courteous nodding bow and a

"*Buona sera, signora*" every time I passed. I felt like a celebrity. I was a blue-eyed blonde with a roundish face and sensuous lips, 5 foot 4, and slightly overweight. I was nothing out of the ordinary, but in that moment, I felt like a star.

The following day, I strolled under the porticos that lined San Marco Square to take in the ambiance of the famous piazza and browsed through tiny shops. I wandered along the narrow *calli* and found myself sitting in a tiny shop barely bigger than a closet, sipping fiery grappa with an old taciturn vendor who was helping me select a bottle to buy to take home. I awkwardly tried out my Italian, which I had begun to learn in anticipation of this trip, but language was not required. It was a sweet, shared moment between the elderly man and me, a moment to silently sip and experience. A bottle of grappa went into my suitcase.

Another day, I went in search of the small Chiesa San Raphael that had been the subject of a novel I loved called *Miss Garnet's Angel.* But after a lunch with too much wine served by a pushy, grumpy waiter who insisted that a half bottle of wine was not too much at lunch and to whom I couldn't say no, I got lost looking for the church. I wandered, a little freaked out, over countless bridges, along calm boat-lined canals, and through sun-baked streets that were deserted of people in the glaring midday sun. I eventually found the simple, square white church of San Raphael with its modest bell tower standing in a silent square. The church is known for its painted doors depicting the biblical story of Tobias, who went on a quest with a dog and Angel Raphael as companions to find the woman he loved.

What did I love? What was I searching for?

The next day, I noticed I had bedbug bites from the bed in my hotel room. My hotel was a bit tattered with age but quaint and proud of its connection with the opera house across the way. A portrait of Pavarotti, who had recently died, was displayed in a place of honor in the lobby. *Never mind the bites,* I thought. I didn't want to break the spell of Venice by being a rude tourist complaining in my hotel.

I headed out for a second day and walked the entirety of it. I toured ancient churches that smelled of dank stone and housed famous sculptures and paintings. I meandered through museums filled with beautiful but gloomy art that I had only seen before in books. Names of cathedrals, artists, and art blurred. All day, I was just another body in the throngs of tourists flowing through endless confusing streets that wound around jagged turns and bordered endless canals. I loved it all. The dank. The dark. The light. The beautiful. I was an utter romantic, and Venice crept into me like a lover in the night.

After two days of racing around a touristy foreign city without the comfort of being with anyone I cared about, I had had enough time alone. Being alone meant there had been no one to talk with or distract me from being permeated by Venice. It was as if I were naked and open as a newborn. Now, I was feeling restless and ready to leave. The following day, I would be taking the train from the city to the mainland and then on to Tuscany. Tonight, I would treat myself to a lovely dinner out.

I put on my nicest dress for my Farewell to Venice dinner and found an elegant outdoor restaurant overlooking the lagoon near Piazza San Marco. I have no problem eating alone in a restaurant, but as I was something as unimpressive as a mature woman dining alone in Italy, the maître d' instantly assessed me when I showed up at the entrance and, snapping his fingers in the air above his head as an order to the waiters, called out, *"La señora, la señora."* The waiters jumped. I was seated at a table in the section of their least senior waiter.

A tuxedoed young man served me an exquisite meal with a composed, almost disdainful professionalism as I stared over my plate into the undulating ripples of the lagoon. He was handsome. His looks reminded me of my daughter's boyfriend at home. Tears welled up in my eyes.

When I saw my waiter notice my tears, I simply explained, "I miss my family."

He was gentle and solicitous after that, though no word was spoken between us. I smiled to myself as I left him a 40 percent tip on the bill for his kindness. A tip not to be expected from an ordinary señora dining alone.

Chapter 2

Italy: Potential for Love

I loved to paint and draw as a child but gave it up to pursue my interest in music. After years of giving private music lessons, I had recently taken up painting again on a whim. I took classes in basic drawing techniques and acrylics. My love of creating art became a new passion. Now, here I was in Italy to take a painting course for fun with two professional American painters as my instructors.

As a painter, I was an amateur. The word amateur is related to the Italian word *amatore*. A lover. I would be painting in the luxurious beauty and peace of Tuscany, just south of Siena, on an *agriturismo* or working farm with guest accommodations. I would take instruction and paint for six days with a group of other painters from America. That sounded like love to me.

We painters made a chatty, friendly group. There was a couple from Pennsylvania, two women from Baton Rouge, a woman from New York, a man from San Francisco, and others. And me, the lone Canadian. Each morning, we met over a Tuscan breakfast of rustic breads, meats, cheese, and fruit on the long table in the enormous dining room. The room was on the second floor of the house, where three large arched windows gave us a view over the countryside. After breakfast, the group gathered outdoors for instruction on structure and form, underpainting, fat-over-lean paint application, perspective, and color theory. The remainder of the day was spent standing in the fields and vineyards to paint *plein air* in silent, meditative focus.

We painted the soft rolling hills in autumn green and gold around our *agriturismo*, the sunrise landscapes where mist flowing over pale blue-mauve land bathed in hazy morning light, the verdant vineyards with rows of leafy vines and dangling wine-red grapes where workers were beginning the *vendemmia* harvest and the simple *pieve*, or local parish church, with its amber-colored courtyard surrounded by arches. We broke at midday to dine *al fresco* under shady trees and ate evening meals in Buonconvento, a quaint little commune near our *agriturismo*. We took day trips to paint in nearby hill towns famous for their wines and toured the gracious city of Siena, home of the world-famous *palio*, or bare-back horse race, where brazen riders spurred their horses through the winding city streets.

The week flew by. Masterpieces appeared on painters' canvases. Friendships were made. I departed feeling enriched by more than the satisfaction of painting lessons, wonderful Tuscan landscapes and warm Americans. There was a sense of peace in my soul.

* * *

It was a long trip from Canada to Italy. It seemed to justify a stay of more than one week. So, I booked a second painting course with a Slovenian woman in Puglia, the heel of the boot of Italy. I caught the train from Buonconvento to travel south. It would be a long day of travel from Tuscany, and I had a day to spare between courses. It seemed a great idea to stop overnight somewhere along the way. I chose the town of Caserta, famous for its royal baroque Bourbon castle and gardens comparable to those of Versailles. There was a festival going on. It was an event for the whole family, complete with lots of entertainment and fireworks. It was something not to miss.

I arrived at the Caserta train station and planned to walk a few blocks to my hotel but spotted a taxi in front of the station. It had been a long train ride from Tuscany. I was tired and not interested in pulling my suitcase three blocks. A taxi would be lovely.

The taxi driver spotted me and leaped from his car to take my bag.

He caught the eyes of two elegant older gentlemen who were standing and talking outside the station. The three men exchanged pointed glances. An awareness of the exchange niggled in my head, but I was too tired to care. I got in the front seat of the taxi beside the driver, and he pulled away from the curb.

He was young and handsome in that sexy, virile, southern Italian way. He looked intensely and directly at me and pointed to himself as he drove, saying, "Massimo. *Trentadue.*" He was 32.

He motioned to me as if to ask my name. I gave him my name, then searched for the words to give my age in Italian.

"*Quarantanove.*" 49.

He gave a low whistle. Yes, I was 49 but barely looked 40. I was dressed in a youthful beige floral print skirt and a simple white T-shirt. I looked young. Massimo tried to speak to me in Italian, eyeing me and leaning toward me. He had Italian-style buzzed hair and intense brown eyes that pierced me. His eyes made rapid shifts between the street and me as he drove. There was an insistent intention with his glances, the way he leaned toward me, the way he openly stared, trying to look directly into my face and penetrate my eyes.

His presence was overwhelming. It seemed the space in the taxi shrank. I pressed further back in my seat toward my window, my heart racing. Why had I taken the front passenger's seat? It was not unusual to do that at home in Canada. But here? Had I sent the wrong message?

We stopped in front of my hotel. It had only been a drive of a few blocks, but I was utterly rattled. I quickly jumped out of the taxi and went around to the trunk to collect my bag. Massimo lifted it out and handed it to me. He waved my euro away when I asked to pay the fare.

He said repeatedly, "*La sera, la sera,*" looking at me determinedly.

I realized he wanted me to go out with him in the evening.

I said, "No, no, thank you," threw my euro in the trunk of his car and raced into my hotel.

I paced in my room and tried to shake off Massimo's intensity. I called my daughter at home and told her the story. She burst out laughing.

"Mom, you're hilarious. You don't need to worry about the taxi driver."

That helped a lot. Still, I didn't go out to the festival that evening as planned. I was nervous about leaving my hotel at all.

I asked the staff at the front desk for a suggestion for dinner nearby and was given the name of a family restaurant a block away. As I left the hotel, I stood at the entrance before going out and glanced up and down the street, then skulked down the block to the restaurant. As if Massimo were going to suddenly reappear.

Oh my god. I was being ridiculous. After 25 years of marriage, I felt so very, very green. I had forgotten how to be nonchalant about repelling a man's unwanted come-on. My imagination ran away with me. That was all it was. Just my imagination. By the end of dinner, I was over it. Yet I had a steamy dream of Massimo that night, as if being rattled by the sexy taxi driver had shaken something loose.

The next day, I caught the train to a town named Fasano in Puglia. Talia, my Slovenian painting instructor, picked me up at the station and guided her car through the pale ochre roads of the countryside, past silvery green orchards of olive trees standing in autumn-dry grass, then on through the elegant gates of *Masseria Salamina,* where we would be staying for our week of painting.

Masserie were large stone and plaster castles that were built in ancient times and situated on high points on the land to have a view of any invading Greek ships coming across the Adriatic toward Italy. Later, *masserie* became agricultural estates. Today, most have been transformed into *agriturismos* or hotels, as was this one. It was gorgeous with its large, fortified front door, stone turret, elegant swimming pool, spacious sunbathing area, and horse stables.

I was shown to my room, which turned out to be a small apartment just inside an arch-lined promenade. I had a simple but sweet bedroom, bathroom, living room, and small kitchen. As I looked around in wonder, I thought, *What more do I need in life than this? A small apartment and one large suitcase with some clothing, paints, books and a music player.* I left my bags and hurried to the dining room where the painters were to meet over a wonderful meal rich in vegetables and olive oil, for which Puglia is famous.

In the days that followed, Talia whisked us to wonderful painting locations across the countryside while she played sultry, rhythmic

Cesária Évora music in her car. The brilliant sun bleached the powdery earth. The glossy leaves of olive trees shimmered in the daylight. Azure blue seas were contrasted by gleaming white cities. Puglia felt like what I imagined Greece to be like. It was an exotic week of painting and instruction that was completely different from my experience in Tuscany.

We painted in the town of Alberobello with its cone-shaped *trulli* houses. The day we were there, it happened to be a Catholic holy day festival. The baking hot streets were jammed with people and lined with kiosks selling household linens, kitchen gadgets, and food. There was a parade of shoulder-to-shoulder people following a statue of the Virgin Mary held high on a platform above the heads of the men who bore her while a priest said outdoor mass over a loudspeaker that blared through the entire town.

A Norwegian woman in our group became my painting companion. She and I escaped the confusion and found a quiet street to paint. An elderly woman came from her house to watch us. She inquired where we were from. She said she thought she heard of Canada but had never heard of Norway. We were definitely in another world.

Another day, we painted in the white city of Ostuni, where my friend and I set up our easels in an intimate cul-de-sac filled with pots of exotic plants beside the colorful doors of the white homes surrounding us. A husky-bodied, white-haired older man in a tank top and shorts who lived in one of the houses saw us painting and charmed us by serving us tea, then offered to show us his villa. We were interviewed by a couple of local cable reporters who caught sight of us as they were passing by. They were doing a feature on tourism in Ostuni. We made a great addition to their story. As their cameras rolled, we felt like media sensations.

Lastly, Talia took us to paint at the U-shaped marina of the town of Savelletri. I set up my easel at the edge of the boat launch area while my friends set off to look for other inspiring painting spots. I began to paint the colorful rows of boats that were docked along a boardwalk lined with restaurants. The boats bobbed on the steel blue of the Adriatic in a contrasting splash of color—vibrant reds, cobalt blues, lemon yellows, and emerald greens.

A group of men who were standing and talking a short distance from me slowly inched *en-masse* toward my workplace, subtly moving as a unit like something out of a cartoon. They continued to talk while they discreetly made a circle around and just behind me, feigning disinterest in what I was doing. But I could see their side-long glances. I smiled softly to myself.

A boy named Michele, making no pretense, ran to look curiously at my painting and cried, "Bravo, bravo!"

Running behind him, a woman in an Italian house dress came rushing from her home to speak to me in an excited gush of English.

"You are from Canada! Another Canadian woman came to Savelletri. She married a Fasano man."

I had an unexpected thought. "I would like a Fasano man." These were Mediterranean men who were dark and warm of skin, full of body, and not tall but pressed close to the Earth by the heat of the radiant sun. They were nothing like my husband at home. I caught myself. I must have had too many long days in the sun.

At the end of the week, Talia reviewed our work.

"Perhaps you would like to paint professionally," she suggested to me.

I was surprised. *Would I?*

"Thank you, Talia. I hadn't been thinking of that at all."

What did I intend with these painting courses? I was flattered by Talia's suggestion. But I was just an amateur, an *amatore* who painted only for love, no desire for any other gain. What was I looking for here in Italy? I had just been allowing myself to float on a whisper of a breeze and fall in love with Italy.

* * *

I caught the train to Rome for two days of sightseeing before I returned to Canada. Rome had not been on my priority list for the trip. I had included two days in the city as an afterthought, never realizing what Rome would become to me. It was midnight on a balmy fall evening by the time I reached Rome's *Termini* station. I grabbed one of the taxis waiting outside to take me to my hotel. Amazingly, the driver was originally from Winnipeg. Meeting someone from Canada seemed like a very comforting thing to happen at midnight in a foreign city. We shared stories of living in Canada as I relaxed in my seat, thinking I was in good hands, but as the driver neared the *Campo dei Fiori,* where my hotel was located, he suddenly stopped in the middle of the street and said, "I can drive no farther. You will have to get out here."

"Wait! Get out here? In the middle of the street? Is my hotel here?" I scanned the street around me. "Where is my hotel?"

"Your hotel is that way. Just around the corner," he said, pointing forward from the windshield.

The street forward was thronging with weekend partiers from the campo just ahead at the end of the street. They flowed toward us like a surging river, completely blocking our passage. The driver got out from behind the wheel, took my bag from the back of the SUV, plopped it on the cobblestones, and said, pointing, "Go that way. You will see your hotel just around the corner."

I was stunned. Obviously, there was no possibility of driving forward. I had no choice but to pay the man and walk. Thanks a lot, Winnipeg! I begin hauling my suitcase over impossible bumpy stone streets against a tide of partiers in a foreign city in the middle of the night. I arrived at the campo and looked around the square. There was no hotel just around the corner. No hotel anywhere. I made my way around the piazza, weaving through a sea of vibrating bodies, squeezing past young people standing with drinks in hand, laughing and talking with friends. No hotel. I spied a gelato shop in a quiet corner of the square. I hurried over and asked the shop girl to please point me in the direction of the Hotel Campo dei Fiori.

She said, "It's there, just around the corner."

"No!" I groaned helplessly.

The girl laughed and said, "Yes! It's just around the corner."

To my relief, it was!

I had two days in Rome. It was love. Two days in Rome was not and would never be enough. I wished I could stay forever. If there is such a thing as past lives, I certainly lived in Rome before. I felt like I had come home.

I strolled the streets and piazzas in the baking heat and saw every famous sight, from the Trevi Fountain and Piazza Navona to the Colosseum and Forum. I luxuriated in the cool satin bedding and air-conditioning in the room of my chic hotel after sweaty days of sightseeing. In the evenings, I dined on simple but marvelous food as I sat in outdoor cafes in the campo, where people who sat at tables next to me were always eager to chat. There was none of the loneliness I felt in Venice. It was bliss. I found an artist paint shop and fleshed out my palette of acrylics, then painted in my room into the night.

One day, I got my bottom pinched by a man in front of *Campidoglio,* who suggested lunch and an afternoon of love. I practically ran from him, more annoyed than fearful. Funny. I was still alone, but I had lost my fear. Fear seemed irrelevant for me in magical Rome, which felt like home. And I had gotten smarter since Massimo in Caserta. Something in me had shifted.

Rome was an intoxicating blend of ancient and modern. I adored its stony architecture, muggy heat, and lazy spirit that seemed beyond time. I fell in love with *Parco Borghese* with its towering Roman pines and its small, lovely museum. I stood awestruck in front of glorious, luminous sculptures by Canova and Bernini. As I left the museum, I saw two police officers on horseback riding through the courtyard. They crossed the graveled square and rode past a woman pushing a child in a stroller. Did the stroller wheels squeak?

One of the horses got spooked. The officer was thrown, and the horse took off across the park at a gallop, with the second officer riding in pursuit. I went to the officer, who lay dazed on the ground.

"Are you alright?"

He looked embarrassed. "Yes, yes, I am okay," he said, feigning nonchalance and getting shakily to his feet.

After a few minutes, I left him there and headed back through the park for the long walk toward my hotel. I called my daughter while I walked and told her about the thrill of Rome. I described all the sights passing by me as I strolled through the pine-filled park, past the Spanish Steps, and past a shop window where I saw a designer dress I told her would look amazing on her. She was excited about everything I described. I felt I was speaking the sights of the glorious city through the phone, and she could perceive it at home in Calgary. Our call lasted over an hour. It was like she was there in Rome with me, my wonderful daughter who had grown into the best and loveliest of friends.

On the third morning, I checked out of my hotel and caught a taxi to the airport. I felt my heart ache as I flew out of Rome. I had an overnight stop in Frankfurt. I booked a cheap hotel near the airport and spent the night adding final touches to my paintings that glowed with life in that dull little room. I left them to dry overnight and wrapped them carefully in the morning to stow in my luggage. I checked in at the airport. No one groped my breasts in security. The plane took off. Then I was home.

Chapter 3

Calgary: Falling Apart

I returned to my regular life in Canada. *Was I changed?* Outwardly, it may not have been obvious. Some people may have noticed a heightened light in my eyes. I have always been an enthusiastic person, especially about any new life experiences. When it came to the things I loved, like books, music, family holidays, and children, some might say I was annoyingly enthusiastic. A woman once sourly said to me, "It must be nice to have time to be so passionate."

As if passion were about time. And I loved to talk. It was a family trait I inherited and passed on. Fast and excited talk about everything. The good, the bad and the ugly. Funny, though, I never talked about my marriage over the years. Not to anyone.

Now back from Italy, I was enthusiastic to tell of my adventures and excited to display my paintings. People listened kindly and admiringly. I appreciated that. But my travel had been about more than just painting. What that was, I couldn't have begun to express at the time. The truth was I had fallen in love. It was not love for a person but for a place. Italy. Rome. That love of place was not unlike falling in love with a person. It was love that brought a euphoric, alive feeling that surged from the inside.

A shift began to happen as if a part of me that had been closed for years began to creak open. I had a subtle renewed sense of who I was and what I might be capable of. I had begun to come back to life somewhere between Venice and Rome. It brought a new energy and desire to change my life. The knowledge of how I could make a change had been missing as I drifted through the days and years of my marriage. I was eager to bloom outwardly now. I was happy.

My husband said, "You found your happy place." It was very astute and unusual for him to be positive about something to do with me.

My husband was 55 at the time. He was a slim, wiry 5-foot 9-inch man with thinning dark hair that tended to curly and captivating, clear blue eyes. He was a successful lawyer who worked in the corporate world, had a long, rich career, and made lots of money. He was magnetic and charismatic and could express himself with flair, humor, and often irreverence that delighted people he interacted with. People loved being around him. He was fast, physically and mentally, and had an indefatigable energy that I've never seen the likes of. He had been an athlete his whole life, and through the years of our children growing up, he poured himself into coaching sports for young people with skill, passion, and generosity. He drove around town in his Jeep T-J with the top down, music blaring, aviator sunglasses on, and a bandana wound into a sweatband around his head. He was recognized everywhere. He was also a man with some deep-seated, deeply hidden pain.

Why he married me, I don't know. Why I married him, I do know. I adored him. In the early days. Over the years, I was increasingly left with the sense he saw me as so much less than him and a hindrance. He rarely acknowledged me or gave me any clue that he saw anything about me except things that displeased him, yet he would make a big show of giving me gifts or treating me beautifully when other people were around.

As the years of our marriage drifted by, the love we started with 25 years earlier turned decidedly to Not-Love. It was an infinitesimally gradual descent that started with little things like him putting the newspaper up in front of his face when I tried to talk. It grew into contemptuous looks that could have shriveled fruit on a vine. He had a brilliance with language and could cut me to shreds with a few choice words; then, when he saw my dismay, he acted as if he didn't know what my problem was. It was all so subtly done I didn't see it at first. When I finally saw it and tried to address it, any talking between us descended rapidly into intense arguing, for which he always found a way to blame me. "We—meaning me—were not going to scar our children by having them hear us fight." He was so good at making every problem my fault. Then there was the cheating. From his point of view, that was my fault, too.

It was all deeply, deeply painful. I shed a lot of tears over the years. Gradually, the love I had for him was crushed out of me. Yet I stayed in the marriage, thinking I could bring him around, thinking I could fix things by reading self-help books on marriage to find ways to address what was wrong with us, wrong with him, wrong with me. What a fool I was.

At one point, ten years into our marriage, my husband became despondent, and several times, I caught him crying in our home office with the hood of his hoodie pulled over his head. When I asked what was wrong, he refused to talk. The situation got so bad I finally told him he had to leave. He got an apartment. I got the name of a marriage counselor from our family doctor. At the end of the first session, the counselor said to him, "I've never seen anything like it. You really have all your ducks in a row, don't you? Let me tell you, there will be no tap-dancing in these sessions."

I saw what the counselor saw. My husband was a master of control. Control of himself, control of his image and how people saw him, control of emotions, control of words, control of agendas, control of life. He made it look so easy and so admirable. But how could there be room within that control to let a wife into your heart, especially a wife who somehow seemed beyond control?

My husband had once said to me, "You are such a romantic girl."

It almost sounded nice. Except I heard the subtle hint of sarcasm and distaste in his voice. I replied with narrowed eyes and wryly pursed lips, "Not anymore."

Maybe the problem with having a romantic wife was that romance was the opposite of control.

The counselor concluded our first meeting, "Next session you will both come with individual lists of what is good and what needs work in your relationship."

Next session, my husband brought no list. I was dismissed from the counseling session. The counselor said he would begin with a few meetings with my husband alone.

We were in counseling for eight months. We arrived at a reconciliation. My husband said he was ready to return to the family and our marriage. I was overjoyed. The day we began to plan his return, a nagging indistinct thought appeared in my mind, and an unexpected question slipped from my mouth.

"Before you come home, is there something you need to tell me?" I felt awkward and couldn't explain, even to myself, why I was asking that question.

"No," he said quickly.

"Are you sure?"

"No, there's nothing," he said with a flare of annoyance.

"Okay. But if there's something you need to tell me, and you don't tell me now, there will be a heavy price to pay."

"There's nothing," he said more shortly.

I should have paid attention to what my gut was telling me.

My husband returned to the family home. The next three months were wonderful. Our children, who had been devastated when their father left, were ecstatic. My husband and I found renewed passion and sexual excitement. I was thrilled we had come through our difficulties.

Then, one day as I sat at my kitchen table to open our cell phone bill, a strange impulse made me run my finger down the list of phone numbers it displayed. There was one number that appeared again and again, a number I did not recognize. I picked up the phone and dialed. I got the home answering machine of a woman from my husband's office. I crumpled over the kitchen table in shock.

When I confronted my husband, he admitted he had been carrying on an affair for years before we went to counseling and sneakily continued it throughout the sessions and his return to the family. He had lied. Somehow I knew there had been something he needed to tell me. I cannot say how I knew. He had lied at the most critical point of our reconciliation. A lie at a time when the truth was imperative was even worse than the affair. I felt like I had been stabbed in the gut.

In the shock of the betrayal, I froze. You may think that, of course, I instantly threw him out. I didn't do that. I thought of my children's heartbreak when their father left before and their joy when he returned. Our family life had been happy for months. No! There would not be a revolving daddy-door! I couldn't endure the idea of seeing the distress on my children's faces if he left again. What about me? Was I ready to throw him out at that moment? No. I decided that my husband and I would have to be responsible and resolve the matter between us. I made my choice that quickly. The marriage went on.

I was frozen in pain for a long time. My husband was a mess of his own distress over what he had done. It took a long time for us to heal. We talked, argued, and hashed out the events around the affair. My husband wanted to recommit to our marriage. We agreed to move on. We took holidays together. We moved to a new house to make a fresh start. Things got a lot better for a couple of years. Then my husband's old behavior began creeping back in, sometimes with a hint of something darker, something cruel. It was like a gradual creeping sickness we could not stop. Years went by. I know I should have ended the marriage, but I felt stuck with no sense of how to get out of it or change it. I saw a counselor on my own. It didn't help. I was still frozen.

The entire story of our marriage is a tawdry, boring one. Lots of miserable behavior. Lots of stupidity on both sides. If I told you all, you would see that for sure. I saw it so clearly, myself, years later. On the surface, my husband had glaring issues. I saw I was his outlet for the pain of an ugly childhood he had locked tight inside. I tried to get him to open up to me. I tried to save the marriage many times. I was trying to keep my family whole. Wasn't I? I've since had reason to look more carefully at the role I played.

Now back from my painting trip in Italy, I set up a workspace in a spare room in my house and began painting daily. My memory and camera were full of glorious images of places I had been. Landscapes appeared on my canvases, and flowers bloomed under my brush. I framed my paintings from Italy and the new ones I did at home. I surrounded myself with happy place images as I renewed the responsibilities of daily life. Was it the stark contrast between the joyful, alive me and the dutiful, unhappy me that created the movement toward the end? The state of the marriage was just not tolerable anymore.

One day in early November, a month after I returned from Italy, I was standing by the counter in my kitchen making breakfast when I began to cry. At that moment, my husband walked into the room and stopped in surprise when he saw me.

"I can't do this anymore," I said.

I didn't turn to look at him but felt him as he stood silently a short distance from me.

"The only thing stopping me from leaving right now is that our son is graduating from high school in eight months. It's his Grade Twelve year. After all these years, I can't leave now and do that to him in his Grade Twelve year! I can't."

Without looking at him, I could feel my husband start to shake.

"No. No, you can't leave now. Wait until he graduates in June. We can re-evaluate then."

The air was thick with thoughts and unspoken things as if all the arguing, problems, and distance of 25 years had accumulated, and now it was impossible to know where to start.

After a resigned breath, I said, "Okay. We'll wait and re-evaluate in June," then, after a short pause, my words rushed out, "But you have to see a counselor."

Quickly, he said, "I will. I'll go to a counselor."

I turned my head to look directly at him for the first time and repeated more emphatically,

"You have to go to a counselor!"

"I will. I will."

I took another deep breath. "Okay. Then, we'll wait."

He turned and left the kitchen. I buttered the burnt toast.

In the months that followed, I asked my husband a number of times if he had gone to counseling. The answer was the same each time I asked.

"No. No, not yet ... but I will."

Months went by. By the end of January, when I asked again and got the same response, anger in me flared. It exploded in February when his answer was still no. I was so angry I could hardly stand to be in my own skin. When no one was around, I raged, I paced, I roared my anger aloud. I had been careful about giving an ultimatum before because I know an ultimatum is only good if you are willing to follow through. I had given him one in the fall. He had promised to see a counselor. Another broken promise. My anger was colossal. It was going to be easy to follow through. I said not a word to my husband but thought, *It's over. I don't care what he does now.*

It was still four months until my son's graduation. I was so angry I wondered if I could actually wait to leave until June. Yes, I'd wait. I had come this far. I got busy with spring things, joined an exercise boot camp, and planned celebrations for my son's graduation. I began having powerful dreams. There was a particularly vivid one. I was in Italy, where I fell in love with a full-bodied, dark-haired man who owned a hotel along the Tyrrhenian Sea south of Rome. He was so real in my dream, a passionate man who lived with his teenage son in a breezy white hotel by the sea. The man had a rich family and social life, a life that was soul-nourishing, a life he welcomed me into. In my dream, I basked in it. He loved me beautifully. The dream was so hot and so real it sent tremors through me.

Nothing more was said between my husband and me about counselors or what would happen in June. Graduation came and went. It was lovely despite what was lurking in the future. My son took his Grade Twelve exams. There was a week of beautiful weather where he celebrated with his friends. Then, it was July. I simply said to my husband, "It's over. I'm going away for ten days to a painting class out of town. I'll talk to you about how we go forward when I get back."

I left. No re-evaluating.

My husband called me many times during those ten days, crying and wanting to talk. *Great! You're the one crying now*, I thought. He waited too long. Waiting until we were at a crisis point before being willing to change said a lot. There was no going back. I couldn't trust him. Could I ever? I definitely could never change him. Like every other woman who thinks she can change a man who does not want to change, I had been a fool. Now, I was explosively angry. I saw the anger. I could not miss the fact that I had been unwilling to change the status quo until I was furious. Why did I need that anger in order to make a change? It was like the heat of the anger melted something frozen in me.

I needed a plan, but I couldn't see my next steps. I was exhausted from dealing with the marriage for years. I had nothing left to give. I had to get away from my husband. I couldn't tolerate the thought of going back to our house. His persistent phone calls told me he wouldn't leave me alone. I needed to be far away. I needed space. I booked a flight to Rome, where I registered for an Italian language immersion for two weeks with extra days for sightseeing around the city. It was three weeks to plan my next steps. It would be three weeks in my happy place.

I told my husband, "I'm leaving for Italy. You should not wait for me. I will not be coming back to you."

I was emphatic. I left the third week of July.

Chapter 4

Italy: Falling Under a Spell

I watched from my window on the plane, face pressed to the glass, as we wound down and over the trees and hills of the countryside below decked out in the rich green of summer. Around and down, the plane flew, soaring into Italy. I held my breath and vibrated with excitement as the ground came closer and closer until we landed at Rome's Fiumicino airport. I grabbed my luggage at baggage claim and went to the Hertz location, where I had reserved a car. I would drive in Italy, never mind what people said about crazy Italian drivers. I was a girl from the Canadian prairies and had driven through the worst sticky winter situations. Italians had nothing on me.

I ended up with a spunky, clunky little Fiat Panda with a manual transmission. I got out of the airport and onto the GRA ring road around Rome, which was jammed with traffic that crept along and came to full stops regularly. Perfect. It gave me a chance to acclimatize.

I rolled down my window and stuck my face out to savor the hot Italian air, air so hot the paved road shimmered in the heat. I wanted to feel the heat. All of it!

The traffic moved again. No, I was not going to drive into frenetic Rome. First, I was going to a little hotel I booked south of the city for five nights to have blissful days of sightseeing in the *Castelli Romani* before going into Rome to begin my immersion.

I reached the closed security gate of the hotel and buzzed to be let in. The huge door swung open, and I drove through the gateway onto the crunchy gravel parking area inside. The hotel was a lovely building of pale gold plaster and tiles, lushly covered by ivy and surrounded by gardens with a view of the volcanic lake the hotel sat on, peeking from between the branches of the trees. Through the open front door of the hotel, I crossed the expanse of the fresh, quaint lobby that led to a simple reception desk just beyond it. A plump older woman with white hair greeted me at the desk.

"*Ho une prenotazione,*" I lilted, trying out my Italian to indicate I had a reservation.

The woman checked me in and handed me my key. I had just turned toward the stairs to the right of me to go up to my room when I heard a door open and turned my head at the sound. A man had come out of a room in a small hallway behind the reception desk and had stopped short when he saw me. He was a slim older man with a gentle face, kind eyes, and cropped white hair. He said something to me in English about check-in, and I held up my key to show I was already in. Without a word, I turned and continued up the stairs to my room.

How lovely that room was. Not modern or elegant but cozy and sweet in pale cornflower blue. I set down my bags and rushed to open the large window that overlooked the lake. It was an Italian-style window with a large casement set into the thick walls of the building, so when the window was open, you could sit on the wide ledge and savor the view. I sat for a bit, then got up. There were still lots of hours left in the day. To hell with jetlag. I was off to explore the *Castelli* in my Panda.

I returned later that evening after grabbing a quick bite out and snuggled happily into bed with my laptop and *The Sopranos* DVDs that my daughter had lent me for the trip.

The next morning, I went downstairs with a full sightseeing plan. As I was passing through the lobby, the man from the previous day stepped forward to greet me.

"*Buon giorno*. My name is Giorgio. I am the owner of the hotel."

I gave my name, thinking that, of course, he would have already known my name from the register. He reached his hand toward me, and I reached out my hand to shake his. He did not intend a handshake. He gently turned my hand and pressed his lips to the back of it with a light, lingering kiss. The kiss reverberated through me and down my spine like an internal shock.

I would never have thought a kiss on the hand could have that effect. It spoke of romance and courtly seduction of days past. It was an outdated tactic, yet it obviously worked. It sparked something in me. But I wasn't attracted to this older, average-looking man, Giorgio. Not at all.

I extracted my hand from his and lamely explained, "I am going out for a day of sightseeing in the area," and quickly left.

That evening, I called my daughter.

"I arrived safely yesterday. I'm at the hotel on the lake. It's lovely with its gardens and terrace. I have a view over the lake from my room."

"It sounds beautiful, Mom."

"I watched three episodes of *The Sopranos* last night. While I was out sightseeing today, driving in my Panda, I hummed the theme song all day. It's a fabulous theme. Another funny thing," I added, laughing, "As I was leaving the hotel this morning, the owner introduced himself and kissed my hand. I realize I am going to have to make wide circles around the hand-kisser."

She laughed but later told me she knew then that something was going to happen.

I spent five days at the hotel. Giorgio was always around but didn't approach me again until one hot day as I sat reading under a shady tree on the terrace by the lake. He came quietly, almost deferentially, to serve me a cold slice of sweet watermelon on a tray with silverware and white linen.

He asked with formal graciousness, "Would you like this?"

"Oh, yes. Thank you," I said and enjoyed the cold fruit in the hot sun.

Another day, I asked him for information about travel to the Gardens of Ninfa, the natural garden created in the ruins of a destroyed medieval town an hour's drive south of Rome. Giorgio was excited by my interest in Ninfa.

"Let me drive you on my motorcycle. It is much nicer and faster than driving by car."

"No. Thank you. I like driving."

For three days, I toured the countryside in my Panda, through lush, wooded roads, past volcanic lakes, and up winding streets of small towns barely wide enough for my car. I strolled through the nearby town of Castel Gandolfo, where the pope had his summer residence. I lit a taper candle in his church for our little family cocker spaniel, Coco, who had a health crisis while I was away and had to be put down, a tough decision made by my 18-year-old son, who was home alone at the time. I giggled to think of little Coco's candle burning in the mighty pope's church. Sweet little Coco.

After three days of sightseeing, eating out, and binging on *The Sopranos* in my room at night, I felt like staying in the hotel for dinner. The hotel did not have a dining room, only a breakfast room. If you wanted dinner, you had to make a request.

"Giorgio, I wonder if it would be possible for me to have dinner this evening at the hotel. Could I dine on the terrace?"

Giorgio said with a courteous bow of his head, "Of course. What would you have to eat?"

"I eat lightly and will be happy with whatever is served."

When I came down to dinner, I noticed that the hotel was completely, strangely empty. There was not a soul around except for Giorgio, who led me to a table situated prominently on the terrace where I could enjoy the view. I felt pretty in my flowing capri pants and smart ruffled blouse. I sat in the golden late afternoon light, looking out at the beauty of the view before me, and breathed it in. I had it all to myself.

Giorgio served me dinner in a silent, formal manner. *So, he is the waiter as well as the hotel owner*, I thought. I savored my simple, delicious meal while the late evening sun played on my face. I felt blissful and relaxed in a way I could not recall having felt for a long, long time.

After I had eaten and sat sipping my wine, I longed for someone to talk to. As Giorgio picked up my empty plate from the table, I asked, "Would you like to join me for a glass of wine? I would enjoy a bit of conversation."

He said rather flippantly, "I don't like wine," and carried away my plate to return minutes later with two glasses of limoncello. He sat. There was still no one around except us two.

We talked lightly. I was feeling bubbly and happy with where I was in the world at that moment. Giorgio sat politely, a little reserved. He was a 59-year-old man with soft features and hair that had likely once been dark but was now white and cropped short to stand fuller on his scalp. His nose was long and a little large in proportion to his other features. His lips were full and smooth and stood out pleasingly on his face. He was simply dressed in casual blue jeans and a crisp button-up shirt with the collar loose and relaxed around his throat.

While we sipped our limoncello, I could feel him watching me. When I glanced back at him, I noticed his round eyes were a lovely shade of blue. I was a little uncomfortable sitting next to him. I could feel him feeling into me. I shifted a few times in my chair.

The conversation turned to the wines of the *Castelli* area vineyards, then to art.

"Have you seen the mosaic that hangs at the entrance of the hotel?" he asked.

"I'm sorry. I have not noticed it."

"Would you like to see it? If you come inside, I will show you."

We went inside to see the mosaic.

"This was done by a talented local artist. He lives here in town."

"It's very nice," I lied. The mosaic was not at all to my taste.

Giorgio stood beside me, quiet, observing me. After a moment, he said, "I have a second mosaic done by the same artist. It hangs in my house. Would you like to see it?"

Giorgio lived in a little house at the bottom of the gardens that surrounded the hotel. I thought wryly, *Sure, you have a mosaic in your house*, but said, "Okay. Yes, I would like to see it."

We walked across the terrace, through the gardens, and down the short stone stairway to a little house nestled in the trees right above the lake. Giorgio opened the iron-grated front door and led me inside his home. He took me directly to the mosaic that hung in his living room and pointed out its features. Again, not my taste.

I could see his room, a man's room that did not pretend to be either masculine or stylish. There was a simple, comfy couch. There were books and papers everywhere. I felt awkward being there with him standing near me, silently feeling into me.

After a moment, I said, "I'm going to say goodnight. I'm driving to Ninfa in the morning and would like to make an early start. Thank you for showing me the mosaics."

Giorgio walked me back to the bottom of the steps that returned up to the hotel, then stopped me. He asked, "Would you like to sit in the garden for a while?"

It was now dusk. The night air was still warm but fresher and softer than it had been earlier in the evening. Birds were calling to each other hauntingly over the lake as the sun went down. The garden seemed to bloom in the mystery of the hour. An enormous oak with a massive trunk stood in the middle of a quiet sitting area over which it spread its leafy branches to create a cooling shaded darkness. The branches of the oak seemed to reach out their craggy arms to gently entice me into the strange magic that permeated that dusky space. They seemed to encourage me, "Yes, please, sit in the garden for a while."

I took a seat on a lounge chair under the canopy of leaves and felt the pleasure of being embraced by trees. I breathed in the sweet, floral, herbal scent that wafted to me from the greenness of grass and trees and was amplified by the cool of the evening air.

He pulled up another chair to sit at my feet. I saw him reach toward me in the dimming light. Unexpectedly, he took my hand tenderly to sit in the palm of his and began to lightly caress the back of it, skimming the surface of my skin. An intense bolt of electricity flashed through me. I caught my breath. I got up in a flustered rush.

"Thank you again for dinner and the evening. Good night," I said and fled.

In the morning, as I was passing through the lobby to leave for Ninfa, Giorgio was nowhere in sight despite the fact he always seemed to be around. I got in my Panda and set out driving through the narrow, winding, tree-hugged roads. Whenever I reached an intersection where I encountered another driver and was unsure of who had the right of way, I just waved a friendly wave and gave the other driver the go-ahead. I was treated to big smiles and friendly waves in return. Who says Italian drivers are crazy? Everything about being in Italy was heavenly. I loved the me I was there.

The Gardens of Ninfa is the rambling 250-acre ruins of a town that was sacked and burned in the Middle Ages. Its tumbled-down castle, churches, and waterways are owned and preserved by a private family who turned it into a park. Everything the town had once been was now overtaken by oaks, cypresses, and innumerable kinds of wild flora. The Gardens was idyllic and did justice to its name: *Ninfa*, Nymph and Goddess of Springwater.

I wandered through sunny paths where streets had been, over stone bridges densely covered with vines, and through the remains of buildings completely overgrown with shady greenery. It was serene, beautiful, and magical, as if Ninfa the nymph was still enlivening it with her presence. I left the gardens with a potent sense of mythical romance humming through my whole being.

Dreamy and relaxed, I returned to my hotel late in the day. Upon entering and glancing around, I saw that Giorgio was still nowhere to be seen. Strange. It seemed like a subtle reprimand. Suddenly, I wished to see him. I went to my room, a little crestfallen.

I came down in the morning to check out and found Giorgio busy at reception. With cool professionalism, without looking at me, he asked, "How was your visit to Ninfa?"

"It was lovely," was all I said, matching his coolness.

"I was away from the hotel yesterday," he continued as he occupied himself with paperwork at the desk. "My daughter had a baby girl. They named her Giorgiana after me," he said proudly, finally looking up at me.

I responded with delight. "A baby? Oh, how wonderful. Congratulations!"

Giorgio's eyes lit up when he saw me smile at his news. He beamed back in return. After I paid my bill and turned to go, Giorgio came around from behind the desk and walked toward me.

"This is my business card with my email and private phone number on the back," he said, extending a card to me. "If you like, you can call me, and I will come to Rome to have dinner with you."

I was surprised and could only give a soft, dubious, "Oh. Okay. Thank you."

Giorgio stepped forward, closer to me, until he was only inches away. He tipped his head slightly and bent forward to kiss me lightly on the lips. I was shocked. My lips were tingling and would allow no words to come from my mouth. Giorgio looked at me gently with eyes that I could now see were indescribably blue. Our eyes met for only a few moments until I forced mine away. I couldn't say anything in response to his offer for dinner in Rome. I was shocked and could give no reaction to the unexpected kiss. All I could say was goodbye. Again, I fled.

I returned my faithful little Panda to the Hertz location at the nearby Ciampino regional airport south of Rome and took a shuttle into the city. My week of Italian classes began the next day. It was a wonderful and challenging course. I found it a bit of a stretch to keep up with the other European students, who seemed to have a great ease navigating multiple languages. In Canada, learning a new language is like trying to build a muscle you never knew you had. I loved the course. I adored the Italian language.

When I booked the course, the language school offered to arrange accommodations for students. I was boarding at the home of a woman surgeon from the University of Rome along with two other students from the language school, a young man from Portugal and a woman from Düsseldorf. The surgeon's apartment was a short walk to the school. I felt vibrantly alive each morning as I strolled through the streets of Rome in the golden morning sunshine, making a quick stop to stand at the counter of a café bar for a cappuccino with the locals or pausing here and there to browse at one of many kiosks that lined the streets. How I adored Rome.

When I was not in class, to my amazement, I began obsessing about Giorgio. Seriously? I could hardly believe myself. Was I so naïve after 25 years of marriage that I was this rattled about a man, the first man I met days after leaving my husband, of whom I realized I gave no thought? Giorgio. He had been so forward. I felt no attraction to him at first. Now, unexpectedly, my body was thrumming. Good God! Did Italian men know something about caressing the back of the hand and soft brushing kisses on the lips that I had been unaware of? It was like a switch was flipped. All I could think about was sex.

That Thursday evening, there was an open-air performance of Puccini's classic opera *Turandot* at the *Terme di Caracalla*, the ancient baths of Rome. *Turandot*, one of Puccini's famous operas, tells the story of a prince who tries to win the heart of a cold Chinese princess. Certain that he will win her, he sings the beloved aria "*Nessun Dorma*," "No one Sleeps," made famous by Pavarotti. It was an event not to be missed.

I went with two of the young women from class. The opera began at 9 p.m., just as the evening turned to night. We sat in seats rising up from the stage that was a vision of lights and glowing colors in the near darkness. The music and singing of the voices seemed to float upward and fill the skies. The only word for it is enchanting. The evening had a rare magic to it, I'm sure. As I watched the opera, I could read my program by the glow of the moon that happened to be full that night. Then, a little before midnight, there was a full lunar eclipse. I felt a bit dizzy and disoriented from the music and the moonlight. It was like being in an intoxicating dream.

After the opera finished, we made our way to the bus pickup area. Buses were the only transit option after midnight as the metro was closed. There was already a throng of people at the stop trying to find their correct bus when my friends and I arrived. Crowds of people pressed to get onto the bus we were boarding, then pushed to make their way down the aisle to find a seat.

A very black-skinned man who looked like he might be from somewhere in North Africa was standing stubbornly in the aisle of the bus close to the front as I boarded. He would not let me pass. People were pressing behind me. I kept trying to get past him. Once I finally did, I reached into my purse for my wallet to pay the fare and found my wallet was gone. I looked behind me. The man in the aisle was gone, too.

"My wallet is gone," I cried out in distress.

"Check your purse again," my friend said. "It's probably there. You just overlooked it."

"No, it's not here," I said, rummaging desperately.

A British woman behind me said loudly and angrily, "That man took your wallet. I know it. The same thing happened to me."

I was in a panic. Out of desperation, I called the husband I had just left behind, who immediately called the bank and the credit card company. Once back in my room, I spent the rest of the night on the phone trying to get assistance from International Visa, who gave no assistance at all. I was desperate to get a replacement card. Online banking and e-transfers did not yet exist. I had absolutely no money. I was first told I would have a new card on Monday. Then, I was told it would be a week. I knew I would not receive another card. I was told that, fortunately, no charges had been made on my cards. There was only an attempt to use my Visa in a pay phone for a call to Africa.

In the morning, I told my roommates what happened. The woman from Düsseldorf slipped 50 euro under my door. I went to Friday class in a trance from no sleep, preoccupied with what I was going to do for another week with no money. My roommates were both going to Naples on an excursion for the weekend. I would be alone. I thought about Giorgio's offer to come to Rome for dinner. I would be so grateful for the company. Yes, I would ask him to come.

I hesitated. I was in a quandary. Why was I resisting while at the same time dreaming hotly about him? Good lord, what was happening? I had a strange thought. With the opera, the moonlight, and the robbery, was some strange coincidence of events pushing me toward him?

Then, a realization dawned. I had told my husband when I left for Italy that the marriage was over and he should not wait for me because I would not be coming back to him. I was free to accept an invitation to dinner with a man if I wanted to. I was free to do that. The realization came in with blazing clarity.

I emailed Giorgio, told him about the robbery, and said I had no plans for the weekend. I asked him if he would still like to come to Rome to have dinner.

"Come!" he wrote back enthusiastically. "Come to the lake for the weekend instead and stay at the hotel as my guest. You can have your own room. Your privacy. Take the train. I will pick you up at the station. We'll go for dinner in town."

I agreed.

Chapter 5

Il Lago: Breathed You In

The local train from Rome to the lake clacked and rumbled its way out of the city and wound past tired graffiti-splashed buildings, past small villages with quiet platforms, past sporadic flowering trees rushing by my window in a blur between which I caught periodic views of the gentle hills of the countryside. As I watched the passing landscape and sat with eager anticipation on the worn seats of the old train, I noticed people near me chatting socially with their neighbors. They looked at me curiously, bestowing sweet, friendly smiles when our eyes met.

When I arrived at the station, the late afternoon sun was already low in the sky. As I stepped down on the platform, I saw Giorgio waiting for me, standing in the softening light of day that cast fingers of light and shadow from the trees to where he stood. He looked more manly, self-assured, and handsome than I remembered. He had a grace about him that was suddenly very attractive. He lit up when he saw me. As he reached to take my bag, he greeted me with a "Hello" and a soft kiss that left the presence of his mouth on mine long after the kiss was over. A young man nearby saw us and yelled out, "*Bel bacio.*" Beautiful kiss.

Giorgio looked deeply into my eyes, smiled, and asked about my trip from Rome. He carried my bag to his car and drove. Once back at the hotel, he led me up to the second floor to show me to the room he reserved for me. He softly closed the door behind him and took me gently in his arms, embracing me gracefully and kissing me with a kiss that was somehow both light and deep. I didn't expect to respond the way I did. Or did I after a week of fraught dreams? No, I didn't.

It was a surprise to be kissed by him. It felt so impetuous to just go with that kiss, a kiss with someone who was practically a stranger and somehow felt nothing like a stranger. He felt safe and sweet. He was someone who wanted me. I went with it. I wrapped my arms around his neck and ran my fingers up the back of his head and through his hair. He took me to the bed, sat beside me, and caressed me tenderly, calling me beautiful. I stopped him.

"Giorgio, I have to tell you something. I didn't come to Italy to look for a man. I just left my husband. I came to get away, to have time alone and think about my life."

"Ah," he said softly, nodding slowly as if that explained why I had been rejecting his advances. He got up and said, "I have to work." He left the room abruptly with me sitting on the bed. What? Why had he left so suddenly with no word of explanation? What was I getting myself into?

Later that evening, Giorgio came to collect me from my room and drove us back into town for dinner on the romantic restaurant patio of a friend. Throughout the entire meal, we laughed and talked easily. The connection we dallied with earlier in our acquaintance suddenly blossomed. It was beautiful and effortless. Every time Giorgio looked at me, his smile glowed on me. Every now and then, I saw him give a soft shiver of delight. I had to suppress my laughter. I hadn't noticed his sweetness before. He was absolutely adorable.

After Giorgio drove back to the hotel, he took my hand and led me down to his little house at the bottom of the garden. He lit a candle in his bedroom before coming to me to gently help me remove my clothes and then his, his eyes never leaving my face. He kissed me sensuously with lips so full of desire, kisses that were unbelievably, unforgettably beautiful. Giorgio made love to me with lovemaking that was both passionate and tender. Everything about him had a sweetness to it. He swept me away.

I slept in his arms and woke in the morning, entwined with him as if we had never moved from each other the entire night. My face was pressed to his face. His breath was gentle on my cheek. It was the most rapturous feeling I had ever known. Giorgio opened his blue eyes to look at me and smiled, his eyes glowing into mine. Words spilled over my much-kissed lips before they could pass through my brain and before I could catch them to stop them, "Giorgio, I think I breathed you into my soul."

Such an extravagant, impetuous thing to say! I wasn't embarrassed to have said it. I felt it truly and freely in that moment. Giorgio smiled at me with pleasure. My words hadn't troubled him. He relished them. He drew me in even closer to him and took me in deeply with his blue, blue eyes.

It wasn't until later that I was even more aware of the crazy and impulsive thing I had said. Where had those words come from? There had been no thought involved in forming them as they tumbled from my mouth: "I think I breathed you into my soul?"

And I had given no thought to how, once I had breathed him in, I might get him out again. Since then, I've realized I should be more careful about what I say.

My weekend with Giorgio was a dream. He worked most of the time. Giorgio ran the hotel by himself and generally worked most of the day, every day. Yet, every time he took a break, he came to find me where I was reading in the gardens. Smiling, he asked me what I liked to eat, and when I said my favorite foods were green beans and fish, he brought me a fresh green bean salad for lunch and, later, delicious white fish with sauteed zucchini for dinner.

One afternoon, we made a short sightseeing trip to a nearby state park on Giorgio's motorcycle. Every time we stopped at an intersection, Giorgio would reach his hand back to find my bare leg to run his hand along it. Then we were off again, free and flying on his bike. The soft air of the *Castelli Romani* kissed my skin as we flew on the winding park road through the thick, towering trees, a road that climbed up and around the mountainside until we reached the top to have a hazy view of Lazio all the way to the Tyrrhenian Sea.

We made love at night in Giorgio's little house at the bottom of the garden. The sex went from tender to intensely passionate and spicy.

Giorgio asked me shyly in the middle of our lovemaking, "*Ti piace?*" Do you like it?

"Yes" was my immediate answer.

He gasped in surprise. I loved it all.

After the weekend was over, Giorgio said, "Cancel your class in Rome. Stay at the lake for the week instead."

"No, thank you, Giorgio. I would like to return to Rome. I'd like to finish my class."

Giorgio drove me back to the train and asked me to come back the following weekend after class and before I returned to Canada. That was a definite yes.

I attended my language classes in the mornings and strolled the streets of sultry Rome that swelter in the August afternoons. I dreamed of Giorgio night and day. I was consumed with love and radiated joy. I could feel the glow on my face and hear the effervescence in my voice. My smiles stretched my face to capacity. Delighted laughter made my eyes sparkle. The students in my class stared. I was completely lit up.

Outside of class, I began to hang out with the young Portuguese man boarding with the lady surgeon. We passed time together in the baking heat of Rome in the August summer days when the city empties and Romans flee to the mountains or the sea to escape the oppressive city heat. My smart, young friend was in his late 20s. I was now 51. I could sense his pleasure at being with me and an innocent attraction that I simply, gratefully allowed to be. I saw that I was magnetic, captivating, and alive in a way that I had never been before. It seemed to defy the parameters of age. That's what love did to me.

One day, the topic in class was love at first sight. The instructor told us, "Italians believe that falling in love at first sight is the marker of true, lasting love. Italian men especially believe it. They call it *colpe di fulmine*. A lightning strike. Once it strikes you, you are done. You have lasting love."

Or is it, love has you, I wondered, tickled at my own joke? I wondered if I had been struck by lightning. Giorgio told me that seeing me at check-in that first day in the hotel had been a lightning strike for him.

I managed to arrange a wire transfer from my bank. With relief, I picked up my cash from the Western Union location at *Termini*. Thank goodness I had kept my passport in the zippered side pouch of my purse. I would be fine until I got home. Now relaxed, I finished the week of classes, said an exuberant, grateful, and full-hearted goodbye to Rome, and raced to *Termini* to catch the sweet, bumpy rural train back to the lake.

That last weekend with Giorgio was heaven. The hotel property was a beautiful dream of romance and peace that made my spirits soar. Ivy clung to all sides of the building. The surrounding gardens were full of blooming pink hibiscus and red-flowered bottlebrush shrubs. The main terrace from the hotel led to a second shady terrace under a pergola covered with vines, which led down a short stone stairway to a third terrace for sunbathing that overlooked the lake and ultimately to the shady, treed retreat where Giorgio had taken my hand to caress it. From there, a short stairway took you to the water of the lake.

Giorgio would break from his work to surprise me in the garden. He made my heart dance with his shy smiles and tender kisses. After he returned to work, I found a hibiscus petal clinging to my shoe. Hibiscus. A symbol of romantic love and passion.

One day, I found myself standing in the gravel courtyard. I looked around and thought about how magical this place was. It was like being on the set of a romantic movie from the 50s where love was still sweet and whimsical. Yet as beautiful as the ivy-covered hotel, gardens, and view over the lake were, as much as I dreamed of how life-changing it would be to live in Rome and as magical as the connection with Giorgio was, something whispered to me that I didn't belong here. It was not a place for me beyond this holiday. I heard the whisper, and in some place deep inside me, I knew it was true even though I ignored the message. I did not want it to be true.

Giorgio jokingly told me one day, "The hotel looks like paradise, but it is a trap."

He had an ironic sense of humor that he employed often. I sensed he used humor as a mask when there was something concerning him. I can't say how I knew that.

"I am partners in the hotel with my mother, the woman you met at reception the first day. I want to sell the hotel. She does not."

"That's complicated. What would it be like to sell a hotel in Italy right now?"

"Tourism has dwindled this year since the Iceland volcano eruptions. A sale would be difficult."

"So, how long do you think it will take for you to sell the hotel?"

"Oh ... one generation ... two generations ..." Giorgio smiled at me as he joked.

Giorgio was busy that last weekend. I sensed him withdrawing from me a bit. It was only a short impromptu love affair, after all. Wasn't it? As the weekend drew to an end and I prepared to leave, he asked, "Would you like to write to me? We could exchange emails. I will write in English, and you can write in Italian. I wish to improve my English. You could do the same with your Italian. It would be practice for both of us."

"I would love that. Yes, let's write."

On my last morning in Italy, Giorgio drove me to Fiumicino to catch my flight and said, "*Coraggio. Coraggio.*" Courage.

I got the idea that he meant to tell me to have courage in dealing with my marriage. Did he think I was returning to my marriage or going home to end it? No, that marriage was definitely over. In a matter of weeks, I had become someone else.

* * *

I was on top of the world when I returned home. After this trip, I had not just shifted inside. I was completely changed outside. I had dropped 15 pounds and now looked slim and super sexy. My body felt gloriously vibrant. I was luminous. My body and I had been very well-loved.

I stopped to visit a friend, and when she opened the door of her house to greet me, she gasped and said, "You're glowing!" I laughed. I've never felt so alive. I went for an appointment with my doctor, and when he walked into the examining room, he stopped short and said, "You're glowing!" Yes, I was.

I began to notice how people responded to me. I went for a family dinner in a Greek restaurant and wore a sexy aqua dress with a bodice that was cut a bit low and revealed more of my full breasts than I intended. My blonde hair gleamed around my face. My eyes shone with joy. The waiters who served our table looked at me, blinked, and looked away as if the light was simply too bright.

My daughter was moving from her apartment to her boyfriend's house and suggested I take over her place. It was wonderful to be in a new space and away from the family house where my husband was now living. I had a fresh young person's space for my new life. I launched into reading and peering into my future as the new free me I was.

I began writing to Giorgio in Italian. The act of writing to him was pure pleasure. I wrote about my return to Canada and not having a direction for my life. I poured out my heart in beautiful, expressive language, telling him of my morning walks along the city's reservoir, where I would sit and cry with only the ducks and the blue sky to see me. I told him he was mistaken if he had the idea I would try to work things out with my husband. The marriage was over.

Giorgio didn't answer me for a couple of weeks. He replied that he had been on vacation with his son in Sardinia. He was exuberant about hearing from me. He loved my emails. He said he could hear my true voice for the first time. "My voice?' I thought in wonder. I realized something of me came through in Italian as if I were speaking from a deeper place in my soul. That language was an unexpected gift to me. It was wonderful to hear Giorgio's voice through his emails, too. His voice was a little stiff in English. Then, we began writing in Italian only because Giorgio said he was so busy at the hotel that it was hard to find time or energy to write in English. In Italian, our letters bloomed.

Giorgio wrote and told me intimate things about himself and his past, the suicide of his father when Giorgio was five, his lonely childhood, his mostly absent mother who was unhinged by her husband's death, and his summers with his Austrian grandmother who took him to the sea where he developed a love of nature. Ah, an Austrian grandmother. That explained the softness in his Italian looks.

Giorgio spent years at boarding school, then went to university to study business. He said that somehow out of all of his messy childhood, he managed to grow to be a man. Then, there were three marriages.

He loved literature and writing. He thought he would like to be a writer but had too many responsibilities with the hotel and parenting a

15-year-old son from his first marriage to find the time. His greatest desire was to be free of the hotel and to have his life finally to himself.

Giorgio also wrote to me about his *"fidanzata."* He neglected to mention having a girlfriend before. They had been in a relationship for eight years, and their families had gotten close. She wished to live with him and make a life with him. He wished to end the relationship but didn't know how because he didn't want to hurt her.

He wrote about us, how amazing it had been that we met, and how wonderful it would be if somehow we found a path forward together.

A path forward? I wondered.

We got to know each other through those emails. We were both writers. There was so much pleasure in it for us. I loved writing and receiving his letters in Italian. The language oozed romance, and I was a romantic to the core.

Then, the letters got hotter and hotter. They seemed to reach between us and kindle the fire we lit when we were together. I wrote that I wished I could see him again. Ultimately, we made a plan for me to go back to Italy in October for two weeks. He said autumn is the sweetest season in Italy. I didn't need convincing. I booked a flight.

Chapter 6

Il Lago: Falling Star

The morning I arrived back in Italy, Giorgio picked me up at Fiumicino. I searched for his face in the throng of travelers at the exit of customs until I saw him standing quietly, waiting for me. He stepped forward to embrace me lightly, a little shyly. It had been a couple of months since we had seen each other. Our connection had happened so fast and existed for a few weeks physically, only later to grow exponentially in our letters.

Giorgio looked different than I remembered, a little older and a little more subdued. Or was there a quiet intensity? He got my luggage from the carousel and walked me to his truck. He dropped my bag inside and turned to take me in his arms and kiss me hotly and eagerly before I got in. I kissed him with fire in return. My god, I had not forgotten his kisses. Maybe it wasn't shyness I detected when I first saw him. Maybe it was hunger.

He drove from the airport to a small town by a river not far away. He said he would like to take me for lunch before we went back to the hotel. I was completely jetlagged with no sleep on the overnight flight and could hardly eat a bite. We made the short drive back to the hotel, and Giorgio showed me to a beautiful spacious room. He left to take care of hotel business, and I got into pajamas to sleep.

A short while later, he was back, kissing me, undressing me, and reaching inside my pajamas. He brought his hand out from between my legs to reach for my face, and there was blood on his fingertips. We were both startled. The bubble of our lovemaking popped. He said he had to go back to work and was gone in a flash. I was crushed.

Late that night after I had slept for the day, I dressed and went downstairs. I found Giorgio silently working at the front desk. There was no one around. He stood when he saw me, pulled me to him, kissed me, and we stumbled together into a little bedroom through the hallway behind the front desk, his place to rest when working overnight. Quickly, he began undressing me.

"Giorgio," I said, taking my lips from his, "I'm sorry about earlier!"

In answer, he kissed me long and deep as he pulled off my clothes. The sex was a longing unleashed.

In the two weeks that followed, we fit seamlessly together. Giorgio took me with him when he went to the market to purchase supplies for the hotel. I loved looking through the piles of fresh vegetables and scanning cases of famous Italian salamis and cheese that could be bought in Canada but at triple the price. We shopped and talked easily. I told him I was planning a new life of my own.

We drove everywhere in his Toyota Tacoma truck, which he playfully called his bus because he used it to collect guests from the airport. We drove his son, who lived with him, to school in a nearby town. Giorgio calmly navigated his truck through the narrow, winding streets that were definitely not designed for a truck. I just laughed at the delight of it all. All of it!

One day as we were driving back to the hotel, I told Giorgio, "You remind me of someone. I'd like to tell you who, but I don't want to offend you."

He bowed his head in a nod and said gently, invitingly, "Go ahead."

"You remind me of my grandfather." I smirked softly to myself, but Giorgio gave no reaction. He waited for me to continue.

"My grandfather was my favorite person. He was always happy. Every day, he walked through the town where he lived and whistled while he went. He was always whistling. He was friendly with everyone and greeted enthusiastically by everyone everywhere. He was a man who had homesteaded the land in Canada when there was nothing else on the prairie and no one for hundreds of miles around."

Giorgio said, "Not even the Indians?"

I said laughing, "Yes, Giorgio, not even the Indians," which wasn't exactly true, but, oh well. He was adorable and caught up in the exotic idea of early Canada.

"My grandfather was my favorite person."

It was true. There was something about Giorgio that reminded me of him.

Giorgio silently took in my words. He glanced over at me, and his eyes softened. I could feel his heart melt, and it melted with mine. He reached for my face as he drove, cupping my cheek sweetly in his hand, and held it there the rest of our drive back to the hotel. I could have died for the joy of such sweet love.

Giorgio invited his best friend, Joe, to the hotel one evening to meet me. They were already having drinks on the terrace when I came down from my room. Joe's eyes opened wide when he saw me. He took in my blonde shoulder-length hair, my simple, elegant black dress, and the red polish on my toenails. He looked at Giorgio and said in awe, "She's a star that's fallen into the lake."

Giorgio replied, his humor quick, "No, she's the volcano."

Later, I overheard Joe say to Giorgio that I would be a beautiful chatelaine for the hotel. Something pinged in my mind about long-lasting decisions lightly made.

* * *

During those two weeks, as the days extended out and my connection with Giorgio deepened, I had surges of joy and energy so intense that I would simply have to go out and run. There seemed to be only two ways to discharge that massive sky-rocketing energy. Sex. Or running. There was a walking trail that began behind the hotel and ran around the lake. I would appear from my room in shorts and runners and Giorgio would laughingly ask, "Where are you going?"

"For a run."

"Again?"

"Yes, again. I just can't sit still."

I was full of joyous, over-the-moon, in-love energy. I had dropped 15 pounds on my first visit with Giorgio in the summer. This trip, I dropped another 10 within days. I was consumed with happiness. I would run, often twice a day, on the fragrant path that started at the back of the hotel and passed through woods that were still lush green in October. The sun that shone through the foliage sent sprinkles of light to illuminate my path as if showing me the way. I felt myself grow lighter and lighter with every step. Happier and happier as my shoes skimmed the surface of the ground of that light-dappled path. I felt miraculous and magical as my feet took me higher and higher off the ground. For moments at a time that seemed to stretch into longer and longer moments, my feet inexplicably did not touch the ground. I was flying. Flying in sunlight and joy.

Some days, I painted on the terrace with the traveler's watercolor set I had brought with me. On other days, I played the piano in the hotel lobby. Giorgio warned me before I sat on the bench, "The last person who played that piano died right after."

"I don't care about that."

'Okay," he said, laughing. "The truth is, the man was 90."

I laughed and brought my hands to the keys. Giorgio came to sit beside me to listen, appreciate, and tell me his favorite of my songs. A Debussy *Arabesque* was mine. A bluesy arrangement of Loewe and Lerner's "I've Grown Accustomed to Her Face" was his.

One day when I was in my bedroom, I glanced out my window and caught sight of Giorgio walking through the parking area below. He caught sight of me at just the same moment. We smiled at each other, our smiles glowing with the pleasure of our love. I felt like Juliet on her balcony looking down at her Romeo. Everything about Giorgio and I had a sense of timeless, eternally romantic love. When I saw him later by the lobby cappuccino bar, I rushed to kiss him while he beamed with pleasure. We weren't teenagers in love like Romeo and Juliet. Were we? No, we were both adults, and we were both utter romantics. We were a romantic match.

We had afternoon cappuccinos on the terrace when Giorgio took a break from work. Our conversations flowed. Giorgio's father had been from Ravello on the Amalfi coast. He built the hotel and then committed suicide; no one knew why. Giorgio said his father's death was like a wall he could never get beyond. Still, he felt his father's presence always around him in the hotel.

I said, "Your father would have been proud."

Giorgio was so faithfully dedicated to the hotel his father had built and to his family. It was as if he were fulfilling some kind of sacred vow. He did it with his full heart.

* * *

One day over cappuccinos, Giorgio told me about his first marriage.

"We had a baby daughter. She was two years old when she died of brain cancer. That was 18 years ago."

"Oh, Giorgio, I'm so sorry. What was her name?"

He shook his head in answer to my question, no longer able to talk as he choked back the emotion. After a minute, he said, "My wife and I tried to make the marriage work afterward. We had a son to try to take away the pain of the loss of the baby. It didn't work. This is the son who lives with me now because he refuses to live with his mother. Now, I am both father and mother.

Giorgio adored his son. He was 15 years old, sweet and gentle like his father. Often, while Giorgio was working, I would sit in the lobby at a table with his son and write on my laptop while the son did his homework. It was like we were high school friends hanging out. Giorgio would walk by and, laughing with pleasure at seeing us, would ask what we two were doing as if we were teenagers misbehaving.

In the evenings, Giorgio and I would snuggle on the couch of a little room off the lobby where Giorgio watched TV with his son. Giorgio relaxed back on the couch and draped his legs over my lap, not minding if his son noticed. When his son would get up to go somewhere for a few minutes, Giorgio would lean over me and kiss me deliciously. I would simply melt into him. I just couldn't get enough. I wondered what the son thought about me being there. What had Giorgio told him about me, the Canadian woman who had first come as a hotel guest and was now a guest of his father's? I never asked.

Some days, Giorgio and I sat together on another couch in the lobby where Giorgio could be near the reception desk. He read to me in

Italian, his voice smooth and melodious with the love of reading aloud. He read an Italian translation of Lebanese poet-philosopher Kahlil Gibran on love, of all things. It made sense. Giorgio had a curiosity for the profound and the mystical. Yet Gibran's version of love seemed to include the certainty of pain. Pain and love did not fit together. I was certain of that.

Giorgio and I talked about taking a holiday together.

Excitedly, he asked, "Where?"

Tantalizingly, I said, "Morocco."

Smiling with pleasure, he called me "*Amante.*" He said, "You are the sweetest woman."

It was wonderful to be adored.

Giorgio called his mother and his son to join us in the lobby one night and asked me to teach them a Canadian card game. Oh my gosh, he didn't know what he was asking. I love playing cards and am a fierce competitor. There was a trick-taking game for two sets of partners that my family played often. It took most people a while to learn the game. To my astonishment, they picked it up right away. Giorgio partnered with his son. I was stuck with the mother, who really was a bit odd. Giorgio and his son dismissed the mother as not understanding the game when she misplayed a card. The old bird knew exactly what she was doing. She didn't misplay cards. She was cheating madly. To the guys' dismay, the women won. I said nothing about the cheating but smiled to myself.

* * *

Giorgio said softly to me one day over cappuccinos, "The very first time you arrived here, it seemed like a little bird had flown into my hotel, and I just wanted to take care of you. Now ..." He trailed away, looked away for a moment, then looked back at me, "You don't know what you've done for me. I feel like a boy again." He looked at me fully with surprised love in his blue, blue eyes.

"Giorgio," I said in return, "You don't know what you've done for me. You've made me feel alive, like a woman again after my marriage. My marriage was a wasteland."

I stopped. I saw the blank look on Giorgio's face. I realized we hadn't talked about my marriage much, and I could see he had no sense of what I meant or why I left my marriage. It had never mattered between us. I couldn't adequately explain the years of indignity. No suicides or babies who died of brain cancer, just grinding belittlement until I was stripped of enthusiasm for life, and it seemed I had lost myself.

Truly. What did all of that matter at this moment in time? It held no significance for me as I soared in this heaven with Giorgio.

Chapter 7

Florence: Not a Lily at All

One day, Giorgio told me he was going to drive to Milan on family business for a couple of days. An uncle required his help. Someone always needed him.

He said laughing, "Someone always comes to the hotel of Giorgio." Hmm. What did he mean? I let his words echo in my mind.

"You are going to Milan? Wonderful. While you are in Milan, I will go to Florence for two days. I've never been to Florence."

I was excited. I dressed in an elegant black pencil shirt, sheer leopard print silk blouse, black satin jacket and heels. I had a romantic idea of traveling to Florence looking somewhat Italian chic. Giorgio eyed me appreciatively when I appeared ready to go. He drove me to catch the small local train to Rome, and then I took the hour-and-a-half express to Florence. From Florence's Santa Maria Novella station, I took a taxi to Grand Hotel Cavour and checked into my lovely little room where I'd stay for the next two nights.

It was late in the afternoon of a glorious autumn day as I left my hotel to stroll the narrow streets to the famous *Piazza della Signoria* a short walk away. As I rounded a corner into the piazza, the square opened wide. There before me was the replica statue of Michelangelo's *David*. And there was the entrance to the world-renowned Uffizi Museum. I saw the numerous outdoor restaurants lining the sun-soaked square. They were full of people dining and rapt in enthusiastic conversations at their tables. This was truly *la dolce vita* and the Florentines were living it to the full. I strolled past restaurants and glanced at menus, then continued walking into adjoining streets to look in boutiques. I eventually came back to the piazza, where I spied a flower shop and went in.

As soon as I opened the door and stepped inside, the scent of flowery freshness filled my nose. My eyes gravitated to a display of white lilies in a bucket on the floor in front of me. They were so clean, simple, and beautiful. Lilies are known as a symbol of purity, love, and valor. The lily is the accepted symbol of Florence. In Italian, it is *il Giglio Fiorentino* that was chosen as the city's symbol. Turns out, what was taken to have been a lily was not a lily at all but a white iris common to the city. Strange how mistaken appearances can be.

Did these flower shop lilies winking from the bucket in front of me care about symbolism? They seemed only to desire to entice me with their dazzling simplicity. I decided to buy a bouquet for my room. As I was paying, I realized I had nothing to put them in. The lady of the shop guessed my dilemma and offered to lend me a vase to be returned before I left Florence.

I was touched by her thoughtfulness and said warmly, "*Grazia, Grazia.*"

She replied in the Italian formal "*Grazia a Lei.*" Thank you, Lady.

Beautiful manners were an important part of Italian life and a fitting part of the '*giving graciousness*' of Florence.

I left the shop and walked back to my hotel through the cobblestone streets of Florence with my arms full of bright white lilies swaying and flirting from the top of the flower shop wrap. I felt wonderful. Like someone I didn't know. Yet I knew I was completely me as I've never been before. I loved being that me with a fervor.

Back in my room, the lilies with their white heads and black centre eyes seemed to watch me from their spot on my bedside table and joyfully agreed, "You have never been as marvelous as this before."

* * *

The next day, I went shopping and sightseeing. I bought a beautiful hand-made red leather handbag and a silver ring clasping an enormous pale citrine stone, a birthstone, handcrafted by a *Firenze* artist. I walked past expensive designer boutiques toward the famous *Duomo Santa Maria del Fiore* with its egg-shaped dome and intricately patterned black and white stonework. It was astonishingly beautiful. Yet, I couldn't help but think it showed itself best when viewed from a distance to get the full effect. Sometimes, you need distance to see the whole picture.

After the Duomo, I had no other destination in particular. I began wandering deserted side streets until I passed a tea shop. I stopped and decided to go inside to find a gift for my daughter, who loved tea. The shop was quiet and empty of people except for a man behind the counter who greeted me and responded to my request for suggestions of tea my daughter might like. I was standing by the counter considering which of the options to buy when the Tea Man began speaking of my daughter intimately as if he knew her. He talked for a bit, then finished by saying, "Your daughter's mission in life is to teach people the meaning of life."

Okay, I thought, amused. I decided which of the teas I would buy.

The Tea Man continued. He began speaking of my son. Did I tell him I had a son? No.

"Your son is trying to decide whether to pursue a career in music or finance."

A very good guess.

"There is an Apollo influence around your son, which gives him his love for music, food, entertainment, and the good life." Then he added, "Tell your son, whatever he chooses as a career, to remember that money is the shit of the devil!"

I suppressed the laughter that wanted to burst from me. Yet, I had to admit, the whole conversation was very strange. My 18-year-old son was a guitarist and passionate about music, yet had an interest in business. He was wrestling with the choice between exactly those two career paths. I could imagine the wry, skeptical expression on my son's face when I told him of the advice of the Tea Man and the shit of the devil comment.

The Tea Man pulled a deck of divination cards out from under the counter and began to shuffle while occasionally glancing at me. Did I ask him to read my cards? No. Yet, he dealt them, studied them, then looked at me with a hint of a frown and said, "There is a lot of sex in these cards."

After observing me for a moment, he went on in a matter-of-fact way, "You love music and art, but your mission is none of these things. Your mission is to teach people the meaning of love."

He laid down another card and said "Eros" and, with furrowed brows, gazed at me briefly. He looked back to the cards, still frowning at them as if the sex they told of was a little too much and mentioned a man hinted at in the cards.

I said, "Yes, I am here in Italy visiting a man."

The Tea Man stopped, eyed me darkly, and said sternly, "This is not your husband?"

"No." I said, surprised by the energy in his question.

He seemed to take the information in, then his eyes got big as if some awareness came to him. He looked at me fiercely.

"This is a karmic relationship!" Then firmly, "In life, it's a good idea not to make the same mistake twice."

It was like he delivered a sharp rap to my brain. I could not make sense of any of it, but yet I knew that I *knew* exactly what he meant. The only thing that I saw clearly at that moment was that the Tea Man had confused Giorgio and my husband.

Giorgio and my husband? How were they the same? Giorgio was so sweet and tender. My husband was definitely not that. How were they the same mistake? And what was the Tea Man so disapproving of? I didn't really care what some man in a tea shop thought of me, but his words had my mind spinning. I couldn't get clarity on what he had just told me. Something in me knew he was telling me something important.

How were they the same?

I paid for the tea for my daughter and abruptly left the store. My thoughts were swimming. It took me some time to wind my way back to my hotel. When I reached it, I realized I had wandered and found the tea shop in an area of Florence completely different from where I thought I had been. My inner GPS is usually unfailing. Where had I been?

Now back at my hotel, I had no idea where the tea shop was, how I got there, or how to get back to it if I wanted to. I searched my cell phone satellite map and Googled it but couldn't find the tea shop anywhere.

That evening, I showered and dressed to go out to dinner. I had seen an advertisement for a concert of famous opera arias to be held that night. It sounded like the perfect romantic thing to do on an evening in Florence.

As I got ready to go, my mind tried to unravel the Tea Man's meaning. How were they the same, and what was the mistake I should not make twice? I somehow knew it should be obvious, that it was staring me in the face, but my mind wouldn't let me see it. Or was it that my heart wouldn't let me see it? Never mind, I knew I'd get the meaning in time.

I caught a taxi to *Chiesa di Santa Monaca*, the small Renaissance church where the concert was to be held. It was very early, and the doors were still locked when I got there. I noticed a trattoria down the street and decided I had plenty of time to stop for something to eat. A waiter seated me in a small wooden booth and took my order for a simple plate of pasta. I felt wonderful and pretty sitting there in my lovely pink silk blouse with its small ruffles and my face shining with happiness. The waiter served my pasta, calling me the Princess of the Trattoria. I beamed with delight.

I went back to the chapel. Inside, it was small and so narrow that it could only hold 3 or 4 chairs on each side of the central aisle. There were lots of empty seats, and I took one in the front row to have the full view of the concert right in front of me.

A young man and woman in classical opera attire appeared ten feet directly in front of me and prepared to sing. An accompanist sat at the piano and began a vigorous introduction that was so unexpectedly powerful that the music seemed to shake the entire room and penetrate my whole being. The young man and woman began to sing with such beauty that their song thrilled and throbbed in my chest and sent waves of ripples racing across my body.

My eyes opened wide in astonishment. Involuntarily, I turned to look at a woman sitting next to me who had simultaneously turned to look at me with the same expression as mine on her face. The singing and piano accompaniment were gorgeous, astounding, and almost overwhelming. After the first aria and without a word, I got up from my seat, as did the woman beside me and the man with her. We three discreetly moved back two rows. The concert went on, and my shivers of delight continued through each aria.

At the intermission, I turned to speak to the woman beside me and discovered that she and her husband were from Gatineau, Quebec, Canada. What fun to have a chance meeting with other Canadians in Florence at a concert like this. As the music continued, we smiled happily at each other after each aria. When it was over, we said our goodbyes and parted, please by our chance meeting in the glorious city of Florence.

I left the concert feeling as if all the molecules of my body had been shaken loose, and I was floating in bliss. It was a deep, satisfied feeling. I felt cleansed, expanded, and restored by the beauty and power of the music. The Tea Man's words left my mind.

I told Giorgio about the concert when we were back at the hotel. We were having a family dinner in the kitchen as usual. I had come to dinner with damp hair combed back smoothly from my face. It had been a hot fall day and I had gone for a swim in the October-cool water of the lake. I hadn't brought a swimsuit with me, and Giorgio said, "You don't need one. This is Italy." He swept his arms wide as if he wished for me to have all that Italy offered.

So, I went skinny dipping for the first time in my life. I loved the way the water glided silkily over my back, legs, and naked breasts as I swam. The fall day had been hot, and the water was cool, not cold. I could see the bottom of the lake where it receded sharply below me to its volcanic core. As I emerged refreshed from the lake wearing only the sheer, clinging black panties I had kept on out of a modicum of modesty, a man passing by in a canoe ogled me, not bothering to conceal his glances. I didn't care. There was a sweet uninhibitedness to that, nothing to hide or be ashamed of.

Now sitting at dinner with damp hair, I happily told Giorgio about Florence, the concert I attended, the Canadians I met, and the thrill of the music.

"I had goosebumps the entire concert."

"*Pelle d'oca*," Giorgio said. He smiled at me, appreciating my love for the music.

After a moment, he said, "You are leaving in two days. Change your ticket. Stay longer."

I sat still in my chair, not knowing what to say. With my hesitation, Giorgio continued, trailing away.

"Stay if you want to."

Did I want to? Would a little longer be enough? Or would it ruin everything this had been? Something had subtly shifted since Florence. Somehow, I knew it was time to go.

Later, Giorgio's mother, who spoke no English but who had been listening to the conversation at dinner about Florence, took me aside, looked at me directly and suspiciously and asked if Giorgio and I had gone to Florence together. I wondered what Giorgio told her about me. I was surprised to be questioned so bluntly and feigned innocent surprise at her question.

"*A Firenze? No.*"

Later still that evening, as I sat in the lobby with Giorgio's son while Giorgio was busy at reception, his mother stood solidly, almost defiantly, beside him by the desk and looked pointedly at me as if to say, "You will not have him!" Believe me, if she and Giorgio were a package deal, I did not want him. I had a pretty clear idea of just how miserable that would turn out.

Chapter 8

Il Lago: Falling from Heaven

Giorgio and I had one more day. We went for a walk on the path in the woods that began behind the hotel. We were holding hands. I loved the sensuous feeling of his hand holding mine. The sun was bright, and the air was fragrant with a scent blend gifted by the rich nature around us. I was wearing a sleeveless turquoise sports top with a mandarin collar and deep front slit. Other men who approached and passed us on the path eyed my cleavage, and I adjusted my top to close it, but Giorgio said "No" and flicked it free again, smiling at me. I was pleased with his pleasure at having other men appreciate me. Why wouldn't I be confident and happy to look sexy? That was not something that had been okay where I grew up.

As we walked, I told him of my experience with the Tea Man in Florence.

"The Tea Man talked of my son and daughter. Then, he surprised me by talking about us. He said our connection was a karmic relationship."

Giorgio asked, "What's a karmic relationship?"

"I'm not sure." I mused for a moment. "I think we are supposed to learn something."

We continued walking. While he held one of my hands, I brushed the tops of the tall waving grass growing along the path with my other hand. I stopped and took a blade of grass to make a whistle between my thumbs the way my grandfather had taught me. Giorgio looked at me keenly.

"I haven't heard anyone do that for a very long time. My grandmother used to do that when we were at the sea when I was a boy."

He looked at me as if trying to decipher some meaning that was hidden from him. We walked a bit farther.

"Giorgio, you've always joked that you were my springboard to a new life and my guru. Maybe I am your oracle," I said, teasing. He caught his breath. How I loved him. I wanted him to be more than a springboard.

"Giorgio, I adore you," I said, laughing, and kissed his face.

We turned around on the path to head back to the hotel. There was no one around now, and the woods were dense. Giorgio stopped to kiss me. He looked at me deeply as if he were trying to comprehend something, thoughtfully taking me in with his bright *occhi blu*. So blue. I ducked into a secluded spot in the trees, laughingly pulled my top over my head, and flung it playfully from me. These were the woods where I first felt the sensation of flying. I wanted to fly with Giorgio.

Giorgio followed me, waving his hands in protest and saying, "Oh, no-no," but stopped, looked at me, then began helping me with my clothes, peeling off his and backing me into a tree. There in the dusky darkness of those magical woods with small shafts of sunlight shooting down towards us through the branches like falling stars, we made love as a culmination of everything we were together at this beautiful, blissful moment in life.

"You are the sweetest woman," he said gently. "You are a woman who should be loved."

We went to Frascati for dinner that night. Our last night. We ran into Giorgio's ex-wife and the mother of his son in a restaurant. He told me who she was, said he would speak to her for a moment, and went over to where she sat with friends. She looked up at him as he appeared and stood respectfully beside her chair. She looked at him with contempt. I knew what contempt was. My blood boiled. How dare she treat him that way? Well, I didn't know her or know what their marriage had been. So many things I did not know.

Giorgio and I finished dinner and took a *passeggiata*, the Italian post-dinner walk. We walked through the town that was filled with the laughter of people socializing on a Friday night. Older couples strolled, families laughed together, children ran, and teenagers eyed each other flirtatiously. Giorgio and I walked up toward the famous *Villa Aldobrandini* above Frascati. From a balustrade in the park of the villa, we looked down upon the town, which was a scene of glowing, flickering lights in the night. The evening had turned autumn chilly, and Giorgio pulled me close to him and inside his heavy fall coat. He spied his son with friends down in the town below us, teenagers goofing around. He watched them delightedly for a while.

"Giorgio, are you spying on your son?" I poked him in jest.

Giorgio laughed. He adored his son. He brushed off my comment and said, "Let's go find him."

We went back down into town through crowds of bustling people until we caught up with Giorgio's son, who looked at me with shy, gentle eyes and greeted me with a kiss on each cheek. My heart swelled in gratitude. The wonder of that sweet son of Giorgio's, so much like his dad.

After Giorgio and I strolled a while, we stopped in a quiet corner of a narrow deserted street and sat on a low stone retaining wall in darkness except for the saffron yellow glow of a single street light. He drew me to him and wrapped me inside his coat again, so close and warm, away from the chill of the evening. In that silent, deserted place with both of us snuggled inside his coat, neither of us speaking a word, Giorgio began to rock me in his arms.

I wondered, "Who is he trying to soothe? Me? Or him?"

* * *

The last morning, I woke up in Giorgio's house in the garden and knew I would be leaving in a few hours. I walked out of the bathroom wearing only my lavender bra and panties, and there was Giorgio in front of me quietly dressing. He softly spoke some small practicality of my departure, but I couldn't hear him. I was suddenly overwhelmed by the distress of knowing I was leaving. I didn't want to leave him! I couldn't leave him! Tears started in my eyes, and shockingly, I felt on the verge of a tantrum. A tantrum is so unlike me. I flicked him petulantly with the shirt in my hands. He said, "Don't be a baby." It stopped me cold. I would not ruin this with a scene.

I dressed and emerged from his house. I could feel the sorrow pale on my face, and the joy drained from my eyes as if the tears had put out a light. My hair was tousled and unbrushed, which didn't matter because it was a cool, gusty morning, and the wind tore at my hair. I pulled my sweater closer and made my way up to the hotel via the terrace. I could see Giorgio's mother through the hotel windows as she walked toward reception. I changed direction and wandered in the gardens for a bit, then entered the hotel as if I had been out for morning air. Giorgio's mother looked up at me cooly from the desk. There was a brief *buon giorno* between us. Of course, she knew.

Giorgio called me outside to the front of the hotel. He took a pot with a blooming cactus and a trowel from the back of his truck and said, softly inviting, "Come. Help me."

We took the plant and knelt in front of the flower bed beside the entrance of the hotel. Taking my hands in his, together we planted the cactus in an empty space in the bed. It was a pretty blooming cactus, and I lightly brushed my hand along the tickly points of its needles. Giorgio said, "No!" worried I had pricked myself and lightly brushed my hand, but I smiled and held my palm up toward him. Look. No marks. He smiled gently back at me and said again, as if amazed, "You are the sweetest woman."

We finished planting the cactus. I noticed there were other plants in that flowerbed, and an unanticipated thought whispered into my mind. Some men have notches on their belts. Giorgio had flowers in his garden.

It was time for a last drive to Fiumicino. We were silent as we started out. To make small talk, Giorgio brought up the topic of his friend Joe whose wife had finally given him an ultimatum. Joe had to choose to leave his girlfriend of ten years or leave the marriage.

"You know, this thing of Joe having a girlfriend that everyone knows about, including the wife, is an Italian stereotype."

Giorgio protested passionately, "No! There are lots of nice people in Italy."

"I know that. I'm just saying ..."

We were quiet again for a bit, and suddenly, Giorgio looked at me, holding his open palm upward and gesturing in a gentle arc toward me, indicating the space between us, "This love ..."

He stopped for a moment and then said like he was summoning the will to say something difficult but necessary, "I can't."

He paused. I waited.

"I don't have my legs under me," he said in a rush of words. "I don't know where I'm going. And I've made so many mistakes before. I don't want to make any more mistakes. I don't even think I want to love again." And after a pause, he said more softly, "Maybe the truth is, I'm afraid to love again."

"I know," I said gently, filled with knowing.

"I can't see my horizon."

"And I have nothing but horizon."

We rode in silence again until we reached Fiumicino. Giorgio took my bag from the truck and came to stand in front of me on the bustling sidewalk outside the terminal. He stepped close, took my face between his hands, and began kissing me, passionate and hungry kisses like he wanted to draw me in and keep me inside of him. I melted with his kiss, not caring about people passing by or my impending flight but wished only to stay with him forever. When he pulled away, he looked deeply into my eyes as if trying to fill me with something he couldn't express but wanted me to fully understand.

"Thank you! Thank you for everything."

Then he was gone. I couldn't watch him go. I turned toward the terminal doors pulling my bag behind me. I heard him call my name. I turned back to see him standing and looking at me through the driver's side window, where he paused before getting into his truck. He was waving goodbye, smiling a dazzling smile, his face filled with love and his white hair lit by the aura of the glowing sun behind him. I put on a big smile and flamboyantly blew him a kiss, then turned to continue into the airport.

I fought tears as I waited at my gate for my flight home. Once airborne, I felt I couldn't breathe. I felt trapped and compressed in the hollow tube of the aircraft. I wanted to claw the wall beside my window seat, to break through and jump from the plane. I had to get out!

I was fully ready to jump. I didn't care about the consequences. The urgent need to stop flying away was a need that scared me more than the horrifying terror of falling helplessly from the sky. I struggled with something wild and desperate inside me, but there was no escape. Wretchedly, I shrank into my seat. I cried behind my dark glasses all the way home.

PART II

A Hard Landing

Chapter 9

Calgary: Clipped Wings

Winter began. Gone was the glorious exhilaration of summer. Gone was the gentle abundance of autumn, the sweetest season. Gone. Winter could not be resisted or denied. It spread a dormant cloak over the world, calling for the ending of a blooming season before the time came to blossom again. My letters to Giorgio slipped into a quiescence, too. A rest after seasons of splendor.

Giorgio and I continued writing for another five months after I returned from Italy. I wrote to him about wanting to jump from the plane after leaving him that last day at Fiumicino. He wrote back. He felt terrible. He thought he had hurt me. He thought he had done a bad thing. I could hear the dismay in his words.

"No, Giorgio! You have not done a bad thing," I wrote. "The time we spent together was wonderful, and I will never see it as bad."

My head was full of memories of blissful, romantic days of being with him, basking in loving him and being loved in return. My body remembered it all, too, the sensual beauty of the lake, Rome, the hedonistic sun, the wonder of Giorgio's touch and love shining in his blue, blue eyes. Eyes do not lie. It had been a beautiful love. I had an email inbox full of passionate Italian love letters. Everything about knowing

Giorgio had been a miracle. It brought me back to life and then some. Now, it seemed those days were gone, like the petals of a summer rose that dropped after the bloom.

Over the next months, our letters stayed within the realm of friendship. So many things remained unspoken, yet unwritten. We shared stories of Christmas traditions and wished each other well for the new year. In January, I went to a personal development weekend in Chicago. I wrote to Giorgio and told him it would have been fun to talk together about it. I said that I was sure he would have found it fascinating. He wrote back, "I miss you."

Ah. It was the first time he gave a hint of his feelings for me since I left. The love and longing of many months exploded from the winter where it had been sleeping in me. I wanted him. He knew it. He must have known it. I told him I wanted to jump from the plane when I left him. Finally, he could say he missed me.

He said it, and, of course, I knew it was true. In my mind, I could see him walking through the hotel where the winter winds of Italy cooled the passion of summer. I could perceive how very empty the hotel was for him now that I was not there.

In his email, he said, "I remember how we were. I remember our love in the woods. Maybe you have someone new in your life now."

My jubilation was boundless. My reply to him was very direct. "Giorgio! You miss me!" My joy could not be restrained. "No, Giorgio, there is not someone new in my life. Your song is the only song in my heart. I cannot have two songs because, for me, that only makes noise. There is only your song."

It was a song demanding to be sung. Sung, heard, and answered.

"Giorgio, I want someone present in my life, not a dream man far away across an ocean. I will feel the same about you always. Even if I don't see you again until we are 100 years old. And if we ever see each other again, I will throw off my clothes and love you again the way we did in the woods behind the hotel."

What he would make of my words, I couldn't say, but I had to tell him. You may say my letter to him was too much after his simple "I miss you." You may say he was afraid to love, and now I would scare him off. You may say that if I had been less direct, more patient and played my cards right, he may have eventually said yes to love. Or you may say it was obvious I was saying goodbye. I considered all of those things, too.

Giorgio had told me he was afraid to love again, and in this moment of my life, I was fearless. I could not play games or try to convince him to choose love. Nor could I twist in the agony of waiting for him. He was thousands of miles away across an ocean. To sit, pine, and wait for him when he said he didn't want to love again would have been pathetic. I was only interested in him knowing the truth of my love for him.

There could be no doubt about what my letter was saying. "I love you and will love you always, but I cannot live only loving a dream." He had a choice. Giorgio, what will your answer be? Will we go forward, or will we end?

I had written what was true for me. He would choose what was true for him. I knew his capacity for love. I knew his heart. It was glorious. Would he choose that? He had to be the one to choose love now. Or not. I realized that's the thing about mature love or what you hope mature love will be. You have to be able to love and see the full truth at the same time. You have to know your truth and allow the other person their truth, even if that means letting that person go.

From some wise place inside of me, I knew that. Yet my longing for him plagued me after I sent the email. I ached for him, body and soul, and yearned for him to write back to me and say, "Let's see where this love between us goes."

There was a stark difference between what I knew was the truth and what I longed for. There were many times I knew. I knew from the start, from the day I stood in the courtyard of his hotel, that the life he lived was not for me and there would not be a future for us. Yet here I was, spinning in the turbulence between my head and my heart like I was on some mad ride at the fair. The clear, sensible me knew that I had to let him go. The yearning heartsick me rebelled vehemently at the thought.

The voice of the Tea Man in Florence came to me. At some point, I saw he had been right. "Do not make the same mistake twice." Finally, it became clear. Do not try to make a relationship work with a man who doesn't come to you freely and gladly, who doesn't truly want to make a life with you, who doesn't have the courage to say yes to love. That man will become more challenging as time goes on. I tried to make a marriage work with a husband who really did not want the marriage and all that went with living with a partner. He did not want to let me inside the protective walls he created around himself to lock away his pain. I had a strange sense now that after the honeymoon bliss was gone, Giorgio would have been the same.

Giorgio had been clear on our last drive to Fiumicino that love was not the thing he really wanted for himself. He tried love and had three marriages end. There were sorrows he had not resolved. He talked of a need to be free to find himself. That was more pressing for him than falling in love again. He was right to claim that.

I tried to be thankful Giorgio had been honest with me. I rationalized to try to move on. It didn't stop me from hearing the tone of his voice passing me in the voices of people on the street. I caught glimpses of his hands, his face, the shape of his body, and a brief hint of his blue eyes in people I encountered. I saw him everywhere, and he was not there. I waited for an answer to my email. None ever came. I knew there would not be another email.

I cried for a month, knowing it was over. I grieved for the loss of that love and the bliss of the dream, a dream so intoxicating it left a sick, hungover feeling in the waking and a wish to never have had the dream, no matter how beautiful it was. Did I wish I had not had it? No. I only wished to have it still.

I laid on my bed when I was too heart-sick to move, then tossed and flailed because the physical pain of not being able to touch him was excruciating. This could not be the end! I wanted him so badly. Why, oh why, had I breathed him in?

I discovered that the thrill of falling in love in middle age was no different than the rush of falling in love at 20. If anything, it was even more powerful. Had maturity brought me a fuller knowledge of love? I hoped it would give me a better ability to cope with the loss of love. It didn't.

At some point, the memory of my dream of the Italian man in the hotel on the Tyrrhenian Sea appeared in my mind. It startled me. It was as if it had been a premonition of Giorgio. The dark-haired Italian man, the hotel, the teenage son, and the sea became, in actuality, a white-haired Italian man, a hotel, a teenage son, and a lake. Had I conjured

Giorgio? Had I foreseen that future? Was it some whisper from the universe about an experience I required to open me to life in a greater way?

I would like to say I chose to use the experience to open to life, that I moved on easily and was grateful for what I had experienced. No, I tormented myself. I had an endless longing and nagging thoughts that everything I had experienced with Giorgio in Italy was too beautiful, too uncanny, too magical and that I had flown too close to the sun. My dismal, distressing fall from that heaven was a result of vain over-reaching. Where those thoughts came from, I can't say. It seemed like a scolding from some dim, faraway past.

* * *

After a month of crying, I knew I had to pull myself together. I had to do something to move ahead with life, despite the misery that churned inside of me. I put on a happy face. I applied all the logic, physical exercise, and affirmations I could come up with. I looked for something I could put on my calendar to move me forward. My horizon was wide open. I felt a little lost. I was like a teenager on the brink of launching into adult life with no clue of what that meant or how to get where I was going, a teenager at 52 with no clue of what to choose for my life. A teenager has a youthful innocence and an optimism that carries them forward, even when they have no clue. I was a very youthful, optimistic person. I could start again and make a new life for myself. The gift of the mature me was that I knew that starts by taking one step. And then another.

I happened upon an article in a magazine offering a unique holiday idea of taking a class creating mosaics in Ravenna, Italy. Perfect! I might have had to give up Giorgio, but I would not give up Italy. I would drown out my longing and his song with new music. I found the school website and booked a class to start in May in a little over a month.

I made a trip to my doctor to address the matter of occasional spots of blood during sex. It was a polyp. The wait time for an appointment with a specialist and treatment for any kind of woman's issue in Calgary was more than a year. I would not wait that long. Sex was a joy I would not forgo again. I found a private hospital in Vancouver that could remove the polyp quickly and easily. I booked an appointment and set up a trip to go. I called my sister, who lived in Vancouver, to ask if I could stay with her for two days to recover as I had been instructed. Everything was set. I had a plan. A first step.

My Vancouver Sister was in the middle of a huge falling out with my brother and his wife, who also lived in Vancouver. It started with a big blowup between them in the fall around something my sister's guy said to my brother's wife over a dinner the two couples were having in a restaurant. My brother's wife had been insulted. My brother was furious and yelled at my sister, demanding an apology from her guy. My sister had called me crying while I was in Italy. Giorgio had been tickled when I got the call because he liked the idea that he was not the only one who got called by people in need.

I told my father that I was going to Vancouver. Dad knew of the fight between my brother and sister and asked me to see what I could do to help them resolve their differences.

"You are the oldest woman in the family. It's like you stand in your mother's shoes."

My mother had died in a car crash 24 years earlier. Yes, I was not just the oldest woman in the family but the oldest sibling. It seemed to me that my dad had given me a commission. I was indifferent about following through. I had personal reasons for my trip, but I would see what I could do. Once in Vancouver, I phoned my brother to let him know I was in town and see if we could get together. To my surprise, after a few minutes of talking, he hung up on me. I was on my way to the hospital and put it out of my mind. Back at my sister's house after surgery, I made a second call to him, thinking we would clear things up.

The call was a disaster. My brother's wife got on the phone and shrieked at me.

"I know what's going on. You've come to Vancouver to connive with your sister to break up our marriage."

My brother roared, "You need to be accountable for what you are doing."

The call exploded in my world and completely blindsided me. My heart was pounding. I felt blood from the surgical site begin to flow.

Shaking, I cut the call short. I had never had a problem with my brother before. My brother was a gentle, funny, wonderful guy. How was this happening? How could he think I would have any thought of interfering in his marriage? The whole incident was completely shocking. In my distress, I called Dad, who was horrified he might have gotten me into the middle of the mess between my brother and sister. Later that night, my brother called my sister, whom he had not talked to for eight months, and in an hour on the phone, did a hate-filled attack on me. My sister repeated every word to me. The words burned.

What the hell just happened? It was like reality had warped. It made no sense.

When I got home, I sent a text to my brother to say that I thought there must be some misunderstanding. If we talked, I was sure we could clear things up. Could he call when he was finished work? I waited for a response and got none. My trip to Ravenna was in a week. There was nothing more I could do.

Chapter 10

Ravenna: Putting Pieces Together

I flew to Europe and landed at Gatwick airport in London at midnight for an unappealing six-hour layover before the final leg of travel to Ravenna. I had barely exited the plane and turned off airplane mode on my phone when a text came in from my brother. All it said was, "Stay out of my marriage!!"

I was dumbfounded, tired from traveling, and unable to register this text as his response to my previous one. It was all incomprehensible. I took it hard, layered as it was over the loss of Giorgio. I sat in Gatwick crying with my sunglasses on at midnight in an airport that was silent, lonely, and almost empty of passengers. I was alone and crying again behind dark glasses.

At 6 a.m., I flew to Bologna and then took a train to Ravenna. The day was gloomy and dull, with pouring rain when I arrived. Was the Universe trying to match my misery? I took a taxi to the bed and breakfast I had booked in the home of a woman who lived on the second floor of a quaint older apartment building wedged between other buildings and shops on the street. The bed and breakfast was only a short distance from the mosaic school. After checking in, I went for a walk in the heavy rain to find the location of my class. I wandered the bland, narrow streets of Ravenna that seemed nothing like the romantic Italy I had known. Why had I thought it would be a good idea to come here? Something in my inner compass was not working.

The next morning, I arrived at the mosaic school as the session began. Ten students were participating. They were from various places in Europe, and, to my surprise, three of the ten were women from Toronto. They were women who worked for a newspaper and had come together at the suggestion of the woman who was the apparent leader of the three. We smiled and acknowledged each other. Canadians in Italy.

The instructor was a widely respected mosaic expert and artist. The history of mosaics and the lessons she gave were interesting. The topic was entirely new to me. Normally, that is exactly the kind of thing that excites me, but I was jet-lagged and profoundly unsettled by my brother's text. I sat silently at my table and took in the class, subdued and turned inward.

The rain continued all that day and the next. I walked to class each day through the cold early spring rain, huddled under my umbrella. I attended class half-heartedly. In truth, I was feeling completely wretched. After two days of class, any desire I had to stay in Ravenna and continue the course evaporated. I hated Ravenna. I was just going through the motions in the class. I knew I was a little depressed. I loathed the direction my life had taken. I wanted to go home. A talk with my daughter and an email from an aunt later that day got me past my distress. Fine. I would see the week through.

The next day after class, I went by myself for a drink at a neighborhood café bar called *I Fratelli*, "The Brothers." I sat down at a table on the small, cramped patio squeezed between the sidewalk and the street and under an awning that kept off the chilling rain. The café was packed with customers, almost all men. The "*Fratelli*," I guessed.

I had just begun sipping my wine when a waitress brought me a second glass and said with a tone of dry distaste in her voice and a tip of her head toward a man standing and looking at me from a short distance away, "It's from *that* man over there."

The next moment a slim, short, well-dressed man with steel grey hair and wearing a grey designer windbreaker and dark blue jeans appeared at my table. He raised his glass of wine to greet me with a toast and gave me a well-polished yet slightly silly smile. I smiled weakly and thought, "Oh my god," exasperated by his pretentious intrusion.

At that moment, my phone rang. I ignored the man and took the call. My daughter was calling to see if I was feeling better. Yes, I was better. That was mostly a lie. I was just going through the motions until I could go home. But I didn't want her to worry.

When I hung up, the man was still there. He raised his glass again, persistent if nothing else, and said, "*Sono Gian.*"

I gave the Italian version of my name, *Cinzia*, and he indicated a seat at my table by way of request to sit. I nodded. I was really not interested in this man coming into my space, but there was absolutely nothing good going on in my life at the moment. A distracting conversation with a stranger was better than nothing.

Gian leaned forward toward me eagerly. I shrank back in my seat and began to converse with him, half-interested, even speaking with a cool annoyance, hoping it would deter him. It didn't. Gian spoke no English, so we began speaking in Italian. That, at least, was fun. What the hell. If nothing else, this was a chance to practice my Italian.

We talked for a while. Yes, I was Canadian. I was only here for a week for a course in mosaics. He smiled and almost swaggered at me. I had the impression he enjoyed the idea of being a bit of a playboy. He struck me as amusing in a boyish kind of way. I finished my glass of wine, and when he offered another, I thanked him and said I was ready to go back to where I was staying. Before I left, he invited me to go for aperitifs with him the following evening at 5 p.m. I wasn't really interested in seeing more of him, but with my tanking spirits and the need for something to get me through the week, I said yes.

The next day in class, I began a mosaic project of reproducing a small 10x12 section from the ceiling of the *Basilica di San Vitale*. The section contained three simple pears on a background of green leaves and a deep blue sky. Instructions were given for the task ahead, and I spent the rest of the class picking through *tesserae,* or quarter-inch square ceramic tiles that were separated into containers by color. It was a quiet, meditative task of choosing the correct shades of greens, whites, browns, and blues that I required. It soothed me. The day of class passed quickly.

I returned to the room in my bed and breakfast and changed my clothing to go out. The sky was still cloudy, but the rain had finally let up, thank God. I walked to *I Fratelli* and found Gian waiting for me.

He led me out along a wide pedestrian street past shops and cafés. We chatted. World Cup Soccer was on. There was lots of enthusiasm around us. Gian was all smiles. He walked beside me, then walked backward in front of me to look at me while we walked, then returned to walk beside me. He was so excited he almost bounced around me like a happy puppy.

Gian took me to a chic, dimly lit lounge. We sat and ordered drinks. I was starting to feel pleased by his high-spirited attention and delight at being with me. We talked and then began laughing a lot. He had a great mischievous sense of humor. I told him of the end of my marriage and the problem with my brother. Leaning across the table toward me, he said in a playful, conspiratory voice, "Sisters-in-law are always the worst."

He was turning out to be rather cute and funny.

Gian told me, "I have a daughter who is pregnant and having a boy. It's the thing I look forward to most in life, being a grandfather and taking my grandson to the piazza to play soccer with neighborhood boys. I will sit and talk with the other grandfathers while the children play."

He told me, "I have a wife who has a big, important job with the government. She makes lots of money. I am planning to retire from my job when summer comes. And I have a girlfriend."

Did I care? Not really. But he was amusing.

What was I doing with a married man who had a girlfriend and who I found so very unappealing at our first meeting but now rather liked? It was as if I were in some strange universe as a new me that didn't seem like me and certainly was not me as the good little Catholic girl or committed wife I had been. In the low state I was in, had something been unlocked? Or was there something I had lost?

Gian got up to speak to someone at the bar. When he came back to the table, he came up behind me and softly, silkily kissed the nape of my neck. His breath was warm and electric on my skin. Another erogenous zone. How could I be a 52-year-old woman and not know these things? Obviously, Italian men knew.

I froze in surprise at the kiss. Gian sat down again, smiled softly, and a little shyly at me.

"Will you go with me for lunch tomorrow at the sea? There is a restaurant I like that I will take you to?"

I didn't answer at first as I pulled myself out of the impact of the kiss. For a moment, I silently mused on the idea of seeing him again and having lunch with him at the sea.

"Gian, I won't be able to have lunch. I have class during the day."

He shrugged and casually said, "Okay," as if it didn't matter to him if I turned down his offer and chose to go to a boring class rather than a lovely lunch at the sea.

"I will wait for you at *I Fratelli* tomorrow at noon. If you come, we will go. If you don't, that's okay."

* * *

The next morning, the rain was gone. The sun came out in dazzling glory. I went to class and began arranging my *tesserae* in my frame, returning to the tile containers to pick through them to find just the right shade of tile I needed. When we broke for lunch, I told my instructor that I had been invited to lunch at the sea. As the rain had stopped, I didn't want to miss the chance for a day of sun and sea. I would not return for class in the afternoon. She nodded. It was okay.

When I arrived at *I Fratelli*, I saw Gian standing inside in the middle of the cafe, waiting for me. He was not what you might call a beautiful Italian man, but he was certainly very well-dressed. He was average-looking, short of stature, with a slightly square, stony-looking face and cool grey eyes. Yet, when he caught sight of me, his eyes lit up. In English, he called out, "Beautiful girl!" to call me over to him. Well, he knew something in English. The playboy! Still, I smiled at him as he led me out to his BMW SUV.

Gian drove rapidly through the streets of Ravenna that wound so maddeningly I lost all sense of direction. From the outskirts of the city, he continued a short distance farther and pulled over at a seaside restaurant with an outdoor patio overlooking the Adriatic.

We were seated on the terrace that was filled with potted plants and surrounded by a white plaster half-wall over which we could see the expanse of the beach leading down to the sea. Gian ordered our lunch of grilled fish and vegetables. He said he would have only one glass of wine for himself and mysteriously left his comment dangling.

I sat at the table and savored the light breeze that played with my hair, the view of the sand glowing in the sunshine, and the stretch of the broad deep-aquamarine sea that disappeared to the horizon where it blended with the dark blue sky. It felt wonderful and healing to be sitting in the sun by the sea. I let the beauty of the day lift me.

After we finished our meal and sat sipping our wine, unexpectedly Gian said, "Kiss me," then quickly, shyly retracted, "You don't have to."

I thought, *Italian men! So forward. Well, I guess if you don't ask, you don't get*. And another thought, *He's not as confident as he pretends*.

I said, "I will kiss you."

I leaned forward across the table full of empty dishes. His mouth landed hard on mine. What was he trying to prove? I kissed him back softly, determinedly soft, feeling the unexpected loveliness of his mouth on mine, and drew him into a melting kiss. After a moment, I leaned back in my seat and smiled a sunny, pleased smile at him. He looked surprised about the kiss. I had a sudden sense of some power that I never realized I had before. Or was it control? I liked the feeling of power, not powerlessness. Maybe I need it. Whatever it was, this could be fun.

After lunch, we took a walk from the restaurant across the beach and along the sea. There was a soft breeze and spring sun to warm the cool air. Gian put his arm around me as we walked along the low seawall that stretched far out into the calm of the water. When we reached the end of the seawall, Gian drew me into him and kissed me again, beautifully this time, his hands beginning to move to touch and caress me. We walked back to shore, his arm still around me, and got into his BMW to return to Ravenna. When we reached town, he asked softly, "Can I come to your room?"

I said, "Yes."

I had warmed to him. Yes. Suddenly, I wanted to be with him.

I didn't know how my B&B host would feel about an unregistered guest in my room, but there was no one around. Gian and I snuck into my little room on the second floor of the house at the very top of the apartment building. Once the door to my room was closed, he began undressing me, throwing off his clothes, then his mouth was between my legs. He took me to the bed, covering me with his body, embracing me, moving with me, and calling me *"Tesoro, Tesoro"*—darling, darling —while we had hot sex in that sweet little attic room with the roof that sloped above the bed.

Afterward, I went into the bathroom, and he followed me, grasped me from behind as I stood at the sink, and pressed into me again, kissing my neck. After a moment, he stopped, embraced me more gently, and said, "This is why I only have one glass of wine. More wine, no sex."

He held me close and caught a glimpse in the mirror of us together.

"We look good together."

We did. His steely greyness against my sunny blondeness. Our nakedness with him tanned and me fair. I liked how we looked together, too, a study in contrasts, but somehow we made a complementary set. Like salt and pepper. I liked how I looked, someone new, someone I was only getting to know, someone dazzling and pretty.

We snuck back out of the B&B. Again, no one was around.

The next night Gian and I met at *I Fratelli* again. With Gian's arms firmly around me and my hands clasped tightly in his, we had drinks and the typical Italian aperitif snacks. He vibrated with excitement to be with me.

"You are leaving in a few days. Don't go!" he said fervently.

"Yes, I am going to Pisa," then added a thought, "Come with me!" I said playfully.

He laughed with delight at my request and said regretfully, "I have to work."

"Tell them you have to go out of town. Tell them you have to visit a sick uncle."

Gian burst out laughing. "Everyone at work knows all my family. I have no sick uncles."

We smiled at each other, enjoying the risqué idea of sneaking away together. Ravenna was a small town. Of course, everyone knew each other. Like the men I saw socializing each day at *I Fratelli*. Like the waitress who said "that man" with distaste as she delivered his gift of wine the first day I met him under the rain-pocked canopy on the patio. Like the waitress we now noticed scrubbing the floor nearer and nearer to our table inside the café. She seemed to have one ear cocked.

"Gian, look at the waitress. Are we being spied on?"

We laughed together at the titillation of our affair. Yet I felt the way he eagerly held my hand. There was something he needed. Something I needed.

Gian asked me if I would like to take a drive with him tomorrow after class to have a late lunch in Cervia, a small city a short distance down the coast. Of course.

The next afternoon, he picked me up at *I Fratelli* and handed me into his SUV.

He said provocatively, "I have a surprise for you."

He drove again around the winding streets of Ravenna until he stopped outside of an apartment building.

"This is the apartment of a good friend who's at work right now. I have a key."

He led me up a half-flight of stairs and into a small one-bedroom apartment. We were barely in the door when clothes started coming off. Gian gasped when he saw me in my sky-blue bra and panties. He moaned, grabbed my hand to pull me into the bedroom, and pushed me onto the bed. The sex was intense. I wanted it to be. I asked him for more. The heat increased. It was delicious. There is something wonderful about the uninhibited enthusiasm Italian men have for sex. Or maybe I had been married for a long time and didn't know men at all. I loved the joyful, unabashed lustiness of Gian. And me.

We dressed, Gian straightened his friend's bed, and we got back into his SUV to continue the drive down the coast to Cervia.

Gian told me, "Cervia is a holiday spot for lots of rich people from Milan."

Its central core was definitely upscale. It had a classy, affluent Rodeo Drive vibe.

"You should come to Cervia to live, get an apartment, and I will come to you."

Live in Cervia and wait for him to come to me? As what? Another girlfriend? I was not interested in that at all. I wasn't even interested in seeing more of him beyond the time we were spending together right now. I loved being where I was with him now. Nothing more.

Gian parked the SUV and said we would have lunch. We walked

along the boat-lined canal that extended from the sea, then stopped at an outdoor café for fish and chips and wine.

"Just one glass of wine for me," he said, smiling. He handed me one of the paper napkins with the name of the restaurant on it. "Keep this so you can remember after you go back to Canada."

Not likely I would forget.

We finished lunch and took a stroll along the canal from the sea, past expensive boats floating on water glinting with sunshine. I was suddenly intoxicatingly happy. The breeze tossed my blond hair catching the light of the sun shining brilliantly around us. I smiled radiantly at Gian, threw my arms wide and told him, "I feel like a piece of sunshine. *Un pezzo di sole.*"

Gian gave me an aching look, pulled me close, and kissed me passionately. He took my hand to run it down his shirt from his chest to the top of his blue jeans, then stopped and unexpectedly said to me, "You were married for 25 years. Things are not the same as they were before. Now, when you have lovers, you have to be safe," he said looking into my eyes. "It's okay. You are safe with me."

My heart fluttered out to him. His caring filled me with gratitude to be in this place with him in this brief passing moment in my life.

We got back in his SUV and began driving out of town.

"My mother lives in Cervia in a nice senior home I found for her."

He looked at me sadly, almost apologetically, and said, "She's my mother."

Oh, I know something about Italian men and their mothers, I thought.

He said, "When I retire in the summer, I'm going to do nothing, absolutely nothing but lay like a rock on the beach."

"Gian, you really don't want to do that, do you? There are a lot more things you could do with your life."

"No, I will just be a rock on the beach."

He pulled the SUV into a deserted roadside park and drew me on top of him as he sat in the driver's seat. Lips connected, clothing came loose, skin met skin. The skin on his chest was smooth and dappled with freckles from the sun. Beautiful skin like flecked Italian marble. I ran my lips over him, savoring him while he moaned under me.

Afterward, I said teasingly, "Ah, Gian. Twice today. So. It's not the wine."

We continued the drive back to Ravenna. Somewhere along the way, I said, "Gian, don't be a rock on the beach. You could start a business. Maybe open a restaurant. You could travel. There are lots of wonderful things to do in the world."

I paused, then turned in my seat to face him directly and continued, "My father is 82 years old. He says when he looks in the mirror, he asks himself, "Who is that old man?—*Chi é quest'uomo vecchio?*"

Immediately, Gian said, as if struck by clear understanding, "Ah! I see! You only look old. On the outside."

"Yes, Gian. Yes!"

Wouldn't my Catholic Dad have been shocked to know his life experience taught something valuable to an Italian playboy his daughter was having an affair with?

I reflected on the juxtaposition of my dad and my illicit lover, of strict Catholicism and the taboo pleasures of an affair. In Italy, I encountered more liberal attitudes to sex and relationships than I was used to. Was that wrong? Was this thing I had with Gian wrong? Not any more wrong than staying miserable in a marriage for 25 years. That much was very clear. How could I have done that to myself?

What is the point of staying in a marriage when the marriage is broken? Had I stayed in mine because I had some Catholic residue holding me to the idea of being good, a good little girl? I think that is part of the truth. Now, here I was doing something bad. Was this thing with Gian truly bad? What was right and wrong anyway?

As Gian continued to drive, he began to talk of his wife.

"With my wife, it's easy for me to do whatever I want. She makes lots of money at her job, and she only cares about work. She doesn't care about what I do or know about the girlfriend I have for casual sex."

"Gian. The wife always knows."

He looked at me, eyes wide as he registered my comment.

Now, we were back in the city. When Gian dropped me off, we made plans to meet the next evening at *I Fratelli*. It would be my last night in Ravenna.

* * *

On the last day of class, we unveiled our projects. The tiles we used to create our images had been pressed into soft plaster on a wooden base set within a wooden frame. When the tile arrangement was complete, the works were set with a fixative of traditional mortar glue made of rabbit skin. The frames were then wrapped in cloth and set in a kiln to dry. When the instructor's assistant unwrapped my pear mosaic, he said softly,

"Ah ... a small masterpiece."

It was lovely. Not two-dimensional as ancient mosaics were but modern with a sense of depth created by the gradient shades of colored tiles I used. The pears looked round and luminous, as if they were popping out of the mortar. I loved it. Despite how half-hearted I had been when the class began, the experience had turned out to be beautiful.

After the last class, I changed my clothes in my room and put on the designer shoes I bought a day earlier. I got to *I Fratelli* at the time Gian and I had agreed upon. I did not see him anywhere. I looked outside and inside, but he was not there. A thin, dark-haired mousy man came up to me, handed me a folded piece of paper, and simply said, "From Gian." I was speechless. I took the note and began wandering back down the street, then stopped at a bench to read. Gian wrote that he would not be able to meet me. He said he didn't like goodbyes. He included his phone number. If I ever wanted to call.

I was feeling a little discarded. Maybe Gian truly was just a shallow playboy who had gotten what he wanted and was done with me. Or maybe he was disappointed that I was leaving and was too much of a coward to meet me to say goodbye. Or maybe he had been hit by lightning.

No! It would not end this way!

I found some notepaper in my purse and wrote, "No problem, Gian. I also don't like goodbyes. Thank you for everything. I will not forget."

I walked back to *I Fratelli* and found the little man who had given me Gian's note. I handed him mine.

"Could you please give this to Gian?"

"*Certo*!" he replied immediately.

I turned to walk away, then turned back and said playfully, "And you won't read it?"

"Oh no, senora, no!" he said as if appalled at the thought.

I flashed a sunny, flirty smile and left. I could feel the eyes of all the townsmen in *I Fratelli* following me as I walked away.

Was I worried that the townsmen might judge me? Not at all. Let them judge. Did I still feel discarded? No. I was happy. Gian had taken me from the miserable place I had been in when I arrived in Ravenna and given me something fun, sexy, and memorable. I know it was that for him, too. I adored him for what he had given me.

I didn't see until much later that in my affair with Gian, I had gone from being cheated on in my marriage to someone involved in cheating, from having my heart broken by an Italian lover to being the heartbreaker of another Italian lover. There was a lot of learning about how I saw myself that I got from knowing Gian, along with the sexy fun. Affair or not, Gian had been a gift.

When I thought of Gian after that, I thought of him tenderly. I hoped I had been a gift to him, too. I imagined that one day when he sat with the other grandfathers in the piazza while their grandchildren played, he might find pleasure in confiding, as some Italian men do, the story of a brief but wonderful love affair with a "*canadese bionda,*" the way many of us relish or retell the stories of our loves.

Chapter 11

Calgary: This is Not Love

While I was back and forth between Canada, Italy, and love affairs, there was still the matter of ending my marriage to address. I yoyoed between delicious optimism for life, fleeting thoughts of Giorgio, and the gloom of situations with my brother and my husband. My husband and I would get together to talk divorce, and every time I saw him, he'd wrap his arms around himself, and tears would well up. This was an enormous change. It confounded me. I saw he never wanted to talk about divorce. It was just an excuse to meet me.

One day, he said, "You were the one person in my life I could count on."

I was stunned. After 25 years of giving me to believe the opposite, he tells me he counted on me? I couldn't believe it. Maybe what he really counted on was me taking the worst and staying.

"I never thought you would leave."

Even after I told him I had to leave?

What would it have meant to me if he told me he counted on me while we were married? I wasn't interested in hearing it now. I couldn't comprehend anything he was saying. The flimsy connection between us had been severed like a disconnected phone service. No words were getting through.

My husband went to visit a good friend in Arizona. Surprisingly, while there, he signed up for a workshop about love, relationships, and self-love. When he returned from Arizona, he told me he spoke to the counselor about how badly he had treated me and how long I had stayed. The counselor had said, "Well, she's a trooper." There had been a lot of suppressed pain my husband took out on me. I'm sure he never intended things to be that way. That was not the truth of who he actually was.

My husband wrote me a long letter. Pages and pages of recollections of miserable things in our marriage, along with memories of things I said to him. "Remember when this happened, and you said this? You were right. And remember when you said this? You were right." Pages and pages. His letter didn't have the effect he might have hoped. It only annoyed me. I didn't want to be pressed or told I had been right. The whole thing made me feel a little nauseous. I certainly hadn't always been right. I didn't want to read that in his letter.

I remembered the day he proposed to me. We had known each other for one year and lived together for another. There had been red flags. I knew they had not been addressed. There was a whisper of knowing something was off. I could have listened to that whisper but didn't. If I am completely honest, I didn't want to hurt him by saying no to his proposal, and I didn't want to create a question mark on our relationship that might have brought things to a crisis point. I hated confrontation. I rationalized instead. I did love him. I adored him. Living together was a commitment we had made about our future. I didn't want to lose him. I said yes to his proposal. I see it was a cowardly choice.

I now saw a change in my husband after decades of no change. I had long labored under the crazy idea that I could reason with him to get him to open up and argue with him to get him to change. Try arguing with a lawyer. Worse, I had been a fool to think I could change him in the first place. I wondered what had happened to the love we started with. How had Love turned to Not-Love? What was love anyway? A rush followed by a bunch of expectations of happily ever after? Had we ever really loved each other? Had we each known who we were individually and wished to become? Or had we only lived from the image of who we thought we should be?

We did all of that, for sure. And I played the game.

I never spoke to anyone, not even friends or family, about the state my marriage had been in or what life had been like inside the home. Not once. People were shocked when we separated. As individuals and as a couple, we were admired. My husband was widely admired in his job, friendships and the community. That admiration was completely deserved. Our life looked perfect. From the outside. My husband and I both played the perfection game.

I realized that whatever state a marriage is in, it takes two people, interacting or not interacting, to create it the way it is. No person is off the hook for their share of responsibility because, without both people, the relationship would simply not exist. I was not absolved of responsibility for the end of the marriage, no matter how badly I thought he behaved. There is a truth that comes out of that. Being angry or blaming someone else is not a road to personal power, but owning the truth is.

My husband had a favorite saying, "The truth shall set you free." I didn't see many truths about my marriage until later. Now, after love affairs that showed me something about myself that I hadn't known and only wanted to know more of, it only irritated me to even think about the marriage. I had exhausted all I had to give. I just wanted to be free.

In the spring, I asked my 20-year-old son if he would like to take a trip with me to Italy. I had a deep, rich relationship with my daughter. But my son—that sweet, funny little boy I had adored as a child who had become a smart and handsome young man—was someone I hadn't spent much time with in recent years. Of course, that was easy to understand. He was a young man getting on with his life. Still, I wished I had more time with him. Travel was something we both enjoyed. I suggested the trip. To my surprise, he said yes.

We flew to Rome, where my son was overtaken by a virus that began just as we left home. He stayed in bed for two days while I roamed the streets and let myself be romanced by Rome. On the third day, we made a whirlwind tour of the city's most famous sights. We only skimmed the surface of the city with no chance to feel its true essence or for me to share with my son the things I loved about Rome. That was okay. One day, he could go back on his own.

We picked up a rental car and began the lovely drive south from Rome toward Naples and the Amalfi coast. I had no intention of driving into Naples. My plan was to park at a train station just outside the city so we could transfer in for a day of sightseeing. But somehow, as we neared the city, I got swept along on the autostrada, and I found myself driving through chaotic Naples in a too-large-for-the-city Opel rental car.

I got pulled into the net and snared by the mad traffic of Naples. The city was in the middle of an ugly garbage strike with monstrous mountains of garbage piled 10 to 15 feet high along the streets and protesting picketers with placards blocking roadways. The main thoroughfare I was driving on had three marked vehicle lanes, but cars jostled, jumped spaces, and squeezed between other cars, so there were anywhere from three to five lanes at any given time. A person needed eyes all around their head and then some to keep from having a collision in the swirling melee. My senses ratcheted up to high. Suddenly, I was in the core of the city, *il Centro*, where the main avenue was a dense, overwhelming web of narrow one-way streets, dead ends, fearless jay-walking pedestrians, no parking, and no stopping.

My son and I were lost in Naples for two hours. The whole time passed in a stress-induced blur. I found myself driving in circles, trying to find the way out of the city with my son, who was barely beyond his virus, trying to help me find and follow the confusing directional signs to the autostrada. Each time we thought we found our way out of Naples' labyrinth, we would discover we were right back where we started in *Il Centro* in the middle of the chaos.

I finally managed to get out of the city with the help of a gas station attendant who ran out to stand in the middle of the busy roadway to stop traffic so I could make a U-turn to the Autostrada ramp with its nearly invisible posted sign that I had missed multiple times. Once safely on the road south to the Amalfi coast, I pulled the Opel over in the graveled parking lot of a roadside restaurant so my son and I could get out and shake off the tension.

"Naples is an armpit!!" I yelled in a loud explosion of stress.

"Mother!! Be quiet. People will hear you," said my son, noticing people walking past us.

"I don't care. I'm sure they know it. Naples is an armpit!!"

"Stop! You are insulting their home!"

My son and I had a stress-generated fight as we stood in the parking lot. There is something very Italian about passionate outbursts, even while you stand in the midst of the glorious beauty of Italy around you. Naples had grabbed us by the throat, and somehow our fight seemed appropriate, standing as we were with a view over the blue Tyrrhenian Sea that sparkled along the cliffs below us in the inimitable Italian sunshine. It was a view neither my son nor I noticed.

Heated exchanges occasionally occurred between us. Sometimes, we butted heads. There was something wonderful, even about that, too. Within the intensity of those moments was a deep mother-son bond and a knowing we both had. We were a lot alike.

My son later said of me driving through Naples, "I don't know how you did it. Naples was insane."

It made me happy. I'd take the praise.

We continued south of Naples and along the narrow serpentine roads of the gorgeous Amalfi coast. The roads hugged vertical rocky cliffs, skirted colorful towns stacked up the slopes, and offered stunning views of the sea. I guided the Opel a little past the famed town of Positano until we came to the town of Praiano and the lovely Hotel Tramonto where we checked in for a night. The hotel hung down from road level along the cliffs to the sea. There was an elevator on the ground level that counted down to the floors instead of up. The rooms had large white arched doors leading to balconies with breathtaking views of the sea.

Down the precipitous cliff from our hotel on a twisting stairway that seemed to be made up of a hundred steps, we found a magical restaurant hovering precariously over wave-washed rocks. We ate delicious fried fresh sardines and pasta while sun-touched water sparkled around us and the late afternoon sun glowed into the restaurant. It was the most magical meal I've ever had. It was something truly special I shared with my much-loved son.

After Amalfi, we drove farther south to Calabria and stayed at a resort in the sweltering town of Tropea to sunbathe and swim, then headed back toward Rome for our flight home. For our last night, I booked into a hotel in Castel Gandolfo on the lake near Giorgio's hotel.

In the morning, my son wanted to spend some time on his laptop. I went out to walk. The town was one end of the wooded path I knew so well that wound around the lake to Giorgio's hotel at the other end of the path. I began to walk and talk to Giorgio. It was sometimes a rant, sometimes an expression of the love I had had. Why could he not have chosen to see where our relationship might have gone? Tears poured down my face. I told him I missed him. I needed to let him go and hadn't been able to. I felt haunted. Could he please, please release me? Could I allow myself to release him and leave him here on this path around the lake?

I walked half the distance around the lake, very aware I did not want to get too close to Giorgio's hotel. I did not want to unexpectedly encounter anyone I knew. I could feel my body begin to tremble the closer I got to where Giorgio lived as if it had a longing of its own to contend with. I could not get too close. I stopped halfway around the lake and turned back. Enough! I was being ridiculous. No more. I finished crying and went back to my hotel to go for breakfast with my son.

Chapter 12

Calgary: This is Love

I started looking for something new to put on my calendar. Again. Another step toward the horizon. I got the idea of returning to university and studying Italian language and culture. I love the whole vibe of university and studying. I had loved writing in Italian to Giorgio. I imagined how amazing it would be to be fluent. I registered for classes in the fall. I began to shop in an Italian market in the city. It was owned by a middle-aged Italian woman and had all the feel of old Italy.

One day in the summer, as I shopped in the market and stood looking in the cheese refrigerator case, a man working in the store passed by behind me.

"*Señora*, may I help you?"

I didn't turn from the case but simply said, "*Grazia, no.*"

I moved on to browse in the produce section. The man came by again.

"You are making something nice for your husband?"

"I don't have a husband."

He went away and came back a third time to where I was looking through the plethora of jarred olives and antipasti on a shelf.

"Excuse me, *señora*. May I ask you something?"

"Yes."

"Are you Italian?"

I turned to look at him for the first time. He was dark-haired, dark of skin, and husky of body, standing confidently and solidly on his feet in front of me.

"No, I'm not Italian. Are you?"

He said proudly and standing taller as he spoke, "No. I am from Kosovo. My name is Rio. *Señora*, may I ask you another question?"

"Yes."

"Will you have dinner with me?"

He asked. Just like that in the middle of the market. My jaw dropped.

"I don't know." I floundered, looking back and forth from the olive shelf and him. "I'm just here looking at olives," I said weakly, gesturing toward the shelves.

"There is a restaurant here next to the market," he continued. "We could meet to have dinner there."

He stood looking at me and waiting. Kosovo. I rather liked his confidence in asking me. What the hell was going on anyway? I wasn't in some foreign place, in Italy, where I had gone along with unexpected things that sprung up with men I didn't know. I was home. In Canada. This was my ordinary life where I had been a wife and mother and was now a 52-year-old woman. How do I navigate the dating game after years of being out of it? How should I answer an impromptu invitation to dinner like this?

"I will keep shopping," was all I could finally get out. "I will let you know before I leave."

I turned and went down another aisle. I was thinking, *Kosovo. I've never met anyone from Kosovo before. It might be interesting to have dinner with him.* And it was nice that he suggested a meeting at the restaurant next door. If I didn't like him, I could just leave.

When he came to find me again browsing in the aisle of dried pasta, I said, "Yes, I will have dinner with you."

We set a time to meet the next day. I paid for my things at the till and left the store, smiling to myself at the thought that if I changed my mind about going to dinner, I could stand him up. He did not have my phone number and had no way of finding me. Then, there he was, casually leaning on the hood of a car in the parking lot, looking a bit like a rebel with his dark, sexy Albanian looks. He asked for my phone number. I gave it to him, thinking, *Oh, he misses nothing.*

The next evening, I met Rio at the Italian restaurant he suggested. He was waiting for me at a table inside by the fireplace. He greeted me with a polite European embrace. I sat, we ordered our meal, and I began peppering him with questions about Kosovo like I was on a fact-finding mission.

He said, smiling at me, "You can ask me anything," opening his arms wide to show me that everything was on the table.

I told him, "I wasn't completely truthful when I said that I didn't have a husband. I am separated and getting a divorce."

He said, "I don't have a wife either."

Rio was completely gracious and comfortable to talk to. I gradually relaxed. It felt easy being with him. We enjoyed our food and talked non-stop. It was mostly me doing the talking and him smiling and answering my questions. After we finished our meal, he asked me if I would have dinner with him again. I liked him. He was polite and respectful in an old-fashioned way. He was definitely direct but with none of the boldness of Italian men. I said yes to another dinner. He suggested a restaurant two blocks down the street. We agreed to meet in two days.

I arrived to find Rio waiting for me at a table outside on the small narrow patio of the restaurant. In the daylight, I glanced at him surreptitiously and began to see him more fully than I had in the muted lighting of the restaurant during our previous dinner together. He had thick dark hair that was short on the sides and longer on the top, styled back from his forehead that had a number of scars around his thick dark eyebrows. His eyes were warm and brown, an almost golden brown that softened his overall darkness and drew me in. He had a prominent nose and the most beautiful lips I had ever seen on a man, a mouth that was broad and lips that were smooth and sculpted in flowing, graceful peaks under his nose. He had a broad chest that was full under his T-shirt and the lovely strong fleshy hands of a man who was used to work.

After we had placed our order with the waiter, Rio pulled a small Swarovski gift bag from under the table and handed it to me.

"For you."

Speechless, I opened the package and found a small box with a silver chain and crystal pendant inside. Instantaneously, unexpectedly, I was flooded with memories of a Christmas when I was 16 years old, innocent, and dating a boy who gave me a necklace as a gift. I had a strange and vivid sensation of air and space moving around me, of time warping, shifting, and blending until it seemed as if this man had just wiped out my past.

"Thank you. It's beautiful," was all I could manage.

A man sitting at a table across the aisle from us leaned over. He asked in a hushed voice as if he were stirred by seeing and overhearing us, "Is this your first date?"

"No. Second," I softly replied.

I began seeing Rio almost every day. There was something about him that told me he meant to be with me, not just to casually date but for something more meaningful, something lasting. How I knew that, I can't say. I just knew. There was a sense of being beyond time with Rio. It was strange. It was obvious he was interested in sticking around.

As Rio sat beside me on the couch in my condo one day, I told him, "I'm not ready for this. I fell in love with someone in Italy not long ago. I'm not ready for anything more right now."

He said, "That's okay. Take your time. I'll wait."

He would wait? What was going on? Men were crawling out of the woodwork. It was almost laughable. I didn't have this many advances when I was twenty. Truthfully, I never had a desire to be a woman who drew men like a siren in a myth. I would rather have been Marco Polo sailing the seas. What was I to make of the parade of men now that I was a woman in middle age?

I looked at Rio as he sat beside me and said he would wait for me. A recollection came to me of the day I spent painting in the marina in Savelletri. I remembered the Italian woman in her housedress who told me of a Canadian woman who married a Fasano man and the thought I had that I would like a Fasano man. Rio could certainly pass for a Fasano man.

Here he was. And here I was, not ready for him. There had been the romance of two love affairs compressed into a space of a year. This would be the third. People would say, "Oh, she was on the rebound. She went a little crazy." I hated being defined and simplified. Giorgio might be considered a rebound, but he was not just a rebound. The playful distraction of Gian had not drowned out the aching for Giorgio. Some days, I wondered, "Was I longing for Giorgio, or was it for Italy? Or something else I could not name?" I was a bit of a mess. I was not ready for Rio.

Nevertheless, Rio and I began spending our time together when he wasn't working as a butcher in the Italian market. We had long conversations on the balcony of the condo I had just purchased. He told me of his impressions of our first meeting. Another bolt of lightning story. He said it was like someone had taken him by the arm, shaken him, and said, "Look. Over there," so he would notice me standing by the cheese case.

Rio told me many stories of his life in Kosovo. He was a great storyteller and always had me laughing in delight. I loved the tales of his childhood, where he had been a devilish, hot-headed scrapper and defender of the family. He told me about being a mischief and getting kicked out of the mosque for poking the bottom of the kneeling man in front of him with a pin. He told me how at the age of 10, he challenged the *hodja,* or Muslim leader in his town, about the teaching around not eating pork. The man had honored their family by coming to dinner. Rio's challenging questions were a little too uncomfortable. He received a sound beating for that.

Rio told me of being poor and hungry and of leaving home at age 14 without telling a soul. He got on a bus to travel the long distance from Kosovo to Croatia to find work because there was no work in Kosovo. No money. His family was large. Parents, brothers, aunts, uncles, and grandparents all lived together. Winter was coming, and there was no money to buy flour and oil. He got on a bus late one night with only enough money in his pocket for two hot dogs and found work in Croatia as a farm helper for a man who saw how young he was and took him in. He worked hard and slept in the barn. A few months later, he went home with enough money to support the entire family for the winter. Rio said that on his return, he strutted through town like a prince, loaded with money taped in a plastic bag inside his underwear as the Croatian man had taught him to prevent being robbed.

Rio's father had been furious. His parents had been sick with worry, but one of Rio's uncles said, "Why are you angry? He is a man now. You should be proud. I would be proud to have a son like this."

Rio told me many stories of the horrors of war. He fulfilled his year-long conscription with the Serbian army when he was 18. Kosovo was still part of Serbia at the time. When Serbians began attacking Albanian villages a year later, killing men and boys, and nearing Rio's own village, he took to the hills with a group of other men to form a resistance to protect the town while his family hid in their home. That's who he was. A Protector.

Rio had a lot of stories and told them with flair. Besides being a farmhand in Croatia, he had been a dealer in gold jewelry in Turkey, a boxer in Bulgaria, a bread-truck driver, a recruit with the carabinieri in Italy, a truck driver transporting livestock and butcher in Kosovo. He did whatever he had to do to make money. He spoke six languages fluently. He spoke no English when he came to Canada three years earlier, only Italian which was fine for his job in the Italian market. Now he spoke English effortlessly, if not perfectly. He told me that at one time, he thought he would have liked to become a translator, but there never had been an opportunity for that in Kosovo. He was gifted with language.

Rio was thirteen years younger than me.

I told him, "I do not like being older than you."

"Sweetheart, with the life I've lived, I'm much older than you."

I was 52 but could pass for a woman 10 years younger. We didn't look like there was a big age difference between us. Still, it took me a long time to get the age thing out of my head.

Eventually, Rio moved into my condo with me. Being together was sweet and easy. Rio was smart, funny, playful, and more big-hearted than anyone I had ever known. I could almost see the potent power of his heart beating in his chest. He loved to dance uninhibitedly to Albanian music. He was a most generous, passionate lover. He oozed romance. He was so tuned into me he could read me in an instant and only wanted to please me. I basked in his warmth when he held me close to him at night, skin on skin. It was like he had a fire burning inside. He was mesmerizing. The darkness of his eyes, skin, and body felt foreign and a little unsettling to me. When I told him I was not used to being with an Albanian man like him, he said gently, "Give me a chance."

His words struck a note in my heart and reverberated like a hammered gong. Give him a chance? I could do that.

New women friends I met at the time thought he was hot with his dark, foreign, and slightly dangerous looks. A couple of women tried to move in on him, only to be met with Rio's cold disdain for their forwardness. He was not interested. He saw only me. People saw us together and said, "You are the most romantic couple."

When Rio looked at me, his eyes glowed like amber embers as if seeing me lit him up from the inside. I adored being with him. He made me laugh. He listened and heard me with a depth I had never experienced before. He never failed to text me every day from work that he loved me. He treated me with such honor and devotion; there is only one way to describe it.

I was *The Beloved*.

Being The Beloved carries the sense of timeless love you read of in old romantic poetry or stories of chivalry. Rio held me in a place of honor and love. There are many men with whom you have to struggle to know their true feelings and intentions. That was not the case with Rio. What I meant to him was crystal clear. Rio said he had a strange feeling he had known me before, a long time ago, maybe lifetimes ago. Something like that had been pushing into my mind, too. Somehow, our relationship seemed familiar and beyond time, as if we had known each other forever.

Rio had first come to Canada three years earlier on a work permit to fill in as a butcher for an uncle who was working in the meat department in the Italian market. He had been here one year when his father died. There were stipulations with the work permit that he could not leave Canada and then re-enter. It meant if he went to his father's funeral, he could not return to Canada on his current permit. His family needed the money. He could see no way to go home for his father's funeral. He didn't go. He told me he was torn apart. He told me he raged and drank.

Now he sat on the balcony of my condo and wept. He cried for his father, who had also been his best friend. He hadn't shown his respect at the funeral as he should have. He cried for his mother, to whom he had given a lot of heartache. He thought he had been a bad son. He wept because he had been in Canada for three years, missed home, and had no idea when he would go home again because the money he sent from every paycheck was much needed. He had to stay in Canada.

He was a favorite of the Italian woman who owned the market because of his exhaustive work ethic. She kept his work permit going and organized applications for permanent residency in Canada. His applications had already been rejected twice. He said he planned to stay in Canada on work permits as long as he could, maybe forever.

I once asked Rio, "How did you know how to treat me as beautifully as you do?"

He shrugged and said, "I don't know. My father was always good to my mother."

The memory of the Tea Man in Florence whispered to me again. I had had a marriage and love affairs with men who never wanted a future with me, not a future right for me or one I desired. Now, here was a man who wanted to give me all. I knew it. Rio completely and profoundly drew me in. After a few months, I made a choice. I surrendered to it.

I introduced Rio to my children.

My son said, "That guy's a hero."

My daughter was cooler. She idolized her dad, and Rio was nothing like her dad. Rio was a simple caring man.

She told me, "Rio is just like your dad."

I wanted to introduce Rio to my father. I asked Dad if he was ready to meet Rio.

"Do I have a choice?" he asked dryly.

I laughed. "Yes, you have a choice."

My dad liked my husband. The most terrifying thing I've ever had to do was tell my stern Catholic father that I was ending my marriage. There was no divorce in the Catholic church. I grew up believing that it was a terrible thing to end a marriage. Dad listened to my reasons and surprised me with his full support. Now, he would meet Rio. How does an 82-year-old Catholic man reconcile the kind of changes I made in my life? Somehow, I knew Dad would support me whatever I chose. I always had a sense he approved of me. He met Rio and liked him. Rio said my father was the first real man he had met in Canada. Dad accepted my choice. I have always been grateful to him for that.

My daughter and her boyfriend got engaged in the fall. We planned an engagement dinner with our family and her future one. I called my husband to tell him I was inviting Rio. He objected vehemently.

"If Rio comes to the dinner, I will not go."

"You won't go to your daughter's engagement dinner? Rio has gotten to know our kids. He's helped them a number of times. He helped our son move. He's part of my life, and I will not leave him out."

"If Kate were here, would it be okay with you if I invited her?"

My husband had been traveling to Australia the past year to search for his happy place and learn to scuba dive in the Great Barrier Reef. He met a young woman with two small children and started a relationship with her. He expected me to say no to his question.

"Yes, it would be okay with me if you invited Kate. People should not be left out."

After two days of thinking, my husband called me back.

"Alright. He can come. I will come. But I want to meet him first, before the dinner."

"Great. I'll ask him. When and where shall we meet you?"

"Not you. Just him. Just before the dinner."

"Oh. Okay, I'll ask him."

Rio said, "I didn't break up your marriage. I will go. It's better that way. Better than if your husband and I sit and look at each other all night like a wolf and a goat."

I laughed. "Who's the wolf, and who's the goat?"

"Oh, I am the wolf for sure."

The meeting between Rio and my husband happened at a bar down the street from the engagement dinner. Guests were seated for the dinner when the two men walked in together. Eyes popped. My husband went to sit at one end of the long table. Rio sat beside me at the other end.

"How did it go?"

"It was good. He was nervous."

"What did you talk about?"

"He asked about the war in Kosovo. He was very interested in the war."

"Yes, he loves war history."

"And he asked if I loved you."

"What did you say?"

"I said yes, I was ready to die for you."

I was astounded. "Die for me? I don't like you saying you would die for me!"

I knew what he meant. It was not about being a martyr, which conjures up thoughts of suicide bombers and creates lots of prejudice toward ordinary Muslim people. Rio said what he said because he was a protector and would stand by me, no matter what.

"What did he do when you told him you loved me?"

"He started to shake."

Rio and I had a year and a half of tears, sweetness, and laughter together.

Then things got messy.

Chapter 13

Calgary: Fall From Grace

A little after the engagement party, Rio got good news. His third application for permanent residency in Canada had been approved. A month later, he asked me to come and sit with him on the balcony of our condo. It was a gorgeous summer day. I relaxed into my seat amidst the colorful pots of sky-blue morning glories, crimson geraniums, and orange marigolds. I loved my balcony, nested as it was in the luminous green of trees around it. I sat and looked at Rio, my face to the sun. Rio sat facing me, the sun behind him.

He looked me directly in the eyes and simply, softly, clearly said, "I lied to you."

His words muddled my senses and the lingering pleasure of the sunshine and my lovely pots of flowers. I sat in confusion. I looked back at him, not understanding, but I heard the gravity in his voice.

"You lied to me? When did you lie?"

"I have a wife."

"You have a wife?!!"

I stared blankly at him for several moments, not sure of what I was hearing.

"Where is she?" I finally asked.

"In Kosovo." He paused. "And I have three children."

"You have kids!!" After another stunned pause, I asked, "Where are they?"

In the blankness of my mind, the words *"Where are they"* echoed.

"In Kosovo."

I just stared at him. I had no words. Rio hung his head and simply said, "I'm sorry. I will go."

He got up to leave.

"Wait!"

I sat and looked at him while he sat in silence, eyes cast down. He looked up to meet my stare and looked into my eyes for a long time, fully, not with guilt or avoidance of the truth but with eyes full of sorrow for what he had just done to me. Sorrow. And love.

I looked back at him. I wasn't hurt. I was in shock. I didn't know how to process what I had just heard. The wind rustling the leaves on the trees was the only sound to be heard. The silence between us yawned as we sat. Finally resigned to an unexpected truth, I asked, "Why did you lie to me?"

"When I met you, I thought you would never be interested in a guy like me." He spoke openly now that the truth had been told. "You were smart and educated. I was just a poor guy from Kosovo. You said you didn't have a husband, so I said I didn't have a wife. It just came out without me thinking. Afterward, I didn't know how to take it back. Many times, I wanted to tell you, but it got harder to tell as time went on. Then, I never did."

We sat in silence again, except for the chirping of birds in the trees around us. I knew what it was like to speak impetuous words that you could not take back once spoken.

He said softly again, "I will go," and began to get up.

"Wait!"

I thought for a minute and said, "I don't know that I want you to go. I don't know what I want. I don't know what to think."

I know what I felt. I didn't want him to go.

"Now that I've gotten residency, my family also has the right to come to Canada. I was forced to tell you about them now. Because my applications were turned down before, I thought I would never get approved. I thought I would stay in Canada on work permits and keep sending money home. I thought I would never go home."

Insects hovered and buzzed as if matching the charged energy around us.

"My family needs the money I make. I had to stay here as long as I could. I started thinking I'd have to make a new life by myself. Then, I met you. I told my family I met someone. I told my mother I lied to you."

"What did she say?"

"She said I was a fool."

He didn't leave just then. I didn't want him to. I wanted to sort out the facts. Were there any more lies? Now was the time to be completely honest. No, there were no other lies. That one was big enough.

Friends and family were appalled when they heard what happened. Rio told them the situation himself. He went to both of my kids, told them he lied, and apologized.

"This is not your mother's fault. She did nothing wrong. I was the one who lied."

I talked to my 20-year-old son.

He said, "Mom, I can see how something like that could happen to me. I could say something in the spur of the moment, not thinking it would amount to anything, only to have it come back on me later. This doesn't change what I think of Rio. I know who he is."

I could see how that could happen to me, too.

My daughter was angry. She was worried that Rio had been using me from the start. These kinds of stories turn up in the news from time to time, stories of foreign men conning women with romance and promises. I heard her out. All I could say to her was that I knew Rio. He had not been using me.

Other friends counseled me to run. They didn't know him, either. Or me. I knew the situation looked bad. I had been in a relationship that looked great from the outside and was lousy on the inside. This situation looked very bad from the outside. No one knew what it was on the inside except me. I decided I would keep my own counsel. People would understand in time. What mattered to me most was that Rio told me the truth. Before I caught him in a lie.

Rio got word that his family received their government permits to come to Canada. He called his wife. He told her that she could come if she liked, but he wouldn't be with her.

She said, "I know. You have been gone a very long time." It had been five years.

Rio told me about his marriage.

"It was arranged when I was 23. I didn't want to be married, but my mother pushed for it. She wanted grandchildren. The Albanian matchmakers said the woman chosen for me and I were a good match. I went along with it until just before the wedding, when I knew I was making a big mistake. I did not love her. It was too late. Marriage announcements had been made. Guests were invited. I couldn't change my mind. When the wedding day came, I was so against the marriage that I didn't even put on my best clothes. I wore a sweatshirt and blue jeans to my wedding."

"For all the years I was married, I traveled for work with my father, and the time I lived at home as a married man would add up to about two years out of the seventeen. I never had any connection with my wife. Yes, we had three children. But that was all we had. In all the years I've been in Canada, the only times she called me was to ask for money. She is a good person and has been a good mother, but I never loved her."

I heard him tell his story of arranged marriage. I thought about how we hear stories of how unjust an arranged marriage is for a woman, a marriage with someone you don't choose and don't love. Do we ever consider what that might be for a man?

* * *

The family arrived as winter began. Rio and I had talked a lot. Neither of us wanted to end our relationship, yet we were the adults in the situation. There were children involved. We had to do what was right. If it meant we had to end, we would choose that. Rio asked me if he could go to stay with his family for a week when they first arrived to help them get settled.

"I haven't touched my children's faces for five years."

I could feel his heart throbbing in his chest.

Rio's children, a son, 11, and two daughters, 13 and 15, spoke

English because he had sent money home for them to have English lessons in Kosovo. His wife spoke not a word. The children were too young to manage without an adult who could speak English and get them settled. The family would be lost in a new country.

"I need to help my kids. There is nothing between my wife and me."

"Okay." I agreed. Things were such a mess; what did it matter if he went to stay with his kids? Things would be what they would be anyway. He could not leave his children stranded in a new country. The whole situation took me into completely unknown, unseeable territory. I could have gone into the right and wrong and the morality of the situation. I definitely would have at one time. Now, I didn't. I just let go.

Rio had an uncle and his wife who lived in the city. They could help the newly arrived family. I knew that was a dicey situation. The uncle's wife hated Rio. Rio called her "Anaconda" when he spoke of her. When I asked why, he said, "It's because she is a big snake."

I wondered, "Does his newly arrived family need a snake in their house?" There was a sense of trouble ahead.

Rio went to stay with the family when they first arrived. Anaconda filled Rio's wife's head with lies and deceitful tactics to get back at him. The aunt told the wife she should provoke him into hitting her, then call the police, and he would be sent to jail. She could divorce him, and he would have to give her money as if he were a slave to her. The wife and aunt lied to the kids and told them nasty stories about their father. So many lies. They used the kids as a stick to try to beat Rio into submission. Big mistake. You cannot manipulate a man like Rio to make him stay. It will only backfire. He will leave for sure.

I got white-hot angry at Rio on one occasion and broke up with him. As he was packing his things from our condo, I saw that all the lies and the family drama had not changed what was between us. "*Us*" was just there, like an aura that resonated between us. I told Rio to leave his things where they were. He stayed.

I went on with my studies at university. Rio went to work each day to come home with a lost look on his face. There was always drama going on.

"I feel a goose in fog," he said. "There are only two things I know. I love my children. I love you. Those are the only two things that matter."

I took a trip to Mexico City with a Cultural Geography class I was taking. By now, I had taken almost enough classes to complete a degree to add to the one in English Literature I had taken in my twenties. I planned to do a double degree in Italian Studies and Cultural Geography, both of which I loved. Cultural Geography was a new interest and involved the study of the impact of people on the geography of the planet. I loved those courses. My degree would be completed in the coming spring.

Rio's uncle got a neighbor who was a psychologist involved to counsel Rio and his wife to bring the marriage to a conclusion. Rio's wife wanted a house from the divorce. She had pie-in-the-sky ideas of living in Canada. Rio could barely afford any house, let alone the kind of house she wanted. Rio bought a small townhouse for his family and put the mortgage payments in his name. He said would pay all their bills.

The family moved into the townhouse, which turned out to be in the neighborhood of the uncle and Anaconda. The oldest daughter and the wife were given jobs in the Italian Market. Anaconda continued to manipulate the situation out of sheer malice. She hated Rio. Rio thought she was a snake. I knew Rio. It would be obvious on his face what he saw when he looked at her. She was the anaconda. She could manipulate other people, but she could not manipulate Rio. She hated him for it. Anaconda took her revenge. The ugliness of it went on for years after the divorce, no matter what Rio did to make peace with his ex-wife and be close to his children.

Chapter 14

Calgary: Fallen Angel

One night in the middle of the mayhem of Rio's family's arrival two months earlier, I got a call from a downtown hospital. A woman told me that my husband was in the hospital and asked me to come. It was strange to get that call about "my husband," who I had been separated from for two years now. I got in my car and made a call to my daughter as I drove to tell her that her dad was in the hospital and I was headed there now. When I arrived at reception, I gave my husband's name. A woman took me to a private room, looked at me, and said, "I'm sorry. He's gone."

"He's gone?" I looked at her, confused.

The woman told me, "He was working out at the YWCA downtown. After his workout, he walked to the front door and turned to wave goodbye to someone inside. As he went through the door, he fell to the ground. Staff rushed to him and used the defibrillator they had on site. The ambulance arrived, and paramedics worked on him, too. Apparently, he never once revived. It appears he had a massive heart attack. His death was instantaneous."

I took in what the woman had just told me in the throbbing silence of the room.

She waited as I registered what she told me. She said she would leave me for a few moments and come back shortly to see if I had any questions. Was there anything I needed? Was there anyone I wanted to call? I said I had called my daughter, who was on her way.

A few minutes later, my daughter hurried in.

I looked at her and simply said, "Dad died."

All she said was, "I knew it when you called."

A nurse came to ask if we wanted to see him. My daughter and I both said yes. We took turns. It was peaceful when I went into the room where he lay. His hair was wild, like he had been in a whirlwind. His face was flecked with pinprick-sized blood vessels that had burst with defibrillation. Yet he looked like himself as if he were simply sleeping. Slowly, I sat down on a chair by the bed where he lay and looked at him for a long time. I felt the calm and peace in the room. No heavy emotion. No need to shed tears.

I said to him gently and simply, "I'm sorry. Sorry about the way everything turned out."

Things began to move very fast even though it felt like I myself was moving in slow motion. There were funeral arrangements to be made and all the other things that go with tending to a person's passing. My daughter's wedding date had been set for six months later that coming summer. She and her fiancé considered postponement but decided the wedding would go ahead. There was a lot of planning and preparation to be done for that as well.

There were funeral people, lawyers, and accountants to be dealt with. People called with condolences. They called needing consolation more than to give it. People talked of the shock of my husband's death. He was only 59 and had been an athlete all his life. It was like his death left us all in the fog of an alternate reality. More fog.

Four hundred people attended the memorial service. My husband would have been pleased. He requested in his will that his funeral be a party, no tears. Of course, there were tears. The emcee choked them back as he read the lyrics of the Celtic song *The Parting Glass*. Together, my son and daughter gave a heartfelt eulogy for their dad that was tender, light-humored, and inspired. People were left in awe. There was also lots of laughter. Friends, boys he coached in football, and long-time business associates spoke and shared funny memories that drew bursts of laughter from the crowd. My husband would have been delighted with all of it.

His girlfriend, Kate from Australia, came for the funeral, too. I paid for her flight and accommodations because my kids said she had been someone important to Dad and should be included. Yes, no one should be left out.

My sister-in-law had a Romanian friend who said instantaneous death of this kind is known in Romania as The Death of the Angels. Had my husband been taken lightly by angels? Had he been an angel?

I looked at what our marriage had been. I remembered how angry I had been around the time our marriage ended. I could see how it would be easy for separated partners to continue for years with sadness or anger about what happened. It could take a long time to get beyond unhappy memories of Not-Love and reconcile the ending of a marriage. But when someone dies, the entire perspective refocuses. Images and memories softened. At least, it was that way for me. Gone was the false luxury of being angry. That didn't mean that I regretted my choice to leave the marriage or mentally rewrote everything that had occurred. But, suddenly, all the Not-Love that had plagued me no longer mattered. It just didn't matter. It all dissolved into Love.

Was he an angel? In a sense, he was. Despite everything that had occurred between us, he had lived his life fully. He lived with enthusiasm. He was inspiring, generous, and a shining light to others. He had been a gift to the world. I could leave it at that.

After the funeral, Australia Kate became an unpleasant situation to handle. There had been warning signs about Kate. I remembered some of the very last conversations I had with my husband, who had phoned me because he badly needed advice about Kate.

"I need to talk to you about Kate."

"Do I really need to hear this?!!" I rolled my eyes when I heard his request.

"I've heard about your relationship since you left!"

"Okay," I sighed. "Go ahead."

"I do not want to be in a long-term relationship with Kate or be a father again to her two little kids. The problem is that she just found out she has cancer."

"Sorry to hear that."

"She had cancer six years ago and has just found out it's back. I don't know what to do. I can't break up with her now."

"I see. Look, I know you wouldn't want to be a complete heel and dump her when she's been told she has cancer. But don't you still have to be honest with her?"

"Yes. But she's so in love with me. She actually thought she was pregnant a while ago."

"Didn't you tell her that you had a vasectomy?"

"Of course!" he said with a flash of irritation. "But she thought she got pregnant anyway because she was so much in love."

"Women don't get pregnant after a vasectomy by being so much in love."

"I know that!" he said, again annoyed, then continued. "Later, she told me she wasn't pregnant after all because the positive pregnancy test turned out to be a false positive. Now, there's this cancer diagnosis."

Something sounded false, alright. I thought it but didn't say it.

"Well, if you are honest with her about how you feel, maybe you can offer to continue to support her as a friend. Look, here's my advice: Don't make her any promises!"

Later, Kate said it turned out she didn't have cancer after all. Someone else's test results had been given to her by mistake. When my husband told me, all I said was, "Boy, she has bad luck with medical tests."

He was defensive, "What do you mean?"

"Oh, nothing," I said nonchalantly, "Just, she has bad luck with medical tests."

He scowled at me but said nothing more. He was a smart man. He could figure it out. It was clear. Kate was desperate to snag him.

Not long after, Kate called him to tell him she was afraid of her ex-husband, who was coming to her door and threatening her. My husband was worried. What could he do from Canada? He left the family Thanksgiving dinner we were in the middle of and rushed out the door to phone her to try to help.

Couldn't he see the game Kate was playing? I saw it but said nothing. I had already said all I thought was appropriate for me, the ex-wife, to say.

Well, he wasn't the only one with a messy relationship.

A little while after the funeral was over, Kate wrote to the lawyers for my husband's estate and said she was pregnant with his child and would be making a claim for child support. My husband would have died a second time if he knew what she tried to pull.

In her letter to the lawyers, Kate named her due date as the same day as my daughter's wedding. My daughter was distraught. Of course, Kate knew the wedding date. Merging those events was a nasty thing to do. What was her problem with my daughter? Kate was only three years older than my daughter. Was she jealous of her? I counted the months back from Kate's stated due date to the approximate date of conception. That date didn't even come close to matching the last time my husband had been in Australia, and she could have conceived.

I told the executor about my husband's vasectomy 15 years earlier and Kate's dates not lining up. That set off a flurry of action. The lawyers wrote to Kate about the vasectomy and date mismatch. Kate replied that they had gone to a fertility clinic. The vasectomy had been reversed, and his sperm had been stored for her to use to become pregnant while he was away. They wanted to have a child together.

What kind of soap opera was she living in? No chance my husband would have had his vasectomy reversed or his sperm stored for her to make use of. The whole thing was ludicrous. Nevertheless, I was told by the lawyers for the estate to go to his house and get a toothbrush or hairbrush and put it in a plastic bag to save for DNA evidence in case of any paternity suit she might bring. So, off I went to our old family home to rummage through the bathroom for things that might contain his DNA.

The whole matter was beyond surreal at a time when things were already confusing enough. It was like being in a bad movie. My distressed daughter took it the worst. I guess I was lucky I had been willing to listen to my husband talk about Kate after all. I knew the score. I told my daughter, "Don't worry about Kate. Just wait. We will hear shortly that she's miscarried because that's one way a lying woman gets out of a pregnancy that doesn't exist."

Less than a month later, Kate announced the loss of the baby on Facebook. She lost the child that was fathered by the love of her life, she lamented. Kate milked the situation all she could. She was a shameless liar.

On one hand, the whole thing disgusted me. On the other, I was a little in wonder at the quickness and enormity of her lies. When I ranted about the situation to my son, he said, "Mother, you don't know what her life has been. You have no right to judge her!"

How did my son get so wise? Yes, despite the mess Kate had created, my son was right. Don't judge.

Chapter 15

Waskesiu: La Vie en Rose

After Australia Kate's Facebook announcement, we all moved on. The last two months before my daughter's wedding flew by. When she was preparing her invitations, I put my foot down about sending one to my brother and his wife in Vancouver. There was not to be an invitation. My brother was still not talking to me. My daughter was not happy to leave out a family member. We argued. I knew how she felt, but I was firm. No invitation. We had enough to deal with without opening the door and inviting craziness in.

My brother had called me the morning of my husband's death to extend condolences. He asked if we could talk. Two years had gone by since our falling out. In all that time, most of my attempts to reach out to him were ignored. Nothing between us had been resolved. Now he said he wanted to talk. I had been in the hospital most of the night and replied, "This is not a good time for me to talk. We have not talked for years. To be honest, this situation between us has been deeply painful for me."

He said, "Well, if it's been painful for you, it hasn't bothered me one bit."

I yelled at him, "How can you say that to me right now? Someone has died here!"

He then insulted me with a comment on the kind of sister I had been. I hung up and cried. Where was this coming from? My brother had lived in other cities and traveled for work his whole adult life. He was never around. Our contact had been minimal. Did he have childhood grievances? I could comprehend none of it.

With my daughter's wedding approaching, my brother contacted me by email. Safer that way, I guess. Dad had phoned him and told him that he had always been a respected member of the family but now would not be getting an invitation to the wedding. That was all he said. Good going, Dad. My brother's email was conciliatory, no apologies but a soft willingness to reach out. After a positive exchange of emails, I told my daughter an invitation should be sent. My brother came to the wedding without his wife, who remained in Vancouver tending to her sick mom.

Not a word was ever said between my brother and me about the false accusation. Did he actually believe I would try to break up his marriage? I decided the best course of action was to wipe the whole thing from my mind. Nothing that had happened was at all like the brother I knew. Had I not been a great sister? What did that mean? I'd let everything be water under the bridge. We lived in different cities and rarely saw each other. There was never an opportunity to talk, and I actually didn't care to delve into the problem any further anyway. I embraced my brother at the wedding and lightly kissed his cheek. I had never kissed my brother before. No other words were needed. There was a silent acknowledgment that what had happened between us was over. Sometimes, speaking no words is a good solution.

As years passed, I got the sense my brother and his wife were in a troubled spot around the time of their attack on me. I heard a few details from my Vancouver Sister. Their accusation had nothing to do with me. I just happened to be in the wrong place at the wrong time. I didn't need to know the whys and wherefores. Any problems they had were theirs to sort out, just as my marital problems had been mine. We all moved on.

* * *

My daughter's wedding was held at Waskesiu, one of Saskatchewan's breathtaking northern lakes. The name means "elk" in the Cree language. Waskesiu was where my husband had spent unforgettable summers as a boy. It's where he and I took our own family for idyllic summer holidays with relatives. Waskesiu was a paradise of vibrant blue skies full of fluffy clouds, forests full of wildlife, and rivers teeming with fish. We swam in the lake's clear waters despite them being frigid even in the summer, rode our bikes from our cabin for ice cream in Waskesiu's little town site with its funky laid-back vibe, and watched shimmering aurora borealis at night.

The wedding took place at the beginning of August, outdoors in a wooded glade on a beautiful blue-sky summer day. My son led my daughter down the walking path that formed her aisle. It wound down from the highway higher up to the small clearing in the trees at the bottom of the hill where the wedding guests waited.

My daughter had lights shining in her face as she floated down to us on the arm of her brother, who led her proudly as the stand-in for their father. She was dressed in a long, white satin sheath that draped on her slender body. Her veil floated in the breeze and formed a swirl of white around her long curling brown hair. She was absolutely lovely.

The ceremony was held in a small clearing marking the end of an old, out-of-use highway that ran directly along the lake. We could see the waters glimmering through the aspen trees that lined the road where we sat. The sun shone on my daughter, standing with her new husband, the sweetest, gentlest man who adored her. They took their vows, standing face to face, holding hands while the hushed guests sat in witness and cello music floated through the trees.

Later as that same sun sank lower in the sky, it slanted in through the windows of the old, wood-beam lodge that hosted their reception, dinner, and dance. My daughter's face glowed as she and her new husband danced their first dance to *La Vie en Rose*. She sparkled as she danced, now wearing a simple, short dress with a full shirt and crinoline while her husband held her lightly enough to let her twirl but strong enough to dip her back and make her laugh. She was such a beautiful girl and her handsome husband looked happy just to hold her.

It was one of the most romantic weddings anyone had ever seen. Guests said they were struck by the beauty of it. They talked about it in awed tones for days. It seemed there had been a golden aura around the whole day. My daughter said it was her dad.

* * *

Waskesiu was where my husband's ashes were scattered. His love of Waskesiu made it the obvious place. My son and daughter chose a location on the far south shore of the vast lake. It was a private spot with a view, reached after a long walk through the trees on a nature trail that skirted the shore.

We began walking, a small parade of nine people that included my husband's three sisters. We silently wound through the trees until I suddenly felt prompted to play music on my phone. I chose the song "That's the Way of the World" by Earth, Wind & Fire, a group my husband loved. The music was laid-back and bluesy but hopeful and upbeat at the same time. That song captured something of my husband's essence.

Everyone remained silent as we walked. I'm not sure they liked the music. They may have preferred a more contemplative walk in the woods. Yet, I could feel my husband's presence there. I had the sense he would have loved our excursion through the forest to remember him and would have definitely broken the seriousness of the walk with one of his famous irreverent repartees that would have gotten us all laughing. He would have loved the music playing in the quiet forest. That's what mattered.

We reached the spot my son and daughter selected to spread their father's ashes. It was marked by a bench above an embankment a few steps from the water. From the bench, you could sit and have an elevated view of the lake framed by the opening in the trees.

My son and daughter climbed down the rocky bank and got into the lake. As they poured their father's ashes from the urn into the water around them, the ashes formed a swirling cloud of grey that colored the water and contrasted the light blue of the lake in the sun and the deep grey-blue of impending rain clouds behind them in the distance.

My son and daughter spoke sweet words to honor their father with his ashes spreading out around them. They climbed out of the water and stopped to dig a small hole in the earth beneath a tree that clung to the bank. From their pockets, they pulled out four *Star Wars* figurines—Luke Skywalker for my son, Princess Leia for my daughter, Darth Vader for their father, and Queen Amidala for me. They placed them in the hole and covered the figures with the soil they had just loosened.

We all laughed. It brought back memories of years of *Star Wars* enthusiasm in our household and summers at the cabin in Waskesiu, where we played poker using Storm Troopers figures as chips from the dozens of figurines my husband and son collected. There was one summer when the Toronto boyfriend of a cousin came to join us on our lake vacation. He loved poker and joined enthusiastically in our evening games. There were so many players at the table that two decks of cards had to be combined. The game was boisterous and fun. The Toronto boyfriend loved the pile of Storm Trooper chips that grew as people placed their bets and were wide-eyed by hilarious outcomes in the game, particularly when someone was magically dealt eight aces in their hand.

That was the magic and mystery of the lake and why my husband had loved it. It's why we all loved it.

Chapter 16

Calgary: Falling Ill

My daughter's wedding had been a lovely interlude in a time of challenge. In the year that followed, I carried on with the practical matters of my husband's passing. That responsibility seems to be endless and took years from my life. At times, I thought it would completely overwhelm me. Where had the exuberant, joyful me gone? I reverted back to being the responsible me.

There was property to sell and my husband's legal consulting business to dissolve. As there had never been any financial settlement or divorce papers drawn up, the entire estate came to me, his wife. I was uncomfortable being called the wife when I thought of myself as the ex-wife. Now, it was worse. I was the widow. Funny how labels play on you. I was not comfortable receiving the entire marital property. Until his death, I had been due half. I solved my discomfort by giving my children each an inheritance from their dad. Solving my money sensibilities made me feel wonderfully, powerfully strong.

As time went on, things started getting unpleasant with family and friends, who began to treat me with disdain. Women who had been friends for years shunned me. Women I loved and to whom I had been close treated me coldly. From some, I got Arctic chill. From others, biting judgment. One woman looked me right in the eyes and told me, "Your husband died because you left him."

My husband once said when he saw women being mean to each

other, "The reason women will never inherit the earth is because of the way they treat each other."

I'm not saying that his words were 100 percent accurate. There could be arrogance in the things he said. But there could also be a whisper of some little truth, and he could be unflinching when he saw a truth.

When I talked to my daughter about the pain of women who spurned me, she said I was not the only one who experienced that kind of thing. Her mother-in-law experienced rejection by her female friends, too, when she left her marriage. It didn't make me feel any better to know I was not the only one. Having experienced what I did, I wondered, with all the complaining women do about what men do to women, do we ever openly acknowledge how some women treat other women?

Truly, I do not wish for you to think I'm putting down my own gender. Look, there's no doubt some men can be beastly. And some are wonderful. Same for women. Why can't people treat each other with decency? What about kindness and love? Love beyond romance and sex? I learned the hard way about the Not-Love women can do. The rejection by those I thought had been my friends was deeply painful. I felt like a pariah.

I looked at my relationships with women. They were never easy, especially if I were too enthusiastic or vibrant. Too passionate, one woman had said. Was that competition? Whatever it was, judgment was never far behind. I hated the judgment. I asked myself what I was doing wrong. I asked myself if I was competitive, too. The best answer I came up with is that I wasn't really interested in competing with other women, and when competition came up, I withdrew. I backed away. I suppressed anything that I thought might be judged.

Then, I saw it. I was pre-judging myself before others could. I was repressing anything I thought might not be liked. I got an image of myself so carefully living my ordinary life. It was the opposite of the exuberantly alive me I had been in Italy. In my regular life, there was so much of the real me that I kept hidden because it seemed I would not be accepted when I so, so deeply wanted to belong. Had I been living a lie and hiding the truth of me? Why would I do that to myself?

I saw it. I was doing Not-Love to myself.

What would truly loving myself be like? I ask you, do we know what truly loving ourselves is about beyond shopping or a day at the spa?

Maybe instead of seeking to belong, I needed to belong to me and love me for everything I was. Maybe that's what Italy and Giorgio had been about. Maybe the person I had fallen in love with in Italy was me!

* * *

The last item to be handled with my husband's passing was the sale of the family home. Rio helped me go through the house, sell furniture, and carry out box after box of junk to prep the house for the market. I spent a day cleaning the room I had once used as my painting room. The paints and the pictures were gone, but the feeling of the space remained. I pulled open a drawer in a bureau and was surprised to see a pile of journals sitting inside. My husband's journals. Had he been writing in the room that had been my painting studio?

I slowly pulled the journals out of the drawer and looked at them as they sat in my hands. He had never kept a journal while we were married. I was the one with that daily ritual. Now, here were his journals, written between my leaving and his death, written in the room that had held the memories of my happy place. I could almost see him there. Sad and alone. It made my heart break.

My husband wrote about his life. A self-examination. He wrote of his painful childhood. He wrote a beautiful creative piece about our family dog, Coco. He wrote a lot about our marriage. He wrote clearly with his famous legal-eagle-eyed view. He wrote his truth. He chastised himself severely in parts. A lot of it was very difficult to read.

No, no!! I would not have wished for him to have had that pain.

I had been talking to him aloud since his death as if he could hear me somehow. I believed he could. I wanted to reassure him. I wanted him to know I held no grudge. I wanted him to know that I loved him, despite all the Not-Love, despite the choice I made to leave. I wanted him to know I appreciated him and knew that the ending of the marriage was not only his fault. It was my fault, too.

I would never, never have wished for him to leave this earth with the pain of thinking about how he had injured me. Injuring anyone was not something he was truly about. He was someone who supported and inspired. There had been a lot of denial within our marriage. Maybe it was too close in, and he couldn't see it with clarity. Maybe I couldn't either. Maybe he did not want me to get too close because I might see his flaws. Maybe his flaws were a distraction from me seeing mine.

Whatever it was that took us from Love to Not-Love, I never regretted the choice I made to leave. But I read his journals and wept. Good God, how stupid we are. Why do we only see things clearly when we stop to look back?

I spoke aloud my sorrow. "Oh my God, I'm so sorry you had that pain. So sorry for it all."

The next weekend, Rio and I spent two exhausting days finishing the job clearing the house of the last of 25 years of family belongings. By the end of the weekend, I was strangely tired, a little foggy, and could barely stand. Something was wrong.

I asked Rio to take me to a walk-in clinic. I explained my symptoms to the doctor, who briskly told me I just had a virus. He wrote me a prescription for cough medicine with codeine and told me to go home to bed. If I had had my wits about me, I would have pointed out that a cough was not one of the symptoms I named. But I was feeling spacey and weak. I followed the doctor's orders and got the prescription for the cough medicine at the pharmacy, where Rio had to hold me so that I could stand. I went home to bed, never touching the medicine.

The next day, Rio had to go out of town for work, and I stayed in bed all day. I got up once to go to the bathroom and fell head-first with a crashing thud on the tile floor like I was a tree felled in the forest. I crawled back to bed and called my daughter to tell her what happened. I was beginning to get a black eye on the side of my face where my forehead and eyebrow hit the floor. My daughter called to check on me a short while later. She was worried. She and her husband were coming over.

When she saw me, she said she knew something was very wrong. Later, she told me I looked translucent. I barely remember the two of them arriving. I was drifting on the edge of consciousness.

"Mom, you need to go to the hospital. Come on. We'll help you get out of bed."

I couldn't stand on my legs even with both my daughter and her husband supporting me and sagged like a rag doll in their hands.

"Mom, we are going to call an ambulance."

I don't remember the ride in the ambulance or being wheeled into Emergency. Once there, I do recall being aware of doctors and nurses rushing around me. I was aware of what was going on as if I were watching the scene as an observer. I vaguely wondered why the lights in the room were kept so dim. Everything was dark. The sound of two doctors talking to each other while tests were rapidly being run drifted over to me.

"Her hemoglobin level is 40. Have you ever heard of a level that low?"

"I think I've heard of it. I've never seen it."

Normal was 120. The danger mark was 80. 40 was something else.

The head doctor of the two asked me questions about my symptoms. I answered her with a voice that sounded clear but didn't sound like it came from my body. The doctor leaned in close to my face, looked me directly in the eyes, and said emphatically, "No one dies on my watch!!"

Her words sounded like an order I should obey. I was immediately given four units of blood. My daughter, who was standing to the side with her husband as the doctors worked, said she saw my face go from translucent to flushed pink as the blood began to circulate through my system. My body had been practically blood-dry.

I spent days in the hospital afterward, having tests to discover what was wrong. There had been massive bleeding in my abdomen. The exact cause was yet unknown. There were moments when my blood pressure dropped so low the nurse trying to take a reading panicked, frantically checking her equipment and retaking my blood pressure again and again. The reading had to be a mistake.

I faintly remember reassuring her from the shadowy place I was in, "Don't worry. Everything is fine."

I watched my kids as they stood with solemn faces at the foot of my bed. I thought of the shock of their father's death a little over a year ago, and I decided, "This is not going to happen. I will not die. I will not do that to them."

I was in a brand new city hospital in a large room that had a sitting area where visitors could sleep. Rio stayed with me day and night. One night, fear crept over me like a malevolent cloud. I called Rio to come and lie on the narrow bed beside me and hold me. A nurse came into the room and looked at us disapprovingly. In a small, quavering voice, I said, "I'm scared." She softened, turned, and left the room. Another night I had a strange floating dream of me as a priestess wearing a flowing red gown and a golden crown with Rio as a big black muscular dog standing protectively and loyally at my side. It had the sense of some strange vision. Even from the state I was in, I had to smile. Well, he once said he was a wolf.

As my daughter was on her way to visit me one day, she encountered one of my friends from the old family neighborhood in the hospital elevator. The woman was someone I considered a good friend, someone I admired a lot. She was coming to visit her own mother, who was in the hospital. My daughter told her I was there, then ran into her a second time in the elevator the next day. The friend never contacted me. Nor did anyone else from the old neighborhood. I never heard from my friend, even when I tried to call and message her later. She was the one who once jokingly and affectionately called me her flaky friend. That didn't seem like much of a joke now.

Someone I met a few years later in a meditation retreat heard me tell of all the people who rejected me. She said, "How lucky you are that you got rid of all those nasty people at once." I heard her, but I didn't listen. I let those losses mess me up for years.

After a lot of tests, specialists discovered I had a rare gastrointestinal tumor. It had something to do with electrical impulses that went haywire between my stomach and intestines. I was told the growth of the tumor had been very rapid, likely within the last two years, and had begun to bleed into my abdomen, causing the crisis. I needed surgery.

The surgery happened a week later. It was successful. There was no malignancy. After only two weeks in the hospital from the start of the crisis, I was sent home with a large vertical scar at my navel. I was told I needed two months of rest to heal, followed by five years of scans at the cancer centre to be sure the tumor did not return.

The specialist I saw gave a fresh perspective to the whole incident. After reviewing the satisfactory results of post-surgery tests with me, he said, "Well, this was a good stress test for your heart."

Yes, my heart kept beating despite having had almost no blood. It filled me with gratitude for my strong, beautiful heart.

From the hospital, I rested for two months as instructed, then went right back into my life without skipping a beat. The sale of the family home was completed. A door closed.

Some people told me they thought the tumor had occurred as a result of too much stress. I told my son I had my own way of how I would look at the tumor.

"My body is trying to tell me something: Don't grow in. Keep growing out."

I had to keep blooming in my own life.

Chapter 17

Calgary: After the Storm

Shortly after recovering from my illness, there was a catastrophic flood in Calgary. Homes, apartment buildings, and neighborhoods were destroyed, streets were impassable, and Calgary's iconic Saddledome arena was flooded to the seventeenth row of seating. Massive amounts of water flow into the city from the mountain spring run-off exacerbated by an unusually heavy downpour of rain. Rio was out of town for work that day. Unexpectedly, just as the storm was just beginning in full force, I got a phone call from the aunt Rio called Anaconda.

Anaconda wanted to invite me for coffee. Would I meet her? I said yes and drove to the coffee shop she named, through wild wind and rain that poured from angry, slate-grey clouds and slashed at my car, past the rivers that traversed the city and overflowed banks to surge violently onto roadways and into homes. I dashed from my car through the downpour and into the coffee shop where Anaconda was waiting for me. As I shook off the rain, I glanced at her. She was a middle-aged mousy-looking woman with chin-length hair that had begun to grey, but she was no mouse. I got a sense of the fierceness packed into her small body.

We found a table and sat. She immediately began to talk.

"I need to warn you about Rio," she said, looking at me sharply with her dark Albanian eyes. "He's a very dangerous man. Very dangerous!"

I had known Rio for three years now. Who did she think she was talking to?

"Rio came from a family of very bad men. All the men in his family are bad!"

I could see why Rio disliked Anaconda. There was always some trouble she was trying to stir up.

"Rio's father was a very bad man," she continued. "He beat Rio's mother."

Was that true? Anaconda's words did not jive with things Rio had told me about his father. What did Rio's father have to do with Anaconda calling me for coffee anyway?

I listened to her talk trash about Rio's family and wondered how a woman could invite another woman she didn't know to coffee to talk this way. Furthermore, her husband was a man in Rio's family where all the men were "very bad men." What was she after?

I listened calmly, sipped my coffee, and smiled as she went on for some time talking about Rio and his family. Finally, Anaconda looked at me and said, "I can see you are a smart woman. Rio is so stupid. SO stupid. I can't even stand to be around him. How can you stand it?"

I said nothing the whole time but continued to smile. She stopped talking to look at me and take me in. I saw a realization come to her.

"Oh! You love each other."

I smiled at her and simply said, "Yes."

At that, it was clear coffee was over. She hadn't achieved her goal, whatever it was. We got up to leave the café. Before we went out the door, Anaconda said, "Don't tell Rio anything about our meeting."

I didn't reply to her request, just thanked her for inviting me for coffee and left to drive back home through the turbulence of the storm.

When Rio got home from work out of town later that evening, he told me about his day and asked me about mine. I told him I had coffee with Anaconda.

"What!!" He was suspicious and leaped from his chair. "What did she want?"

"Wait. Just wait. Sit down," I said calmly. "I'll tell you the whole story."

He sat to hear me out. When I finished talking, he beamed at me. He didn't care that Anaconda said nasty things about him. He was not happy that she spoke badly of his dead father, but that ultimately didn't matter to him either. He only cared that I saw through her.

He picked up his phone and called Anaconda.

"I hear you two women had coffee. Thank you for inviting her. You are the first member of my family to offer her an invitation. Thank you."

Seconds after he ended the call, my phone pinged with a text from Anaconda saying, "You couldn't wait even one day to tell him?"

I laughed at the silliness of it all.

Anaconda was the source of a ruffle between Rio and me a year later. We had gone for dinner in our favorite restaurant which was jammed with customers. I had a couple of glasses of wine. The conversation turned to Anaconda's impact on Rio's family. The wine loosened my tongue, and I began to rant about Anaconda, not noticing people at neighboring tables looking at me. Rio abruptly ended the conversation and said it was time to leave. As he drove us home, I noticed he was driving aggressively but paid no attention. The next day, he asked me to get dressed. He was taking me for lunch.

At the restaurant, I sat at our table. Before he sat, Rio stood before me, hands together, and said, "This lunch is to say I'm sorry. I was angry at you last night in the restaurant and drove home too fast. I shouldn't have been angry at you. I'm sorry."

"No!!" I looked at him in amazement. "Rio, I should be the one who is sorry. I was the one who was talking too loud in the restaurant. I'm sorry."

We looked at each other for a moment and burst out laughing. Rio sat and smiled widely at me. We enjoyed a delightful lunch with lots more laughter and the pleasure of us being who we were together.

I saw what Rio did by taking me to lunch. He could have berated me for causing a scene in the restaurant the night before. We might have fought. Instead, he apologized for something he did that was completely insignificant. It allowed me to see and acknowledge my own mistake myself. Anaconda had been so wrong. Rio was not stupid. He was oh-so-clever. I learned to watch more carefully what I said after a few glasses of wine. And I learned again how generous and loving Rio was. I learned how much he loved me.

* * *

With my body mending and the sale of the family home completed, I found myself living in what seemed like a vacuum. There was the "before." Now, what would the "after" be? The blooming? The next step? Something had to change. What was that?

It was me.

I knew it was imperative to change how I was living. Exactly what had to change or how I couldn't say. Where was the joyful, alive me I had been in those sun-soaked, love-filled days in Italy? There had been a precipitous drop from where I had been to where I was now. I loved the me I had been then. I ached for it. I yearned for it. I saw that all the yearning for Giorgio had grown into a massive yearning for me.

Some days, I was happy, as if a draft of fresh breeze caught me and carried me up for a brief time. But there had been a stream of constant problematic people and events that had been dragging me back down for several years now. I had had enough of dropping and had no intention of letting the falling go on. Something had to change.

I had a powerful sense of a need to go seeking. It pulsed inside of me where the tumor had been, and had the sense of a holy mission or a pilgrimage to find greater wisdom. Something was calling me. It connected with the Marco Polo part of me that felt a thirst to explore the mysteries of the world. It echoed out of the inexplicable experiences I had had and mirrored a part of me that wanted love and magic that was extraordinary. I suspect a desire to seek and see beyond the normal is not uncommon in people who have a brush with death. I had to find something out in the world to answer my need for deeper truths than the ones I had been living most of my life.

I couldn't explain it to myself. I couldn't explain it to Rio. I told him I had to go. Rio was confused about what was going on with me. My crisis had been intense. He knew intuitively that I had to go, yet he had no practical idea of what that meant.

I had the idea that I should go on a retreat. I searched online for one that might get me started in a different direction. I found a seminar that started in a week at Esalen, the famous retreat centre near Big Sur, California. There was one Esalen seminar that still had space available. I didn't even look fully into what the seminar was about when I booked it. I completely winged it. I was seeking with no map, just an inner compass and an inner knowing that I had to take a bigger step. I told Rio I was going for a week, would be back, and left in a completely unexpected direction.

Chapter 18

California: An Uncommon Retreat

The spectacular coastal city of Monterey sat on a peninsula surrounded by wave-splashed cliffs in radiant sunshine the day I arrived in California. Glamorous Monterey. Its famous Cannery Row area was once home to a booming sardine-canning industry and the setting for John Steinbeck novels I had read. Monterey had grown into an exciting seaside destination with restaurants, galleries, posh hotels, and the exclusive Pebble Beach golf resort a short drive down the highway. It had the sunny magnetism of Italy or Spain, but where those countries were steeped in centuries of history and tradition, Monterey was centuries younger and vibrant. This was California, after all.

I rented a car and drove 17 miles down the scenic coast from Monterey to Carmel-by-the-Sea, where I had booked a hotel room. Carmel is a gem of a seaside resort town with lots of artist shops, restaurants, fairytale cottages, and pure-white sandy beaches. It was soothing to be near the ocean. I browsed through Carmel shops displaying astonishing art and dined out on fresh oysters in lively American bars. Each morning, I drove 40 minutes south of Carmel to the Esalen retreat center near Big Sur for my seminar, passing through deep forests of pine, oak, and cypress, over the iconic Bixby Bridge, and along high coastal roads that wound over the cliffs blanketed by the dawn fog that rolled in over the ocean like massive weather fronts skimming the waves.

Esalen began as a retreat centre for alternative consciousness in the 60s and had a bit of a hippy reputation. It was sheltered in the forests giving it a close, intimate feel. It had rich gardens of vegetables that were used for organic vegetarian meals served in the retreat. It boasted some of the most dramatic views of the sea I had ever seen. The seminar I signed up for was given by a man named Paul Selig, an author and playwright from New York. Paul had unexpectedly begun to receive channeled communications from a group of unknown "Beings" from who knows where who spoke to him and gave him a message he was to share. His method of receiving the communication was to hear what was said to him and immediately speak it out loud, at which point it was recorded by a woman who typed as he spoke. The transcriptions were made into a series of books; the first of which was called *I am the Word*.

The idea of channeling may sound bizarre and may not be your cup of tea. I had some inexplicable things happen in my life. I thought of the Tea Man in Florence. I thought, "Channelling? Who knows what is possible under the sun? Knowledge evolves, new things come in, old things are thrown out. Things that begin by being rejected as impossible are later accepted. Like flying. Channeling might be possible, couldn't it?"

I remembered flying on the path behind Giorgio's hotel in Italy. It had been so real to me that I was actually flying. That's not anything considered normal. My thinking has always been, "Don't take the unusual too seriously. Don't let it derail you. Just see what you can learn that is practical in your life." I knew nothing about the channeling topic of Paul's seminar or what I was getting into when I booked it. So what if the topic of the seminar was bizarre?

The seminar lasted six days. Paul was a slightly balding, heavy-ish, quirky, and insecure man who found it difficult to understand why he, of all people, had become the recipient of channeling. It frustrated and plagued him. I wondered, *Did he have a choice if voices insisted on talking to him?* Paul made me laugh.

The people in the seminar were mostly young adults, with the exception of the woman who sat beside me who was closer to my age. During the course of the week, Paul would deliver the messages he heard from the voices, take questions from the group, and give responses from the Beings by hearing their answers and repeating them aloud to the group as rapidly as they were spoken to him.

Paul asked each participant who had a question to step forward to stand in the centre of the room, give their name and ask their question. There were questions about career, love life, and people looking for their twin flame. I hadn't come to the seminar with any idea what it was about and had no questions to ask.

As the days went on, a swirling, muddled interior pain I was not aware I had, began to surface. One day, I said I had a question and stepped into the centre of the room. I stood in distress as helpless sobs pushed out of me. I spoke of my lousy marriage and my worries that my children had suffered because of it.

"I am so worried that something I was a part of might have injured my children."

The Beings answered, "The job of being a mother is the hardest job on the planet. Your children are just fine."

The woman who sat beside me later said, "Thank you for asking that question. I needed to hear that, too."

With me still standing in the middle of the room, the Beings continued, "Please state the full name of your mother."

When I gave the name of my mother, who had passed away years earlier, Paul's face suddenly changed as he continued to communicate the words of the Beings. I saw him sitting before me with my mother's expression on his face, a man's face but weirdly also that of my mother. The look on his face expressed judgment and even resentment of me. It was chilling. I suddenly realized I had always been aware of my mother's judgment and resentment but never truly knew it until I saw it on Paul's face.

My mother had been a hard-working woman. How could she not be? She had six kids to care for and a busy household to manage. She also had a husband who could be sullen and bad-tempered, a man who worked very hard and brought home money that had to be carefully stretched to meet the family's needs. She was beautiful and could be delightfully gregarious in social situations, even though she was the opposite of gregarious in daily life. Most surprising, she was a woman with astonishing creative gifts and musical ability. Without having had a single music lesson, she could sit at the piano and play by ear with startling aplomb.

I loved and admired my mother, but there was not a single time as I was growing up when I felt close to her. She seemed beyond reach. There were times I had the sense she resented me for the opportunities and successes I had from my own musical talent. She had a way of coldly bringing me down when I accomplished something by saying things like, "Don't be a show-off" when I couldn't see how I was being a show-off at all. Still, she was my mother, and I loved her.

Our relationship changed unexpectedly when I gave birth to my daughter. In that shared experience of womanhood, my mother suddenly became a friend. She talked warmly and openly to me. We connected. It only lasted until my baby daughter was two months old when my mother was killed in a car crash. She was gone. Our budding friendship was gone. That loss shook me to my core. It took years to reconcile the violence of her death and the loss of her just when I had her.

As I looked at my mother's face superimposed on Paul's, I got an unexpected awareness about my mother and me and, even more, about me as a mother. With my own children, I made sure I was there for them. I hugged them and listened to them and celebrated their successes. I made sure they knew how much I loved them. I realized my mother had not been what I hoped for from a mother. I learned I was not my mother.

Another day before the beginning of the afternoon session, participants were sitting in the chairs that circled the room, waiting for the session to begin. There were empty chairs across the room from me. My eyes were drawn repeatedly to one of them. I turned my glance to my left to face Paul, who had begun to speak, but my eyes were drawn back again to the empty chair. I went back and forth between Paul and the chair a few times. I had a strange see-sense moment of seeing my husband sitting in that chair. He looked at me as if he were watching me and assessing me with aloof non-emotion. Was he there? If he was there, why was he there? Did he want to tell me something? I turned back to hear Paul and glanced again at the empty chair. The see-sense was gone.

Paul called out, "Wow! Did you see that? Did you see that light fly out of the room?"

Judge if you like. That's what happened.

Things occurring in that seminar were beyond strange, but somehow, I knew that there was something in it that I was looking for. I didn't overthink it. I just went with it. I left the Esalen retreat feeling lightened in an inexplicable way. I bought and read the books Paul Selig published. They had a profound influence on me. The gist of the books was about living life from joy. I thought, *What's so weird about that? What would living from joy mean for the me I'd like to be in the world, for the life I'd like to live, for my future?* Letting go of your suffering was the first step to the joyful life the Word books promised. Yes, I was definitely up for no more suffering.

There were still times when the ache for Italy, Giorgio, and the sensation of flying joy swept over me like an aloha. That thrill had been so all-encompassing it seemed I could not completely move on from it. Don't get me wrong. I loved Rio. He was a wonderful man. Our life together was beautiful. I loved him with a steady, gentle love, different from the flying love I had with Giorgio. How could I stop the aloha and rediscover the glowing, soaring me I couldn't seem to find again? How could I let go of my self-inflicted suffering?

I saw that love for myself had gotten completely intertwined with the dazzling experience of love with Giorgio. I struggled to find a way to tease apart the two threads. No, I'm not talking about twin flame stuff like the people in the Esalen seminar. I'm not talking about karma mentioned by the Tea Man in Florence either. I am talking about reclaiming my own thread, my own love of self, and learning to live in the fullness of everything I could be. There was something I was still not getting. My search to know continued.

Chapter 19

Springbank: A Healing Refuge

West of Calgary, there is a bucolic stretch of countryside called Springbank. Driving to the western edge of the city, you pass over Calgary's high plateau known as Paskapoo Slopes until the road reaches the end of city development. From there, a dramatic view of the lush valley of Springbank opens below you with a jaw-dropping vista stretching all the way west to the jagged marching line of the Rocky Mountains in the distance. As the road sweeps down from the slopes and through the valley, you traverse soft rolling hills past elegant homes owned by affluent Calgarians, past sprawling acreages, and horses running in the fields.

The day my real estate agent took me to see an acreage for sale ten minutes west of the city, I caught my breath as her car flew down the slopes and into the greenness of the valley. When we arrived at the property, we stood on the wide porch at the front entrance of the house, and I looked west over the four acres of the property and the pastureland before me. Something in the land rose up to greet me. I felt it move up from the ground, into my feet, and through my body. A sense of peace flooded me. I told my agent I didn't need to look at any other properties. This was it.

Rio and I moved to the acreage in the spring. The house was a fully renovated 100-year-old, two-story farmhouse with red siding, white trim, and a wrap-around deck with stone pillars and black railings. The house and deck were surrounded by pretty, black mulch-filled flower beds and sprawling green lawns. The entry of the house was a large, vaulted space that rose in a soft white peak to the second story. From there, you walked directly into a warm, creamy country kitchen and dining room. The entire space was wide open but grounded by rustic wide-plank hardwood floors of walnut brown. There were big rectangular windows or glass doors on all four sides of the house so light could flood through the home, turning it into a jewel box, sunrise to sunset. From a cozy sitting room off the kitchen, a dark wood staircase led up to the second floor with a large master bedroom, a marbled bath, and two additional bedrooms. The house was a beauty.

Rio and I moved when the markets were in a bull phase. The investments I now owned were earning well, and the costs of the property were within budget. We were full of optimism for making a life in the countryside which Rio and I both loved. We planted trees. Pink flowering hawthorns, red maples, and hardy varieties of tart cherry trees that had been developed at the University of Saskatchewan. I planted creamy white Beauty of Moscow lilacs and pink Vanilla Strawberry hydrangeas and filled the flower beds around the house with fuchsia foxgloves and blueberry bushes.

We created a garden out of the hard-packed grassland north of the house. I planted seeds in peat pots and filled every window in the house with bedding plants to put in the garden closer to summer. Our house looked like a big, glorious greenhouse with the sun streaming in and illuminating the glowing growing greenery that filled every window. Rio built hot beds out of polycarbonate in the garden for tomato and pepper plants that were too delicate for the chill that came daily, even in summer months, across the foothills from the mountains. Dad told me that gardens generally do not produce well the first year you open new garden land. He wanted to prepare me. That first summer, our garden flourished. The produce we harvested tasted like it came from heaven.

Rio and I enjoyed life to the full. We got a puppy. She was a three-month-old white, black, and brown Australian shepherd-cattle dog mix with puppy ears that flopped down to two points on either side of her head. She was so adorable and had such a captivating lively personality that Rio and I both cried when we first saw her. We named her Bella.

Beautiful Bella. While we worked in our yard, Bella raced around with us, digging in the dirt with wild abandon and sometimes trying to herd us with her big cattle dog spirits.

I tended the garden while Rio worked his job during the day, then spent weekends on the riding lawn mower, endlessly cutting the three acres of grass on the west side of the acreage. Back in the days when the property had still been a functioning farm, a barn and windmill once stood on the now-empty stretch of grass. That barn was long gone but it seemed there was an echo of it still on the land.

I had the idea of building a new barn, one with red siding and white trim to match the house. I thought we could create a retreat and art center to hold classes and rent to other groups or businesses for seminars. Many days, I walked out of my house and could see the new barn I would build sitting in the space of the ghost of the old one. I began to investigate the county requirements for building a barn and starting a business on an acreage. There were many.

Rio and I built a gleaming white two-rail ranch fence to mark the boundaries of our property. The property became even more of a stunner. Bella had run out onto the highway that passed near the acreage one day and had a close call with a car. Once the fence was in place, she miraculously respected the boundaries of the property. She would run wildly at top speed but always stop short at the fence. Bella was pure speed and dog joy on four legs.

As our home was a large one with lots of room for guests, family came to visit from out of town. We started a new tradition of having Christmas dinner cooked solely by the men and teen nephews. The courses were recipes of their choice, which they cooked while the bossy women of the family sat, sipped their wine, and tried not to supervise. Our first Christmas dinner was a roaring success.

We got to know our neighbors, who were delightful, down-to-earth property owners and maverick Albertans. We had a friendly country gentleman living across the road who loved having us as neighbors. He would drop by, always ready to help clear snow in the winter, plow our garden plot in the spring, fill us in on neighborhood gossip, or just chat. Our appreciation for him was immense. We affectionately dubbed him "Our Handy Neighbor."

On some hot summer days, I would look for Rio around the house and yard, only to find him across the road, sitting behind the Handy Neighbor's barn with a bunch of other men from the area, laughing and drinking beer, sheltered from the hot summer sun by the cool shade of the barn. Rio loved the company of those men, and they enjoyed his manliness, his happiness to be included in their group, and his love of a good joke.

Life was absolutely beautiful. No suffering in sight.

*　*　*

A year after Rio and I moved to the acreage, the markets had a major setback. A lot of money was lost from my investments. It was not easy for me to take. At that point, Rio made a modest income from his job in the construction industry, while the money I had was entirely from the investments that had been built up by my husband. I had been a co-partner in his consulting business and managed the books, even though I was a terrible bookkeeper. I had not had another job outside the home for twenty years. I was not used to making all the financial decisions on my own. Managing the investment portfolio was far outside my comfort zone. Especially during the market upheaval. With the markets a mess, I started worrying about money. The idea of building a barn became a question mark. Even if that idea became a reality, the income it might generate was a long way off. What could I do that would supplement our income? I began looking for career ideas that might fit my skills.

I had been a radio copywriter when I was first married. That ended when I had children. I had been a piano teacher when my children were young. That was not something I considered going back to, even though I loved it at the time. There was the painting I had done on my first trip to Italy and the Slovenian instructor's suggestion that I might like to paint professionally. Was there something there for me? No, I had pursued that for the pure joy I got from it. I loved the Italian and Cultural Geography courses I had taken at University. An art history professor offered me a job as his assistant for a project of going to Rome to bring a Leonardo Da Vinci exhibit to Calgary. I was thrilled, but the art history professor died unexpectedly before the project started. The job in Rome was a no-go, my university studies had been interrupted by my husband's death, and my health crisis had intervened to change my life direction. The career trail went cold.

I remember being asked when I was 18 years old what I intended as my career. At the time, I had no idea what I wanted to be. I only knew that I wanted to keep learning and keep growing my whole life, whatever that entailed. I loved being a student and learning new things. I loved being a mother. That was a special and unique type of career for me. I had sampled and tried a lot of different things. Now, I wanted something more.

With all my shifting pursuits over the years, an aunt I loved called me a dilettante. A dabbler. Her judgment of me stung. Is that how people saw me? A dabbler and a flake? There was something true and also something so false in those judgments. How did I see me, the searching, curious me, the deep and knowing me, the passionate, romantic, adventurous me? Those were the things that were most true about me. But what were those true things worth if other people didn't see them or if they did not amount to a reputable career or life purpose?

A thought came into my mind one day. Maybe my life purpose is more like the purpose of a bee. A bee flew and flitted from flower to flower, garden to garden, meadow to meadow as it invisibly carried pollen to fertilize plants, flowers, and the world. No one judged a bee for that. Maybe the life of a bee had meaning for me, and there was a contribution I brought to the world by living and being just as I was. Still, there were those damned financial markets. A bee didn't live in a reality where money mattered.

What kind of work could I do, a woman in her fifties? I scolded myself. Who cares about being in the fifties? My dad was 88, and he just retired from his job as a country plumber. I could start something completely fresh if I wanted to. I could look forward to 30 years of work ahead. I looked for something I could get excited about, do independently from home, and get into while my barn project took shape.

Through it all, the Springbank countryside continued to restore me and hold me in a safe place despite market turbulence and the unknowns of a career direction. I walked every morning down the quiet country roads from the acreage with Bella leaping exuberantly beside me in the tall, swaying grass in the ditch. In the sunrise, fog from the nearby Bow River rolled over the land like a fluffy blanket shimmering in the pastel pink morning sun making the landscape dreamy. I walked miles every day. The Earth never ceased to surprise me with its beauty. The land healed my body and soul as I knew it would from the first day I set foot on the property. Yet despite the family visits, neighbors, Bella and the life Rio and I shared, I was lonely through my days. Women who previously had been friends were gone, and I had not found new friends to replace them.

The second spring we lived in Springbank, I went to a Hay House conference in Denver. I thought I might like to write. I was a dedicated writer of my daily journal. I thought I might like to write something more, maybe write and publish a book. I loved books. I loved telling stories. I had stories to write. I went to Denver in search of inspiration. Many interesting writers spoke at the conference. A particularly memorable talk was from a young woman who wrote a book about her search for God in the world. She had had a heart condition and got a pacemaker that failed. She spoke of what it was like to feel herself dying and draining away from her body. She said she discovered that when she had drained away, all that was left was God. It reminded me of my husband dying and my discovery that when my anger drained away, all that was left was Love.

Chapter 20

Springbank: An Extraordinary Encounter

As the days turned from the cold of spring to the hot sultry weather and brilliant blue skies of summer in Alberta, Rio and I made plans to host a dinner party. We would host my daughter's father-in-law and his wife for the first time since the wedding. They were coming on the night of the Perseids meteor shower in August. We planned an evening of dinner and, later, star-watching from the open lawn on our property.

A week before the dinner, I got a call from my Vancouver Sister. She was four years younger than me and the oldest of my three younger sisters. She was a beauty. People thought she looked a bit like a cross between Jennifer Lopez and Angelina Jolie. She and I had been close, especially in recent years. She told me she and her guy were making a trip to visit Dad and would visit us for a few days as they came through Calgary. I was surprised at the suddenness of the visit but excited. Rio enjoyed prior occasions of socializing with them. We were both thrilled they were coming. They would arrive the day before the dinner party. We thought it would make for a lively evening.

Things didn't turn out that way. My sister's visit was a fiasco. It was like a sudden and unforecasted tornado ripped through our home, no warning sirens, only damage that years did not repair.

It started with a conversation between Rio and her guy while the two men sat drinking beer on the deck on the hot August afternoon they arrived. It continued the next day while Rio was at work with behaviour and things said that veered into the incomprehensible and left me stunned. It overran the dinner party that evening with hostility my sister's guy directed over dinner at my daughter's father-in-law, who went home at the end of the night feeling he had been insulted. It exploded the next day with my sister and her man leaving abruptly first thing in the morning and culminated a few days later with a torrent of shrieking by my sister, nasty threats and ultimatums from her guy, and a bunch of he said-he said about the conversation between the men on the deck the first day.

There was so much drama there was no possibility to talk clearly. Things got twisted, blown way out of proportion, and were sometimes outright false. In the end, Rio was accused of being a liar. I was completely blindsided by it all. The degree and violence of the turmoil left me spinning in shock. It was an ugly, incomprehensible mess.

Rio and I were sitting on the deck a day later. He looked at me directly, openly, and with clarity blazing in his eyes and said, "I can see what's going on here. I lied to you once, and now I am the liar. I did not lie in this situation. Yes, I lied to you once. I will never do it again."

I said, "I know. That happened a long time ago, and it has been forgiven and forgotten. And I know you were not the one who lied in this situation."

I did know. My only thought was that this was crazy. It was so enormous I had no idea what to do about it. I was so shaken I could barely form a clear thought. Then I was outraged. My sister sent me an email with a link to a website with helpful relationship advice, the implication being that my relationship needed help. What was her problem with Rio? Then I remembered the "Muslim immigrant" comment that had been thrown in with the threats and ultimatums by her guy. What was his problem? Who comes to someone's home and behaves this way? Added to my distress, now there was anger. How dare they!

Churning under all my upset was the question of how I would be able to clear things up with my sister. That was me, the oldest sister, the fixer. But I had no answers for this problem. My sister was furious. Where was her fury coming from? I had a sense it was not really about Rio and me but originated with something else, something between my sister and her guy hidden within the crisis. A kind of madness had started, and once it started, it seemed there was no stopping it.

A counselor once told me, "When people are playing crazy music, get off the dance floor."

How could I do that? This was my sister, to whom I had been very close.

* * *

After the fallout from my sister's visit, I needed time and space to breathe and stop the distress that raced through my body like an electrical current. It had been a situation of high stress which was something I was trying to eliminate from my life since my tumor. I had no idea what to do to change things. It was exhausting. The confusion and delusion of it all made my mind spin wildly. I couldn't relax. I couldn't sleep. I needed relief.

I decided to go into the city to join a meditation group I had been attending at a place called Home of OM. Spending time in meditation instead of worrying would be such a relief. I arrived at Home of OM to find there would not be a meditation as usual but a session on how to connect with spirit, particularly the spirit of a loved one who had passed. It wasn't at all what I had in mind, but I half-heartedly went along with it. I'd take any distraction that offered a little peace.

The group instructor, who was a Sensei master, lowered the lights and put on serene Asian music while participants sat on chairs in a semicircle around her. The safe environment of the darkened room began to calm me.

"There are many types of spirit we can connect with," the Sensei instructor began. "The easiest connections are with people we have known who have passed. Because of us, they still have a link with the earthly plane. They are often in communication with us though we may not know it. We receive messages from them which can take various forms. Most commonly, their messages are things that simply pop into our heads. We will prepare for spirit connection with a relaxation exercise."

I listened to the instructor as she walked us through the exercise.

Her gentle voice, the muted lights, and soft music with chimes tinkling in the background made the room seem like a soft, safe cocoon. My breath became gentle and rhythmic as I registered the sound of the chimes.

The instructor asked us to think of a loved one that we'd like to contact. The first person I thought of was my husband. I had done a lot of reflecting and talking to him over the years since he passed. I didn't need to connect to him. I thought of my mother. It had been a long time since I had seen her. Yes, it might be nice to hear from her.

The instructor softly spoke about the process of how to prepare for connection.

"Please, close your eyes and imagine your loved one standing in front of you."

I closed my eyes and looked at the inside of my eyelids to see if I could see anything. Nothing.

The instructor kept talking. I kept looking. It seemed that all I could see was static, the kind of static of an old TV set that was not linked to any broadcast. I looked again. Was there something moving within the static? No. I was just imagining it.

The instructor continued, "Now that your loved one is in front of you, you may ask him or her to take a step toward you."

She had barely spoken the words when there was a massive swoosh of air but not air. It rushed toward me and seemed to wrap me in a light embrace. I felt it physically, but it was not physical. I was encircled in warmth but not warmth, pressure but not pressure. The space around me was full beyond explanation. I took a sharp inhale of breath.

The instructor went on, "Your loved one will now take ten steps toward you, one step at a time. Ten ... nine ... eight ..."

There was no need to count. It was very clear to me that no more steps were required. My mother was already with me. I knew it but didn't know how I knew it. I sat stiff as a rod in her embrace. Was it her? My mind went blank and I could form no further thought. I could only sense what was in the space around me and listen to the instructor talk while the music continued to play.

The instructor suggested, "If you like, you may now ask your loved one a question."

I had no question. I could think of nothing. I could see nothing behind my closed eyes. I simply sat rigid and frozen in what seemed like a soft, pale pink and blue embrace that was palpable. This was so far beyond anything my mind would allow.

After a few minutes, the instructor said, "It's time to say goodbye to your loved one."

In that instant, I caught a momentary flash of my mother from behind my closed eyes. I knew it was her, yet could barely recognize her. She was so different from the mother I had known. She was young and utterly joyful. She flitted away from me like a lovely teenage girl dancing off into the distance. I started to shake in my chair.

The instructor asked us to slowly return to the present moment of the room. She went from person to person in the group to ask what they had experienced. When she got to me, I couldn't talk. I started to cry.

She asked, "Was that your mother?"

"Yes."

"I thought so. You look a lot like her. Only she was very young. Much younger than you are now. She was very beautiful."

"Yes. She was," I mumbled through my tears.

I was crying profusely now. The woman sitting on the chair next to me began digging in her purse for a tissue for me.

The instructor said, "We'll take a break before continuing the next part of the session, where we will talk about other types of spirit connections."

I got up from my chair and went to where she sat at the front of the group. Before I could say anything, she said, "Yes, I know. You are leaving."

In a daze, I walked from the room and opened the front door of the building to go out to my car. As I put my hand on the door handle, I heard a voice from somewhere around me say, "She's your little sister. She just wants to be like you."

I gasped and began sobbing as I walked to my car. This was really just too much. Shock mingled with the distress of the events of my sister's visit. Crying, I began my drive home, wiping my tears repeatedly so I could see the road. I got part of the way through the city when I remembered I had planned to stop at the grocery store on my way home. There was nothing at home to have for dinner. I stopped at the store and wandered through the produce section, then down the aisles in a trance with no clue of what I was doing. At some point, I remembered Rio had unexpectedly asked me that morning if I would make a certain dish he liked that I had only made once before. He couldn't remember what it was called. He described it.

"You remember ... you made the dish once. It had ground beef, red beans, green peppers, and a tomato sauce."

"Rio, I don't know what dish you are talking about." I was short. My stress-packed mind could not be bothered to think about what dish he meant. But now, as I stood in the grocery store, it hit me. Succotash. Rio had been asking for succotash. It was the dish my mother made countless times when I was a child. My mother's succotash.

All the air went out of me, and I started crying silently and helplessly in the produce section. I put my sunglasses back on and walked through the vegetables trying to find the ingredients I needed. I paid for my items and drove home, crying all the way.

When I got into the house with the groceries, I told Rio what happened at the meditation group. He listened intently without saying a word.

"Don't you think it strange that you asked me to make succotash—a dish I made for you only once a long time ago, a dish that was my mother's recipe—strange that you asked me for that dish today of all days?"

I looked at him with eyes that were red from tears. Rio nonchalantly looked back.

"Why did you ask me for that dish today of all days?" I asked.

"I don't know. It just popped into my head."

The meditation instructor's words echoed. "Messages just pop into your head."

"Maybe I am not the only one hearing from my mother," I said softly.

Rio just shrugged. "Maybe," was all he said.

* * *

After any kind of falling out, there is usually a need to go into who was right and who was wrong. It happens with family members or partners. Or with friends. Or enemies. I've come to realize that when a person thinks they are 100 percent right, it is often when they are the most wrong, wrong in some way that may not be obvious. Funny how that works.

I've learned that letting go of the need to be right or the need to fight is a huge gift. Letting go, in general, makes life so much easier. Sometimes, letting go is the only choice when you know the other person is not receptive or ready for reconciliation. This was the situation with my sister.

My sister was so angry, she heard nothing I said in the months and years that followed when I tried to reconnect with her. She has a very hard time letting go. She is difficult to talk to once there is anger. That's true for most of us, isn't it? I knew where the tendency for anger came from. It was a factor in our childhood home. Good communication skills were not something learned and practiced either. Then, there was the need to be right. It was a hidden subconscious theme in my family, where we lived with traditional Catholic ideas of being flawed by original sin and needing forgiveness, the fear of judgment after death, and Sunday chants of "I am not worthy." The upshot was it was dangerous to be wrong because there were dire consequences. You had to strive to be good and perfect and right. You couldn't sin, and you better not even make a mistake.

How could I let go of my need to be right about what happened during that traumatic summer visit? How could I let go of the sick, churning feeling inside? It seemed letting go meant, first, stepping away from thinking I had to be the oldest sister and the fixer. I could be a caring sister, but not in the "I have the answers because I am the oldest sister, so let me care and tell you how to fix the problem" way. Being the responsible oldest sister had been drilled into me as a child. That had to end.

That I cared about my sister was the truth, never mind any childhood sibling rivalry or misunderstandings over the years. Under all the mayhem, I loved her. How could things be cleared up when communication had broken down so there could be love between two sisters? I just didn't know. To start, I could simply keep reaching out and let her reach back when she was ready.

My sister once said to me, "You have no idea how much our relationship means to me."

I had replied, "It's the same for me."

It seemed I had lost my sister. At least for now. It was heartbreaking for me. I thought of painful losses like the loss of Giorgio and now my sister. Can the heartache of losing an Italian lover compare to the sorrow of losing a sister who had been with me for my lifetime? There was also the loss of my mother, who strangely reappeared in the middle of the turmoil with my sister. What did she mean when she said, "She's your little sister. She just wants to be like you?" At first blush, it might seem obvious what she meant, but I had a sense there was something else she was telling me. It niggled in my brain.

The coincidence of events that included my mother, my sister, and me left me with the sense that we three were bonded in some way that seemed to be full of Not-Love when, in actuality, I think it was Love. I sensed a truth in that but couldn't fully grasp it. Maybe you see it. Oh, how mysterious life can be.

Then I saw the wisdom of letting life bring healing in its own time. Things would unfold in the future as they would. I could work with that. In the meantime, there was no right or wrong. What nonsense the idea of right and wrong is. There is only each person doing the best they can within who they are. I could do my best, make no judgments of myself or anyone else, and allow the peace of doing and being my best be more than enough. What if I lived my life from that? Who knows? That just might be the wind under my wings.

PART III

Updraft

Chapter 21

Discovery: Frankincense & Roses

After two nurturing years of sweet life together on the Springbank acreage, Rio and I decided to move back into the city from the country. Our house was beautiful, but it was just too big for the two of us. It was too expensive for what we required, especially with another market upheaval and more money lost the second year. The expense of living on the acreage could no longer be justified.

The acreage had required a lot of upkeep. I started to develop arthritis in my hands, which made gardening difficult. There were other challenges. The young trees we planted the first spring took a hit in the fall from an early September snowfall that was so wet and heavy it broke their branches. The garden that flourished in the first year failed in the second. And county requirements for a barn and related business also turned up many more obstacles than I expected. I was in a program at the cancer center for follow-up scans related to the tumor I had had. The results had been clear so far. I had five years of scans to complete. I hated having to go to those appointments. It felt like my illness was following me and would not let me go, even though I knew in my heart that my tumor would not return. All of the challenges turning up in my life just made me weary. I began to get the sense that maybe the retreat I had in mind when I first moved to the country and dreamed of a barn was one that was only meant for me.

It had been a glorious retreat. Rio and I loved our country life. The views west from our house over gentle sloping pastures blessed us with sublime sunsets and magnificent vistas of the mountains. The serene, pale pink and blue sunrises in the east forever after reminded me of my mother's embrace in the meditation group. We loved the sunny peace, the country friendliness of our neighbors, and the luxurious spaciousness of the rolling ranchland, which was not empty as a city person might think but teeming with life and a presence that was richer and more nourishing to the soul in many ways than the bustle and excitement of the city. It was a different way of life. Now, something told me it was time to go. It was as if there were a new chapter opening and calling me.

The sale of the property happened so fast that we set a record in the countryside. It seemed like a confirmation. The choice to move was the right one. With packing and cleaning, I didn't have time to mourn leaving until the last day when I walked out of the house, closed the door gently behind me, and walked down from the wide front porch. I wept. Then gratefully, I let it go from my life. It had served its purpose.

Rio and I found a house in a peaceful Calgary neighborhood called Discovery on the western edge of the city. It was a quiet residential area set beside the Elbow River with lots of nature around it. Interspersed between the houses were large expanses of grassy hills with treed winding paths perfect for walks with Bella, who was now a powerful, full-grown dog who required lots of exercise to satisfy her high-energy needs. We bought a two-story home with a big backyard. It was pretty and comfortable. Truth is, I never loved our Discovery house the way I adored our Springbank home, but with its abundant green spaces, Discovery seemed a good compromise between city and country. I rather liked the name of the neighborhood, too. Discovery. It spoke of what I wanted in life.

After we got settled, I slipped into a routine of days spent writing in the sunny large office I created in the bonus room above the garage. I lined my walls with my paintings of Italy, filled my bookshelves with all my favorite books, and sat every morning with my coffee, writing by hand in my journal using the glorious colored ink I bought for my fountain pen. My search took the form of joining online personal development webinars, reading esoteric books, and playing with tarot cards. Ideas for books I could write began to pop.

I loved tarot cards. It was a private, playful practice I had had for years. I considered the cards as snapshots of some advice that was good only in the moment you drew the card, not as tools for foretelling the future. That worked well for me. There were cards that I identified with—the Empress, the Sun, and the Fool, who reminded me of seeker Tobias from the *Chiesa San Raphael* in Venice. It was not hard for me to see that I was often the Fool, blithely going through life with an underlying optimism that never failed to keep me moving forward, even in the worst times, even through tears. Yes, I shed a lot of tears over the years, but that was not what I was truly about. My nature was to let nothing stop me and always find a way to return to the optimism of the Fool. Yet, the Fool could be naïve and oblivious. I had been that, too.

My daughter and her husband announced that they were expecting a baby girl in the coming summer. Our new home in Discovery was only 15 minutes from my daughter's house. It was lucky I would be so close to her and the new baby. There would be lots of excitement when the grandchild arrived. She would bring freshness, a new chapter, too.

* * *

Our Discovery life was quiet and pleasant with none of the activity and palpable presence in the landscape we had loved on the acreage. It seemed I had sailed my boat into the calm of the doldrums. Travel was something that always gave me a boost, as it does for so many people. Rio and I decided to take a holiday to Italy. Incredible Italy had been my happy place. I had gone with my son. Now, I would go with Rio.

We flew to Rome and enjoyed a couple of days sightseeing, then rented a car and drove to Umbria for a week on an *agriturismo*. The sprawling stone house was once a family residence and had been converted into apartments for guests. All the windows of our apartment gave serene views of the lush countryside and spring-green olive groves belonging to the property. We had a bedroom, spacious sitting area and kitchen that was a marvel of Italian design. What looked like a simple bureau in the kitchen opened upward to reveal a stove, sink, fridge, and prep area below.

Rio and I cooked simple meals, swam in the outdoor pool, and toured the quiet famous hill towns that dotted lovely Umbria: Todi, Spoleto, Spello, Norcia, and Assisi. Assisi was the destination that called to me the most. I had left Catholicism behind me long ago, but I was drawn to go there because my mother loved Saint Francis of Assisi. She was in my mind the day we drove to Assisi.

On the way there, I told Rio the story of Francis and his origins in a wealthy Florentine family. As a young man, Francis gave up his worldly wealth and began ministering to the poor. I talked of my mother's love for the saint. Rio sat in silence, listening with full presence, a rare thing when so many people listen while planning what they mean to say in return.

As I talked of my mother, unexpected tears welled up, and my throat tightened. They reminded me of the tears that threatened to overwhelm me when my mother died, ones so intense they frightened me so I pushed them down. Here they were, surging up from wherever they had been hidden. There had been so much surfacing about my mother in recent years. These tears now felt like a softening. A loving softening. By the time we arrived in Assisi, they were done.

We parked the car and began to walk. There was a gentle numinous peace in the sun-warmed narrow streets that wound like a maze through Assisi. Stairs took us up, down, and around as we walked in the general direction of the famous basilica. We came upon a small chapel with a sign on the doorway: *Santa Maria delle Rose*. The chapel had a very plain stone exterior with a few small steps under a brick archway leading to two wooden doors. We decided to go inside.

Santa Maria delle Rose was no longer a chapel. It had been converted into an art gallery housing an exhibit created around the Virgin Mary. The pews and all things ceremonial were gone and replaced with an illuminated circle of carvings of Mary. The artist's intent was that when you looked at the carvings from different angles, they showed different aspects of Mary standing, praying, and pregnant. There were small replicas of the exhibit carvings for sale, smooth meditation pieces of sculpted stone that fit perfectly in one's hand. I bought one for myself and one for my pregnant daughter. Something about Mary was pushing into my mind. It was not about her big role in religious history. It was something else.

Rio and I left the chapel and continued walking past quiet lunch places, shops, and silent monks in flowing brown robes until we rounded a corner. There was the basilica, sitting at the end of a long grassy lawn with its back to the verdant valley below. We walked to the arched double doors of the entrance and followed the crowd inside. The musky church interior was adorned with famous frescos, religious relics in gold, and a scant hint of incense. There was nothing there that drew me to stay. Something about it repelled me. After a brief visit, Rio and I left. Once we began driving out of the town, I began to speak aloud about what was pushing into my mind.

"What is bothering me is the fact that Francis was a man who gave away all his worldly wealth, yet here was a large ornate basilica built in his name. That doesn't seem to represent Francis at all. It's about Catholic pomp and opulence. It's the antithesis of how Francis chose to live."

Rio, my ex-Muslim man, just nodded and listened.

"And there was the chapel of *Santa Maria delle Rose*. Maria of the Roses. Such a plain chapel. Such a simple woman. Who was she?"

A picture came to mind of an innocent young woman who gave birth to a child. Nothing more than that. Or maybe she loved roses and loved to tend them. Or maybe she was as sweet as a blooming rose. She had been turned into an icon by a Catholic agenda.

What, then, was all the pomp and ceremony around those two? Who needed that? Had my mother needed something from that? She had been a devout woman. I heard she once wanted to become a nun. For me, Catholicism had nothing I needed, yet as we left Assisi, a wafting scent of frankincense and roses followed me and played in my senses for years after.

* * *

After Umbria, Rio and I drove south to Amalfi. Rio said Amalfi was the most wonderful place he had ever been in the world. Going south from

Umbria and making a wide circle around chaotic Naples, we came to the famous winding Amalfi coast road. I had driven the road easily before, but now it was jammed with tourist vehicles, buses, and the cars of impatient Italian drivers who evidently couldn't understand why tourists could not navigate the road beyond a snail's pace. The Italians vigorously waved their hands out their car windows at vehicles and drivers they passed. "*Che cosa il problema?*" There was almost an inch to spare, plenty before you'd scrape your car on the stony walls along the road or hit a bus that was painfully trying to navigate a tight turn. The passionate Italians made me laugh with absolute delight.

We drove past Positano and Praiano to the *borgo* of Conca dei Marini, where I had booked us into a bed and breakfast named *Ercole di Amalfi*. Hercules of Amalfi. It was situated on the mountainside up from the main road and was reached by a steep narrow winding lane. The B&B was named after the man who built the house and had been a legend in Amalfi for his strength.

An Amalfi taxi driver told us, "That man was known as the Hercules of Amalfi. He was the most powerful man in the area. He could carry massive beams and heavy stones up and down the hillsides without tiring at all. His strength was far greater than everyone else's. After he died, his daughters converted the house into a B&B."

"What a great story," I said. "We love the beautiful B&B." And I thought to myself, *Hercules sounds a bit like Rio, who also has massive, tireless strength.*

The B&B was modern, cool, and lovely. From our room, there were doors that opened onto a sitting area under a shady pergola that was covered with fruiting lemon trees. A few steps down from the sitting area was a terrace with bistro tables for dining *al fresco* with an unobstructed view of the endless blue sea and of the nearby *Monastero Santa Rosa* convent turned luxe hotel and spa sitting on its promontory high above the water.

Rio and I dined on the terrace on salami, cheese, and fresh bread that we tore into bite-sized pieces from the loaf. We ate like peasants and felt like kings. We clinked our wine glasses and smiled at each other at our good fortune of finding this little piece of paradise. Our souls felt expanded by the air, the sky, and the shimmering sea.

That trip did not have the exhilaration I experienced in previous trips to Italy. It was a soft, romantic, soul-satisfying time, like a *dolce* after a mouth-watering, sense-exploding meal. It seemed to heal something in my relationship with my mother. It left me with a sense of the mysterious calling of Frankincense & Roses. It was mostly a shared time of sweet simplicity for me and my loving man and best friend, Rio.

Frankincense & Roses became a whispering presence in my world. Its scent wafted through the days and years after Assisi and seemed to be calling me to something. What, I didn't know. Was it calling me to purpose? I had the idea of getting serious about becoming a writer. Maybe writing was what Frankincense & Roses was about. A book. What was I searching for? If you had asked me at the time, I would have told you I was searching for freedom.

In one of my Italian classes years earlier, I heard a woman author give a talk about being born in Sicily and moving to London to become a lawyer only to also become an author and write all her books about Sicily. I thought, *I could go the opposite direction, leave my English-speaking country and go to Sicily to write.* I told Rio he could do something like become a fisherman during the day while I wrote. We would dine out and sightsee in the evenings. We both loved the idea. There was a choice asking to be made.

Chapter 22

Kosovo: Small Miracles

Early the following year, Rio got an urgent call from Kosovo. A good friend of his, Maxi, had been thrown in jail in Bulgaria. The story was that Maxi had been in the capital of Sofia with another friend who was trying to buy cheap cigarettes from two Bulgarian guys to sell on the black market in Kosovo. Apparently, Maxi wasn't involved in the deal. He was in the wrong place at the wrong time. The men were sitting in a café having coffee over the negotiation of the cigarette purchase when the police swooped in and made arrests. Maxi got scooped along with the others.

Maxi was in jail with no way of getting out except by paying a lawyer 2500 euros to take his case. If he was unable to get a lawyer, he would stay in jail indefinitely. There was no one in Kosovo who had 2500 euros to give to Maxi, so Rio got the call. Rio was upset about his friend's crisis. He didn't have the money available, so he asked me.

"2500 euros is a lot of money to send to someone I don't know," I argued. "2500 euros to get someone out of jail when I don't know him or all the circumstances of how he got there."

Rio and I went around and around the matter of sending money to Kosovo.

"I know my friend is innocent. I've known him for 25 years. Maxi is a family man. His sons will have no father if Maxi is left in jail."

"Rio, I understand that you know him. But I don't. And how can you be absolutely sure he was not involved in the cigarette deal."

"I just know him. He will never get out of jail if we don't help. That's how it is in Bulgarian jails. You have to have money to get out, or you don't. Ever."

I was involved in one of many online courses that I was taking at the time. The current one was called *Awaken the Species* by a famous writer Neale Donald Walsch who wrote a book called *Conversations with God*. Walsch talked about the way we are living on this planet. One of the things he talked about was giving. He said if someone asked you for money, just give it. Did he mean 2500 euros? What kind of strange coincidence was it that I was taking that course at the same time Maxi's dilemma came up?

For me, the idea of sending a lot of money to someone I didn't know seemed like holding out the money in my hand and having my hand cut off as the money was taken. But in the end, I saw how important it was to Rio, and I capitulated. I was shaking when we went to Western Union to wire the money to Maxi's wife, whose plan was to go to Sofia to meet a woman who had a friend in the police force who would help.

A lawyer was hired. The lawyer arranged a call from prison for Maxi. The only person Maxi called was Rio. The lawyer took the 2500 euros, did his work, and a month later, Maxi was released.

Gratitude overflowed from Maxi and his family. I had never experienced anything close to that kind of gratitude before. Rio made sure everyone knew that I was the one who had come up with the money. The gratitude washed over me like a miracle that I was beyond comprehending. No cutting off of hands. In the end, it seemed to me that 2500 euros meant little in the face of that.

Rio and I had planned a trip to Kosovo during our first winter in Springbank. He had not been home in almost ten years and was incredibly homesick. We had booked our flights and told no one except my family and Rio's family in Kosovo's capital Pristina that we were going, but somehow Rio's ex-wife found out about the trip and called her brothers who lived there. Her brothers called Rio's brother for coffee and told him to let Rio know that he had better not ever think of coming back to Kosovo, or they would be waiting for him. Rio's mother was distraught and urged Rio not to come. Our trip was canceled.

This year, Rio and I planned another trip to Kosovo after Christmas. Going home was more urgent for Rio than any threat his ex-wife's brothers could make. I won't pretend I wasn't more than a little nervous about going. Kosovo seemed a little scary. Would his ex-wife's thug brothers be waiting for us?

We booked our flights, and Rio told his family not to tell anyone we were coming. We celebrated Christmas Eve with my family, flew on Christmas Day, and planned to stay in Kosovo into the new year. After 20 hours of flying from Canada to Switzerland to Kosovo, we arrived at the Pristina airport late in the evening of Boxing Day. Rio looked around the airport in wonder. A new modern airport had been built since he was in Kosovo ten years earlier.

"The last time I was here, you wouldn't have been surprised to see sheep being herded through the airport," he said. "Everything is totally different."

Rio's brother was waiting for us. He was an overweight man with a round face, glasses, and thinning hair. He looked nothing like Rio. The two brothers shared a long embrace. Rio's brother didn't have a car and had arranged with a friend who drove a taxi to take us home. Rio stared out of the window at the night lights and busy new thoroughfares of Pristina passing by us. He said he had no idea where we were or where we were going. Everything had changed.

We arrived at the apartment building where Rio's family lived. His brother had an apartment on the second floor. Rio's mother lived in an apartment Rio owned on the third. His mother was standing at the top of the stairway from her apartment, looking down the stairwell, waiting for us to arrive. Rio rushed up the stairs, glancing up to where she stood as he ran. When he reached her, she began to sob and shake. Rio folded her in his arms and let her burrow her head into his chest. She had waited ten years to see her son again. Rio's sister-in-law took the shaking woman into the apartment to sit her down and calm her. She made tea for me and Rio whom she called "Agi" or uncle, a term of respect.

Everyone made a point not to look directly at me. I was the Canadian woman who had absconded with their son and brother. It was okay by me if they didn't acknowledge me beyond a brief greeting. This was Rio's long-awaited visit. I was a stranger from a foreign country. I must have looked a little out of place in their home, the blonde Canadian woman who spoke no Albanian, who was not Muslim, who dressed differently, and who came from a wealthy country. I might as well have been from another planet. That was okay, too. I reverted to an old childhood habit of sitting quietly so I could listen while adults talked. I heard a lot of interesting things people did not intend for me to hear that way. I found out I could make myself invisible.

A day later, Maxi and his wife, Irena, came to visit. They were beyond excited and greeted us like we were their long-lost, dearest friends. They had big plans. They were going to treat us to a trip through Kosovo, Albania, and Macedonia.

We drove south from Pristina to the historic city of Prizren, which dates as far back as the Bronze Age. While we strolled through the city, I got gently scolded for spontaneously dancing to the lively music of Roma street buskers.

Rio told me, "We Albanians had a good relationship with the gypsies until the war with Serbia. We got along. We helped each other. Then, the Roma betrayed us to the Serbs. Most Albanians have still not forgiven them. Better if you don't dance to their tune here in the street."

I wasn't bothered by Rio checking me on my dancing. I only thought *War is just the stupidest thing*!

We continued west, flying on the autostrada at top speed through stunning, untamed mountains to Tirana, the capital of Albania. Driving through Tirana was absolute mad chaos that seemed to me even worse than Naples. Our party was a lively group of people who laughed at the insanity of it all. It was such fun. We stopped in the city for lunch of fresh-caught fish from a vendor in the marketplace in downtown Tirana. We waited while the vendor flash-cooked our fish, then took our steaming parcels to a nearby café to enjoy it over crisp cold glasses of beer.

In the evening, we dined at a dinner-dancing spot in a hotel resort. There was a band with a famous Albanian singer who entertained us with American pop and Albanian music while we feasted on the delicious dishes of Albanian specialties that covered our table. People brought their entire families to the event, even little children, and everyone danced. It was a warm family event like nothing I had experienced before. Irena taught me an Albanian traditional dance where the woman twirled and fluttered a white handkerchief above her head to entice the dancing man near her.

Lastly, we drove through Macedonia to the capital of Skopje, where street signs were written in the Slavic Cyrillic alphabet. I could comprehend none of it. It filled me with a taste of exotic adventure. The whole trip happened in two days. It was a laughter-filled whirlwind with lots of jokes, food, and dancing.

Maxi and Irena also planned a New Year's Eve celebration at a newly built resort outside of Pristina. Their entire family of 30 people or more came to party for the new year and celebrate Rio and me. People dressed in their finest clothes. The ladies were in holiday gowns, the men in suits and ties. We feasted on whole lamb roasted outside on a spit, fresh Albanian cheeses, and a banquet of vegetables, salads, and sweets.

After dinner, there was dancing to a mix of traditional Albanian and North American pop music. Everyone danced, young and old. No one held back. They expressed their full body joy for the celebration. Rio is a wonderful and enthusiastic dancer. He was in his glory and looked super sexy to me. The men in their elegant suits danced arm-in-arm in a line in traditional Albanian style. The women smiled and twirled. More handkerchief waving.

Rio was welcomed by Maxi's family like a long-lost son. I was treated like a queen. The older women eyed me from the corners of their eyes. The younger women who could speak English crowded around, eager to hear about North America. They might have been young women from a poor country, but they were also utterly modern and smart, with a passion for hip-hop music and fashion. They had jobs. With the internet, they knew what was happening in the rest of the world. They had plans. Rio told me that when his grandmother was married, her eyes had been pasted shut with a flour and water concoction for the entire wedding day until her husband, whom she had never seen, washed the paste from her eyes on their wedding night. What a departure it was for these young women from those prior generations. So much had changed in Kosovo.

The evening was a glorious sensation. It had been a very long time since I celebrated New Year's Eve as a major event. Rio's homecoming was a smash hit. I had never seen him happier. We danced and partied until midnight when everyone joyfully wished each other *"Urime,"* congratulations on the start of the New Year.

As our Kosovo visit went on, I made a better connection with Rio's family, thanks to his teenage niece and nephew, who had taken English lessons and were completely fluent. They spoke more polished English than many North Americans and facilitated conversation between the family and me. I was no longer invisible.

I asked Rio's brother, "Do you think Rio has changed since he's been in Canada?"

"Phew! Completely changed."

From the stories Rio told me, I knew he had been an intense young man. I had a sense that he had not been satisfied with the life of poverty and war he had been born into. Now, he was changed. Under all the hot-headedness of the guy he had been, there was the sweetest heart ever to be found in a man. He had both intensity and heart. I loved that.

We settled into daily life with the family. Rio's sister-in-law had the responsibility for all the domestic jobs in the house. She cleaned and made all the meals, simple meals that were spectacular. One day, she made a dish called *passoule*. She slowly baked beans with chunks of beef that had been smoked for long periods over a wood fire. The aroma that wafted from her oven was tantalizing. The taste of the *passoule* was indescribably delicious. It was smoky and savory and tasted like it came from something living.

Another day she made *bourek*, the famous traditional pastry accredited to Bosnia, which was also a staple in Kosovo. I watched her prepare the dough with nothing more than flour, salt, and water, then knead it, spin it, and stretch it in her hands until it was a paper-thin sheet ready for filling. The dough, which had started as a plain lump of flour and water, turned into something glistening and luminous as she worked it. Impossible. I expressed my wonder at her handiwork, and she gifted me with a happy smile.

She went on to lay out the sheet of dough on a large cloth on the table and began adding rows of cheese and leek filling, then rolled the dough until she had a 4 or 5-foot sausage-like strand that she coiled in a pan to bake. The bourek came out of the oven golden brown, cheesy and delicate. It disappeared into the mouths of the hungry family. Did they even realize what they were eating? It was a bit of magic disguised as pastry.

In the evenings, the family sat together to have tea served by Rio's sister-in-law. The living room was small and furnished with three couches placed in a U-shape with a coffee table in the middle. When everyone gathered on the couches, there was barely enough room from couch to table for knees. There were barely enough seats as well because it was common for visitors to drop by and join for tea. Everyone squeezed in and sat face to face, shoulder to shoulder, to sip tea and talk.

The evening conversations often went on until midnight, with Rio's sister-in-law constantly replenishing the ever-disappearing tea in the cups. The conversations were animated. Those Albanian people loved to talk, and they loved to laugh. The conversation was beyond me, of course, but every now and then, after a raucous round of laughter, Rio would stop and translate the joke for me. While he spoke, everyone listened in total silence to watch for my reaction. When I burst out laughing, everyone smiled and picked up their stories and jokes again. Laughter was a valuable commodity for them in a country where other kinds of commodities were scarce. How beautiful is that!

Rio and I received many return invitations to tea from friends and relatives. Each time we arrived at the home of our hostess, we were treated like royalty. The tea table was set with the best she had to offer. There were beautiful cakes, chocolates, nuts and fruit. In every home, we were served giant portions of cake, which were enough for two or three people, in my opinion. But I didn't want to say no to the cake and risk offending the hostess. I ate the cake that was served to me, little knowing that after I ate the first piece, a second would be plopped on my plate.

By the time we had a few teas with generous Albanian ladies, I told Rio, "Of all the dangers I dreamed I might encounter in Kosovo, there is one I never expected. In Kosovo, they could kill you with cake."

Rio roared with laughter.

I know Rio's sister-in-law would have liked to talk to me directly without the necessity of her daughter as a translator. I was like a new sister-in-law for her. She was curious to know about Canada.

"What did I think of Kosovo?" her daughter translated. "We are poor here. What was it like in Canada?" Her daughter passed on my answers.

"There are so many wonderful things in Kosovo even though you don't have much money. You have a close family, wonderful times you spend together, and beautiful food. Yes, in Canada, we have family, but many people live great distances apart. We have money and lots of things. We also have lots of people with loneliness and depression."

How could I adequately explain to her how keenly I appreciated the warmth, liveliness, and gratitude of the people I met in Kosovo? It made Canada seem almost cold.

* * *

One of Rio's greatest regrets was that he had been unable to attend his father's funeral. He wanted to see his father's grave. His brother took us to the cemetery and led us to their father's headstone. He stepped forward first and knelt at the gravestone, bowing and praying. He stood up, and Rio walked somberly forward. Unexpectedly, tears started in my eyes. I knew how much this moment meant to Rio. He knelt and made no prayers or gestures. He said he had no right to do that. He was no longer truly Muslim.

I recalled a similar feeling when I attended Catholic mass with my father. I was no longer a Catholic by any stretch of the imagination, yet I went with him out of respect. When my father got up to go to communion, I hesitated. I had no right to go to communion. I hesitated for only a moment, then got up and went with my father. If there is a God, he or she is far beyond Catholic rules. I'm pretty sure I would be forgiven for going to communion out of respect for my father.

Now at his father's grave, Rio just kissed the tips of his fingers and held them on his father's headstone. I couldn't stop the tears. I wiped them from my face with the edge of the cape I wore. I could feel the sorrow Rio couldn't express. He had been closed in and shed no tears. As we drove from the cemetery, Rio turned from the front seat where he sat with his brother to where I sat weeping in the back and softly said, "Thank you."

Rio, the ex-Muslim man, and I, the ex-Catholic girl, never had a single issue around religion. Rio once said to me he didn't care about following Islam. It was no different in his view than any other religion. God was God. No matter what you called him.

* * *

After Rio and I returned from Kosovo, I took other trips that year on my own, exploring-seeking bee that I am. I had wanderlust. My wanderlust was so intense it made my body ache. I thought of lust, of Giorgio, of aching. Lust is one of the Seven Deadly Sins of Catholicism. Yes, I will confess. I lusted for Giorgio, along with the love. Pride is another Deadly Sin. The saying goes, "Pride comes before a fall." I knew about falling. What about lust for life, for greater life, and for the beauty the Earth affords? What about pride of self and self-love that is essential for a good life? I saw that the only sins are ones that take you from being true to yourself in a soul-expanding way, whatever that means for you. Even if it means being a little bee.

In April, I went to a Writer's Workshop in Las Vegas put on by Hay House Radio. The *piece de resistance* was the keynote address given by a man named Joe Dispenza. His address blew my mind. He gave an impassioned yet gentle speech that was a scientific and eloquent plea for the planet. He talked about the nature of humans and our impact on the Earth, hoping to inspire us to change how we live and work together for our world. I was in awe and leaped to my feet to join the standing ovation he received.

After the last lecture of the weekend, I headed for the on-site bookshop and bought Joe Dispenza's books. I clasped them to me while I continued to browse. Books have been a major part of my life. They seem to call me. I scanned the tables of books and picked up one by a man named Dain Heer. *Being You, Changing the World*. I had no idea who Dain Heer was. He was very handsome, though. I put his book down and wandered along the tables again, only to find myself back at Heer's book. I picked it up, put it down, and finally took it with my other books to the cashier to pay. I went home from the conference and began reading Dispenza while I put the other books on my shelf.

Dispenza had a miraculous story. He had been injured in a car accident and was told he may not walk again. He left doctors and diagnoses behind and went off by himself to heal himself. He developed a meditation technique of using the mind to change the body and came back from his self-created retreat walking. He began holding teaching retreats around the world with a philosophy that was far from ordinary. I went to Barcelona for my first Dispenza retreat, followed by a second in Sardinia. I began meditating for an hour each day using his techniques. I'm not sure if I changed my body with my mind, but the peace I got was a blessing.

That summer, my daughter gave birth to a glorious little girl they named Penelope Rose. Poppy for short. I was given the name Gigi because my daughter knew I did not want to be called Grandma. The name "grandmother" gives me the willies. I was too young at heart for that. I was nothing like my own grandmothers, who had been sad women resigned to the travails of life. I had lots of living yet to do. Gigi was perfect.

Shortly after my daughter and her husband took tiny Poppy home from the hospital, my daughter went through a difficult postpartum depression. As Gigi, I took on the job of babysitting. Those days with an infant were big ones, with no time to meditate, but the time I spent with Poppy was worth every minute. Poppy was a magical force of nature. She had a sky-high energy and sense of knowing her own mind I've never seen the likes of. Sparkling Poppy stole my heart.

What about my own sparkle and vision for life beyond being Gigi and babysitting? Within all the upheaval since my husband died, it seemed I had lost myself. I wanted to glow again! I know what makes me sparkle. It begins with romance. I love the five-senses thrill of being alive, traveling to exotic places, new experiences, new outlets for curiosity and new things to study. With all my searching since my tumor, I realized there were big things I was searching for, not just the meaning of love or the truth about myself. I was searching for the extraordinary in life, in the astounding beauty of the Earth, of the world, of me. I wanted the miraculous magic of life. There had to be magic, didn't there? Otherwise, was life truly worth living?

I found magic many times, especially in those days with Giorgio, which seemed like the ultimate irresistible love that somehow kept sucking me back into a romantic dream. It was a glorious romance that made me soar, yet I could see that love, romance, and sex did not completely satisfy a deeper longing I had. They can sometimes be blinding illusions. I now had a man who adored me and fit my life, but I realized a man's love wasn't truly what I was searching for either. I had to laugh at myself. I was starting to sound a bit like Giorgio, who said no to the love between us so he could find himself.

Oh my God, I loved the magic of all of it. Love and magic went together for me. I saw that living was about the chance to experience love, and love was one experience of magic. I wanted the magic. Not blind illusion. Magic. I wanted to fly again.

"Where are my wings?" I wondered. "I want to be free to fly!" My life may have been chaotic, and I may have been flitting about, but I am happy to live my life that way. It's who I am. It's my life to live the way I've come to live it. I would rather die than live a mundane life. I wanted to know exactly what it would take to have the full magic of life.

Chapter 23

Calgary: A Little Bit of Magic

One gorgeous, sunny summer morning, I drove to Pigeon Lake in central Alberta. I was a little amazed to find myself on this unexpected journey driving north on the four-lane Queen Elizabeth II highway out of Calgary through soft rolling prairies and green fields of Alberta. I vibrated with excitement and wondered at how I got headed in this direction. I was going to Pigeon Lake for my first Access Consciousness class on The Bars®.

Just as summer started, I had finished the last of the books I bought in Las Vegas and scanned my shelves for something I had not read. I found the book I purchased in Vegas on a whim, the book I walked past, picked up and put down so many times, then finally bought with no idea what it was about. Dain Heer *Being You, Changing the World*. *Being you? Changing the world? Okay*, I thought curiously. I opened the book and began to read. After about 15 pages, I turned to the book cover, stared at the handsome man looking back at me, and said to myself aloud, "Good God! Who is this guy?"

I flipped to the back of the book to look at the references and found the name of an organization he was affiliated with. Access Consciousness. A Google search provided a website that seemed vague. What was Access Consciousness? The website mentioned something called The Bars but gave little information on what that was other than it was a hands-on process of touching points on the head.

Classes were offered everywhere in the world. Even in Alberta. I found a Bars class to start in two weeks at Pigeon Lake, a couple of hours north of Calgary, and signed up immediately. I kept reading Dain's book.

I arrived at Pigeon Lake with its broad gleaming waters full of fish, golden sand beaches, and a quaint resort village consisting of restaurants, shops, and a small hotel and spa. I found the home of the woman who was hosting the class in a second summer village near Ma-Me-O Beach, the Cree word for "pigeon." The class was given by a young woman facilitator from Colorado. She opened with a short talk that could have been given in Greek, as far as I could comprehend. We then broke into pairs at massage tables to begin learning The Bars process.

As I was the newbie, the facilitator asked me to take a turn on the massage table first. For an hour, the facilitator talked about hand positions and chatted cheerily while my partner placed her hands on various places on my head to *"run"* my Bars, moving her hands from position to position after many minutes on each spot. It was lovely. I felt peaceful and relaxed and enjoyed listening to the facilitator talk. After more than an hour, she said we would break for lunch and switch partners after that.

When I swung my legs off the table and put my feet on the floor, the room spun. I called out in shock and tried to stand but couldn't. I felt as if I had been on an all-night bender. I grasped the sides of the massage table behind me and launched myself at a kitchen table a couple of feet from me but collapsed and had to cling to the table to keep from falling over. I shouted to the facilitator.

"I can't stand. I feel dizzy, like I'm completely drunk."

She calmly told me, "The dizziness will pass. You should just go for lunch."

I staggered out of the house and down the street with another class participant, grabbing onto cars and fences along the way to support me. At the restaurant, I couldn't eat a bite. I somehow made my way back to the class location.

The instructor asked, "How are you?"

"I am still very, very dizzy. I can't stand. I can't walk."

"It will pass," she said again.

I was astounded at the state I was in. Was this all from someone touching my head?

"Why don't you sit and take a turn running your partner's Bars?"

So, I sat and put my hands on my partner's head in the positions indicated. Sitting quietly was fine as long as I didn't move my head. I listened to the facilitator talk more about The Bars. It's a process that allows energy to "run" between hands and head in specific points in order to allow brain waves to slow and the brain to dissipate the charge of stressful thoughts, beliefs, emotions, attitudes, and ideas we stored in our minds. It might be compared to a massage that releases tension from muscles. The point of running The Bars is to allow you to have more ease in your life, be more present, have a clearer awareness of everything, and recognize how you can live in a happier and gentler way without stress in your head. A Bars session is experienced differently for each person in every session. Each of us is unique. You never know the change you might get. It was always beneficial, and sometimes it was extraordinary.

Well, no one had to convince me that something had gone on when my Bars were run. A fleeting thought flashed in my mind. Just how many stressful thoughts did I have jammed in my head? Maybe that's why I was dizzy when they were released.

After an hour, the facilitator said there was still time to switch with our partner again for a second session each.

I said dubiously, "I don't know that I am interested in another session."

The facilitator laughed and said, "YOU don't want another session, but what does your body want? Ask your body."

I groaned. Somehow "yes" was popping into my head for the second session. My partner ran my Bars again, and we exchanged places for me to give her a second turn. My dizziness didn't change. I sat quietly, only moving my hands. At the end of the class, I spoke to the facilitator.

"I don't know how I am going to drive home. I am still so dizzy."

She said lightly, "Ask your car to take you."

Okay, that was weird! Oddly, I didn't protest. Something had me believe that everything would be alright if I drove home. I imagined driving the quiet country road from the lake back to the four-lane highway, testing how I was behind the wheel. If I was not okay driving, I could pull over and call Rio to come and get me.

It was late in the afternoon when the class ended. While we were busy running Bars, we hadn't noticed a storm had rolled in. The area of Ma-Me-O Beach was still bathed in sunshine while in areas just beyond, a storm churned. We were in the eye of the storm.

I got in my car and, smirking, asked my car to "take me." I was fine driving the quiet country road as long as I didn't move my head too rapidly. I got to the highway and stopped. Continue or call Rio? I decided to go on. I stayed in the right lane for slower traffic so I could pull over if needed. I could always stop and call Rio.

The farther I drove, the more potent the storm became. The landscape became a bold masterpiece of art. There were sweeping views of the wide Alberta prairies stretching in every direction around me, mostly flat land that was shaped with gentle hills here and there, a landscape now swept with fierce gusting wind and lashing rain. Rain drenched the fields, turning them deep green in brilliant contrast to the violet-blue storm clouds that vaulted to the ceiling of sky. An occasional break in the clouds caused intense shafts of glowing sunlight to flood the fields like torch lights and amplify them to vivid cobalt green under the perse ink color of the turbulent sky. I've never seen anything to compare to the astounding power and glory of nature that day. As I drove, I slowly turned my head to look from the corner of my eye in awe at the stunning view outside my car. Oh, how I loved the magnificent, powerful Earth.

I made it back to Calgary easily. Rio helped me into the house. The dizziness gradually subsided over the next three days. I've had my Bars run many times since that day. I've never had a repeat of that first experience. To be sure, my interest in what Access and Bars were about was now piqued.

After that first Bars class, I began taking Access classes with a hunger for the next nine months. The classes included long discussions on everything from relationships, family, money, and body health. The perspectives offered were fresh and often far beyond the ordinary. I have to admit sometimes they seemed beyond strange. But I was no stranger to strange by now. Access classes were wonderfully freeing. Something in them touched on the unusual things about myself and out-of-the-norm things that interested me that I had always kept carefully concealed. Kept secret. I continued taking classes because I needed to find out what the hidden things were. Something changed in my life the day of my first Bars class. It was a monumental change that I couldn't explain. Was this what I was looking for? There was something extraordinary available in the world and in me. I wanted to know how to make life magical. If learning how to do that meant I had to go on an extraordinary journey to find me, I was in.

* * *

I turned 60 that summer, a month after my first Bars class. My daughter planned a special birthday to honor me. The day before, all she said was, "We are not going to tell you anything about what we have planned for your birthday. You are not to try to be in control of anything. You just have to go with it."

"Okay, I will," I said, excited at the thought of an adventure.

Rio woke me at 4 a.m. on the day of my birthday. He packed the car with a picnic basket with breakfast things, coffee, and a nubbly olive green blanket that was a gift from my daughter. He ushered me in and drove south out of the city to an area in the foothills, where he parked and walked me to the top of a grassy hill with an eastern view. He laid out the blanket and put out the breakfast things he brought. We sat quietly in that early morning hour and watched the sun slowly slip above the horizon in the east. Suddenly, the sky was a glorious vision of pink and gold light that cast a rosy aura over the waving grass of the prairie below the hill we sat on. Rio and I didn't talk. We just sipped our coffee, nibbled our bagels, and watched the sun rise until it stood full in the sky. It was inspiring, like a portent of something wonderful to come.

Once the sun was up, Rio packed the breakfast things in the car, and we began to travel farther south. He turned from the highway and drove for an hour along flat grain fields and golden pastures on gravel country roads that were deserted of any human traffic. We reached a farm with a pretty white farmhouse and screened porch. There were riotous gardens of flowers all around the property. My daughter was there to greet us.

"Mom, these are the decades of your life," she said, beaming at me. "It started with your birth at sunrise. This decade represents your childhood on the farm. The lady who owns this farm grows flowers to sell at the farmer's markets in the city. We are going to collect flowers and create bouquets."

We followed the owner of the farm while she took us to gather flowers. She talked of the varieties of flowers she grew, some of them rare, the process of tending what she grew, and the microclimate her house was situated in, which allowed her gardens to flourish. We took armfuls of the flowers we collected into her barn, where she put out tea and helped us create graceful bouquets to take home.

My daughter and I got into her van with our floral creations and headed back to the city for what she said was the next decade of my life. When we arrived at her house, my son pulled up in a white stretch limousine.

"Mom, I'm taking you out on the town. This is your young adulthood." He had a playful, slightly shy grin on his face. I laughed in delight. The limousine driver took us on a scenic excursion to the best lookout points in the city. Many I was familiar with but it now seemed as if I was seeing them for the first time. While we drove, my son and I shared a bottle of champagne. He then picked up his guitar that he had brought with him and sang a song that I once told him was my favorite song. Stevie Wonder ... *If it's Magic*.

If anyone had asked him, my son would have said he is not a singer. I had never heard him sing before. The tenderness and manliness of his singing blew me away. My eyes welled up with tears. The champagne sent fizzy bubbles to my nose. I cried and vibrated with happy awe.

The limo finally stopped outside a pub, and my son said, "Time for lunch. And, most importantly, shooters!"

We had a boozy lunch in that dim, busy pub. After throwing back a couple of shooters, I was flying.

Next, I was picked up and taken to a spa. My daughter said, "You are now in the decade of being a young mother. There's nothing you need more than to pamper yourself."

The spa treatment was followed by a family dinner outdoors in the courtyard of a popular restaurant. It was the next decade, the mature me with my family and now a grandchild around me. To close off the day, Rio and I were sent to a hotel for the night.

My daughter said, "We know travel is a big priority for you in this next decade of your life. Sorry," she grinned, "We are not going to send you on a big, exciting trip out of town," She laughed. "A hotel will have to do."

I crawled into bed that night and relaxed between the cool crisp hotel sheets. I was so swept away by the wonder of the day that I was a little disoriented. I hardly knew who I was anymore. It was the most beautiful thing anyone had ever done for me. I was awestruck at the love my family showed for me. After all the fantastic journeys I had had, this one was the most fantastic one of all. My daughter was the brains behind the day. She knew how to create magic, too.

Chapter 24

Saskatoon: The Family Fishbowl

After my joyful summer birthday, my dad also had a big one coming up. He would be turning 90 after Christmas. It was a major milestone, and the extended family always put on big celebrations for milestone birthdays. Dad was not receptive when it came to having someone celebrate him. He did not like to be in the spotlight. But 90 years old? Surely, something was warranted. I asked him about having a celebration and, amazingly, he said yes.

Dad was getting older. Who knows how long he would still be around? He was a strong, powerful man, and longevity ran in the family. He was doing extraordinarily well for his age, but he lived alone on the farm in Saskatchewan. I couldn't imagine how lonely that life would be or how that might impact his aging. It definitely wouldn't be the life for me, but it was the life he chose for himself, and he stubbornly resisted any conversations about making any move or change.

Over recent years, I had begun speaking openly to Dad about everything, the strange things that happened to me, even my rejection of Catholicism. I had a lot of unusual perspectives that I told lightly and simply, and he always listened. I had the sense it spoke to him of something hidden in himself that he had never found a way to express. He began speaking openly to me, too. My Catholic dad once asked me if I thought there was something to the idea of being psychic. I could almost feel a locked door in him open a crack. Was he having unusual experiences?

I told Dad about my encounter with Mom in the Home of OM. He listened carefully as I told the entire story. He was silent for a while after.

"Dad, life is a fishbowl. We swim around thinking the bowl is all there is, set in our ways of thinking. We don't know what is beyond and don't consider what might be greater than our life in the bowl. We just keep swimming."

Dad sat quietly, thoughtfully, then changed the subject as he always did when he didn't know what to say.

Late that summer, he said to me, "Remember when you told me how you remembered what happened when you went into surgery when you were four? You said you forgot about it until many years later. The same thing happened to me."

I had been desperately ill when I was four and had to undergo surgery to have a kidney removed. I was an adult in my 40s before I first fully remembered that day. A vivid memory had come to me of being wheeled into the operating room. As I lay on the table looking up at the huge theatre lights above me, the anesthesiologist, who was the only person in the room with me at the time, told me that if I was not a good little girl, the boogie man was going to get me. Then, he lowered the anesthetic mask. Everything went black. I didn't remember that incident for almost 40 years. My parents never knew what happened that day. I only told Dad later. He had been outraged.

Now I asked, "What did you remember, Dad?"

"It was the day your mother died. She was in the car, ready to drive to Saskatoon with your aunt. I got in the passenger's seat to say goodbye, and she said, "I'm leaving you." I kissed her goodbye, got out of the car, and she drove away."

My mother never came home from Christmas shopping with my aunt in the city that day. I thought about the shock of the car crash and her death. Her words to my father before she left had gotten pushed from his mind.

Dad continued, "I didn't remember that conversation until lately. What do you think she meant by saying she was leaving me?" Then after a pause, "Do you think she knew she was going to die?" His voice was plaintive.

"I don't know, Dad." I plead ignorance. What could I possibly say in response to that? My mind spun with his question and my memories of the relationships between my parents.

Dad had been a difficult man to live with. I thought of how hard life with him had been for Mom over their 25-year marriage. Too often, he was a closed and very angry man. Yet he adored my mother and remained completely devoted to her, even after she died. He lived for 30 years alone. It never dawned on him that she might ever think of leaving him, even when she said she was leaving. If that's what she meant. Had they had a fight, had she blurted out the words in the heat of the moment, did she actually plan to leave, or was his memory off? It was unsettling to think about how she left him the day she died.

"I don't know, Dad," I said again and added lamely. "Life can be a mystery."

We dropped the subject. It wasn't until much, much later that I remembered there were two Christmas gifts my mother bought in the city, found in the wrecked car she died in. One was a highchair for my baby daughter. The other was a world globe for Dad so they could dream of places they could travel together.

After our conversation, Dad seemed distracted. One day around the same time, he was looking for some of Mom's classical record albums and got upset when he couldn't find them. He confronted the youngest of my three sisters. He thought he had seen her rummaging through the shelf where the albums had been. He accused her of taking them. My sister said she did not take them and angrily insisted he retract the accusation. Knowing Dad, of course, he wouldn't. He would never take anything back or change his mind once he took a stance. Dad and my sister stopped speaking to each other.

I called my Youngest Sister, and we talked about her falling out with Dad.

"I want to call him and clear things up with him, but I just can't do it," she said.

I got a sense of the firm, hard no-go making a call to him was for her.

"Dad told me what happened," I said. "I told him I knew you were an honest person, and if you said you didn't take the albums, you didn't take them."

I told her about Dad's memory of his last words with Mom and asked her to consider the state of mind he was in when they had their argument.

My sister responded with an "Ah!" and said definitively, "I'm going to call him!"

For months after, every time I spoke to my Youngest Sister, she said she hadn't called Dad yet. I could tell she was afraid. I knew Dad. He would never call her himself. That was a huge issue for him, some kind of massive resistance to being wrong or ever making the first move to reach out to someone. She would have to be the one to call.

I suggested to her, "Just call him, have a 30-second conversation, say "Hi" and talk about the weather. Tell him you have somewhere to go and will call him again later and end the call."

"I will. I'm going to call him." She never did. Her final words to me about it months later were, "I can't do it."

He can't. She can't. This was going nowhere, and Dad's birthday at the end of December was approaching, so I got busy making calls to plan the celebration. Then my Vancouver Sister got involved.

For the first time since the fiasco in Springbank three years earlier, my Vancouver Sister and I had been talking on the phone again that fall. We discussed plans for Dad's birthday. We talked the way we used to talk, in easy, flowing, and happy conversations. I was so relieved that the problems of Springbank were finally receding into the past.

One morning a few days before Christmas, I sat down to send her a text to let her know how happy I was that we were talking again. Before I could finish, a text came in from her to the whole family. She wanted to let everyone know that I would NOT be planning Dad's birthday any longer. I was baffled. I called her and walked into the lion's den.

"I was just in the middle of typing a text to you to say how happy I was we were talking again when your text came in. Look, I'm not upset. I'm just wondering why you sent that text?" I tread carefully.

My sister was very, very angry. What had happened since our most recent phone call two days earlier, I don't know. For 30 minutes after— or was it an hour—she tore a strip off me. She started talking about

Springbank, lots of fast, blaming, violent rage that came at me with a hurricane force. When I tried to calm things down and asked that we not fight, she furiously talked over me. She told me bad things family members said about me, the thrust being was I was a terrible, terrible person. She accused me of having had an agenda the summer she and her guy visited us in Springbank. When I protested, she began laughing hysterically. When I asked her to please stop laughing, she only laughed more.

I hung up and threw my phone on the kitchen counter. My whole body was shaking as if I had been hit by a massive force field. I walked around my house, shaking my arms and my body, trying to get the trauma out. It felt as if I had been physically struck. It is said that the pen is mightier than the sword. I discovered that furious words spoken can be like an atom bomb. That phone call blew me up.

The effect of the call stayed with me for a long time. It was still fresh as Dad's birthday approached two weeks later. As I went to join the party, I was so nauseous at the idea of seeing my sister there I thought I was going to vomit. I got to the restaurant where the party was being held and sat at the table. My Youngest Sister arrived and barely looked at me. Her husband looked at me as if to say he thought he had known me, only to find out I was something else, something terrible. I later heard there had been a get-together amongst my three sisters just before the birthday. What had my Vancouver Sister said? I sat quietly through dinner and wished I was not there. I felt sick.

A few days after Dad's birthday, he and my Vancouver Sister, who was staying with him at the farm, drove to Saskatoon for the day. The weather turned snowy the afternoon they drove home from the city. There was an incident on the road. Dad was driving. His car went into a skid. My sister became hysterical. When they got back to the farm, she phoned my brother in Vancouver and told him a story. My brother got upset and called Dad to tell him that he had to give up his driving license. Dad was furious. The next morning as he was leaving the house to go into town to run errands, Dad left a note on the kitchen table telling my sister to take her things and leave.

When Dad got back to the farm, he called me. He was upset. She was actually gone. She had called my Youngest Sister, who drove out from the city to pick her up. Dad told me his version of the events on the highway the day before.

"We were driving from the city. The weather turned. It had begun to snow. Snow was blowing on the road. I noticed a half-ton truck a short way in front of me. I saw the truck begin to swerve and suddenly go into the ditch. When I got to the place where the truck had been, I hit something frozen in the snow on the road, and my car began to swerve, too. There was lots of oncoming traffic. It was a dangerous situation. I got the car back under control and drove on. But something was really wrong with your sister."

"What do you mean, Dad? What happened?"

"I don't know." He trailed away then said vehemently, "I've never seen such a witch!"

"When I had driven a bit farther, and we got to the junction on the highway, I stopped the car and told your sister to drive. She drove 80 kilometers per hour on the highway the rest of the way home. I was thinking there was something wrong with her and maybe I should take her to the hospital, but I didn't. A little while after we were home, your brother called and told me I had to give up my driving license. I knew your sister called him." He added angrily, "Someone went into the ditch on the road that day, and it wasn't me. And I guarantee you, the person in the truck was a lot younger than me!"

He paused. After moments of silence, he continued. "This morning, before I went to town, I left a note to tell your sister to leave the house. Now, she's gone."

We were both silent. I had not been in the car and had not seen what happened. My sister had been upset. Anyone would have been upset by a close call on a highway. But there was something more that went on, and Dad, being the man of few words that he was, could not explain it. He really didn't have to. Something inexplicable had happened between my sister and me, too.

In my mind, I could see my Dad afterward, sitting silently in his living room armchair as he always did, day after day, mulling over in his head what had occurred on the highway when my brother called to tell him to give up his license. He had been blind-sided, thinking about what was wrong with my sister while she was telling my brother a story about him. He had been furious, hung up on my brother, and left the note on the kitchen table the next morning. The best thing I could do now was turn down the heat.

"Well, Dad, it sounds like you did everything you could and avoided an accident. Thank goodness no one was hurt!"

It was the phrase people used in situations of near disaster. A dubious "Yes" was all he said. He was not convinced.

* * *

You may wonder why I told you all these things about my family. Was I looking to have my say or set the record straight? For eight years, events in the family had been painful. It took me years beyond those eight to find enough resolution so I could stop worrying, sleep at night, and address my indignation and symptoms that began to seem a lot like PTSD. This was the heart of the issue for me. How could I get free of the pain of attacks by family members? Believe me, I considered detaching myself from my family altogether.

What was going on with my family anyway, decent, smart, good-humored people who generally got along? Was my entire family going through a midlife crisis? What had started with my brother in Vancouver, flared in Springbank and exploded around Dad's birthday seemed to be spreading into the family like a virus.

A counselor I was seeing said, "This is scapegoating. People are looking for an outlet for their own problems."

Maybe. Counseling helped me look at things with a clearer eye. After a number of sessions, she asked me if she had helped me.

"Yes, you've given me some relief. You've helped me see things more clearly in my mind, but it doesn't stop the hurting in my heart."

She just looked at me with resignation. There are some things even psychology can't fix.

* * *

What is love of family? Families can be great. They can also be a source of a lot of Not-Love. What was the problem in my family? Too many fish in the family fishbowl and not enough love to go around in childhood, so people had repressed resentment? What was behind the lashing out and mean things said or done? What part did I play in all of that?

I had changed a lot in the years since my marriage ended. Maybe others were unsettled by that. Had I disrupted the ecosystem of the fishbowl? Did others have problems in their own lives and need an outlet, as the counselor suggested? Who knows. Nothing is ever black and white. It certainly doesn't help when people are unable to talk without anger or blame. Or are unwilling to talk at all. All you are left with is mystery.

Gradually, I began to see the family fishbowl from beyond the bowl. I began to see things could be different. After the Springbank falling out, there was one phone call I had with my Vancouver Sister where I told her I loved her, that I had always loved her. I don't think she heard me. Maybe she didn't believe me. Was speaking of love too far beyond the believable in my family? I had the idea that speaking with love could solve all problems. It sure didn't prevent her explosion at me around the time of Dad's birthday. Maybe there was something else I didn't yet see.

My daughter said to me one day, "I see what is troubling you. You are grieving the loss of your sister."

She put her finger on the very thing that troubled me the most. The moment she spoke, I knew it profoundly. The grief of loss had been hidden since the explosive phone call with my sister. Seeing the grief began to help to change things for me.

Maybe I tell this story with the hopes of remembering that the Not-Love was not what was real and true about my sister, not true about me, and had nothing to do with the best things between us. What mattered the most was love. I saw the choice between Love and Not-Love is always only a breath away.

There was something else I saw. My heartache could not go on if I truly loved myself. Loving yourself is even more important than loving someone else. It's the beginning of everything beautiful. I had been the oldest sister in the family. It had been part of my job as I grew up to be responsible for my siblings. Taking care of others had been a lifelong job. Yes, I always found things that lit me up. But had I ever really understood what it meant to love myself and not get side-tracked by other people's dilemmas?

What was required of me? It started with being able to fully, completely let go, out of love for myself, first of all. I had to let go of my suffering and live beyond the fishbowl.

That was easier said than done. I didn't change overnight. I'd be lying if I said I didn't do a lot of obsessive thinking. It was as if I were trying to solve an unsolvable Rubik's Cube. I tried to stop myself from analyzing things to death. Sometimes, there is no need to try to understand people's choices. They are just choices. The ultimate truth is I did not know all the ins and outs of the path my sister walked in life or why she chose the things she chose. She was a smart woman. It was her right to follow her own path and discover her own wisdom and truths. I had no right to judge any of it, try as I might to make sense of things. As my son had said, "Do not judge." He was right.

Chapter 25

Calgary: Choices

Access Consciousness helped me more than anything else at this time. It is impossible for me to even begin to tell you all the things I learned during the first five years I participated and how it changed me. Access meant taking a closer look at how we see, feel, and think about the things going on in our lives. Access might be considered a way to learn how to live your best life beyond the normal and fixed ways you think things should be. That was my take on it. Access was about learning to know that *You Know* and know what is true for you even if it's not true for anyone else. It meant seeing that you create everything in your life, everything, and have the ability to choose joyful possibilities instead of problems if you would just look beyond what you've learned to believe. Most of all, Access offered practical tools to get you out of anywhere you were stuck, whether that was your finances, relationships, or health. Or family.

Choice is one of the biggest components in the Access outlook. Each person has an absolute right to their choices. Every choice. Life is all about choice. We have a choice about everything, every thought, feeling, and emotion we experience. We can choose to have them or not and choose something else. If you don't like how something is going in your life, make a different choice. If you don't like a choice someone else is making, you have to know that it is absolutely their choice. Not yours. Don't take the bait and make it about you when it isn't. Don't think you have the right to try to change what someone is choosing because you think you know better, even when you see someone is making a choice that might end badly. How can you know what any other person has come to learn in this lifetime? That was a very different perspective than the one I functioned from. The idea of choice fit my idea of the free will we come to life with, yet I realized how little I knew about true choice.

Access helped me gain a measure of ease about my Vancouver Sister. She was making choices for her life. I had the choice to make things personal or not. I had the choice to grieve, swirl in drama so I was blinded from having clarity and let events take me down, or I could choose to be kind, especially to myself, and turn my focus to the wonder of life. I began to understand that I could choose joy in every moment, not wait for joy to find me. That was a choice that seemed like an act of love.

Much of the time, Access was wild fun, with a lot of laughter, and very unusual perspectives. Sometimes it seemed just plain weird, but I loved it. Other times, it was a bit of a rougher ride, especially when I had to take a deeper-than-comfortable look at myself. Access gave me greater ease with even that. I learned to look at all the truths about me, the good, the bad, the ugly. There was something funny that came out of that. It's seeing the beautiful things about ourselves that we often resist the most.

I absolutely loved Access and participated for years. I can honestly say what I got from Access was clarity about the strength I possessed that I never really understood I had. Some of the things I learned were inexplicable. That's how life is sometimes, isn't it? Inexplicable. Ultimately, I learned to let go of judgment. I let go of the judgment of others that had been a source of so much pain. I just stopped caring. I didn't stop caring about people. I stopped caring about being judged. It felt like wide-open, glorious freedom.

At one point, I realized all the classes I had taken could lead me to a certification as an Access facilitator. I began to get excited about my direction in life again. I told my son that I wanted to have a career as a facilitator. A career was something I had not had before. I wanted to do it, just for me, to prove to myself I could do something beyond the flitting. My son was very supportive of my motives. He also simply said, "You picked a tough business. It's not easy to launch a career as a coach or facilitator. It can take years to establish."

I didn't care. It seemed to be a choice that fit me. I completed the Access prerequisites for the certification and went to Rome for a week of training in the spring. I was thrilled to have achieved that certification. It pleased me that I had done it in nine months. Even better, I got my certification in lovely Rome. I got home, ready to get to work.

That June, my son convocated from Business at the University of Calgary. His major was accounting. When he first told his dad that he was choosing accounting, his dad gave him a surprised and skeptical look. His dad liked to make jokes about bean counters and Dilbert accountants. But my son was not deterred. That's one of the things I admire about him. He follows what he knows is true for himself, regardless of what other people think. Despite the passing of his father in the middle of his university program, my son had been very successful in achieving his degree. He had job offers lined up.

My daughter and I attended his convocation. I've been to many convocations over the years, but this one was special. My son, who had been the funniest, dearest little boy, was now a man, and I was so proud. As we watched hundreds of graduates cross the stage to receive their diplomas, I flipped through the program to pass the time. A page fell open with a list of students convocating from the College of Italian Studies, and there was my name, recipient of a degree in Italian Studies with Honors. In the aftermath of my husband's death, I had hurriedly completed the degree but never applied to receive it until earlier this year. To see my name in the program gave me a little thrill.

I loved everything about doing that degree. What might I have done with it if events hadn't intervened? Maybe the point wasn't about what I would do with the degree but the process of achieving it and some unforeseen benefit it would provide for me later. Was it the same for the Access certification?

As one year flowed into the next, I struggled to get my Access business going. Nothing went at all according to plan. I couldn't get a toehold or a normal, productive, or laudable trajectory. There were times I wanted to bail out. I chastised myself. Not again! The skipping around from thing to thing was becoming an annoying habit. What was I doing with my life? What choices could I make?

* * *

There was a big choice Rio and I were confronted with at this time. Bella, our adorable little puppy of our Springbank days, had grown into a head-strong adult dog who became impossible to manage in our city home despite our attempts to make life good for her. Bella was a fast, intense bundle of energy who loved people and vigorously jumped on anyone who came to the door. Bella was a powerful dog who could not be held back. People were afraid to come to our house. She was difficult to take for walks because she was unwilling to tolerate the leash and would drag Rio and me behind her every time we tried to take her out.

There were days when her head-strong exuberance made me laugh, days I took her to her favorite off-leash park where after an hour of running with wild abandon, she hid in the tall grass to peer at me from a distance, watching me as I tried to coax her back to the SUV to go home. An hour at the park was not enough time for her. She was barely warmed up.

And she didn't like to ride in the back of the SUV. She wanted to sit in the front seat with me, the way she rode in Rio's truck with him. But she was too much of a distraction as I drove. I insisted she get into the back of the SUV. She refused. There was an occasion when I got into the SUV myself with a piece of bacon and tried to lure her in.

"Look, Bella. Have a sniff of this lovely bacon. Hop in, and I'll give it to you," I coaxed.

Bella just looked at me as if to say, "You think I'm stupid?" and turned her head away from me in disgust.

Rio spoiled her by letting her ride in the front of his truck with him. She would bark at cars that passed them as they drove. She hated the roar of other cars and, especially, the spinning of their wheels. One day a woman rolled down her window as she stopped at a red light next to Rio's truck and called to him.

"Why is your dog barking at me?"

Rio said, "She's barking because she's not happy you passed us."

Rio and Bella were quite the pair. He adored her. She was devoted to him in return.

We hired a dog trainer to come to our home to train Bella. When I first spoke to him on the phone, he promised that he could get a dog well under control within the first visit. After his session at our home, the trainer looked exhausted. He couldn't understand how his tried-and-true method had failed. He looked at me woefully and said, "This is going to take a lot longer than a day."

Bella loved people. She loved life. She loved running wild and free. She was joy in motion. She was not meant for city life.

Of all the people who did not like Bella or were outright afraid of her, my granddaughter, two-year-old Poppy, was not one of them. Poppy would come to our house to be babysat and the first thing she asked for was Bella. Poppy toddled around our house with Bella following close behind, with Rio or I close behind them both to make sure Bella didn't knock Poppy down. That never happened. Poppy would deck Bella out in play costume jewelry while Bella stood with adoring attention. Poppy and Bella were a match. Both were forces of nature. Both were spirits wild and free.

Bella dragged me down in the parking lot one day when I took her for a walk at the off-leash park. After our walk, I managed to get her into the back of the SUV and was about to take off her leash when a car drove past. Bella bolted from the trunk as I still held the leash, dragging me and scraping me on the pavement behind her. It happened lightning-fast. I was badly injured from shoulder to wrist and down my leg. That was my last attempt to take Bella to the park.

The easiest place to take Bella for walks was in our neighborhood on the paths that ran through the grassy hills between the clusters of houses enclosed safely in their fences. Those paths wound for long stretches through treed areas until you had the feeling you were no longer in the city. There was an entrance to one of the paths across the street from our house. Once beyond the street and on that path, we could let Bella off the leash to run with glee. She was wonderful then, always wheeling around and returning obediently when called. The only problem was getting her on the leash again to cross the street back to our house.

One day, I thought I would experiment with a suggestion from someone in Access around the idea that dogs are telepathic. I was going out for my own morning walk, and Bella stood eagerly and hopefully beside me at the front door. I had stopped taking her out with me at all after the parking lot incident. My arthritis could not withstand her yanking on the leash. So, I took morning walks alone. Yet Bella came and stood at the door beside me every time I went out. She had been the little puppy who went with me for glorious sunrise walks in Springbank. Running free on the acreage as a small dog had been her joy. Now, leaving her behind broke my heart.

I turned from the door and sat on the bench at the entrance of my house. I called her.

"Bella, come here." Then thinking in my mind without uttering a word, I spoke to her while I looked directly into her eyes, and she looked directly back at me.

"Bella, I am going for a walk. I would like to take you with me but I can't. You yank on the leash, and you drag me down on the road. It hurts my body. But if you would like to try one more time, obey me and not pull on the leash, I will take you with me."

Bella just looked deeply into my eyes with her golden brown ones.

I snapped on her leash and opened the front door. Bella was about to bolt out in her excitement but turned back to look at me and reduced her speed by about 50 percent. How could I blame her for what she was? She was speed. But I noticed how she tried to please me.

We got across the street from our house and began down the path into the trees and hills. I snapped off her leash, and Bella was gone in a blaze of black and white fur, running so fast her hind legs outran her front ones. We had a lovely walk and returned to the street near our house. I put Bella's leash back on, glanced up and down the street to make sure there were no cars coming, and got ready to cross. At that moment, a neighbor's garage door opened, and a car backed out onto the street. Bella hated cars and car wheels. She was fiercely poised to charge.

I yelled in distress, "Bella!"

Bella stopped, turned to look at me standing wide-eyed behind her, then stood and watched the car go by. My God! She never charged. She continued to look back at me as we made our way across the street to the house. When she and I were back inside, I sat with her at the front door, stroking her fur and praising her lovingly. "Good girl, Bella. Good girl."

Rio and I had to make a decision about Bella. Even though I had had a successful outing with her, with my flares of arthritis, my confidence in taking her out was shaken. She was impossible when guests came to the house. She would leap at them with enthusiasm, then howl when we were forced to close her in my office. She was impossible when Rio came from work after a long day on a construction job. She would whine at him all night to take her out to walk, but the one walk a day she got with him was far from adequate. Our home had a lovely backyard, but it was about as useful for Bella as a paddling pool for an Olympic swimmer. She began to get listless and very overweight.

"Rio, this life we live is not fair to Bella. She's not a city dog. She needs a farm where she can run free. I can't stand to see her get fat and stare out the window wishing to be outside. I can't stand going out of the house knowing she is sitting at home languishing on the floor. She needs a farm. We need to find a new home for her on a farm."

"I can't give up my dog. I love her. How can I give my dog away? I'll walk her more. I can't give Bella away."

"You've tried that. We've tried to make things good for her, and nothing has worked. This life isn't fair to her. It is selfish for us to keep her living this way."

For months, we went around and around on the subject. Finally, Rio agreed. Bella needed something that we could not give her.

"Okay," he said, "Look for someone with a farm."

I immediately posted an internet ad with photos of Bella, a blurb about her personality, and her need for a life on a farm. Ten minutes later, a man from a farm an hour from Calgary replied to my ad, saying, "I lost my dog who had been my best friend a while ago. I've been waiting for the right dog to find me. Can I come to meet Bella?"

When the farmer came to our door, Bella rolled over on the floor in front of him so he could rub her belly. I had never seen her do that before. She accepted him.

Rio sat with Bella on the steps that went down into the yard from our deck the day I was to drive Bella out to her new home on the farm. Rio said he could not take her there to give her away himself. Man and dog sat in silence as they stared out from the deck. Rio said he told Bella he would never forget her.

Bella was agitated all the way to the farm. It was as if she knew. I reached the farm where the farmer and his two teenage sons were waiting for us. It was a great situation for Bella to have a home with grown men. But they were a sad, sorry lot. The wife had left the marriage a short while before. Their sorrow was palpable.

Bella leaped from the car and began racing around the farmyard, trying to chase chickens until the farmer grabbed her by the neck and held her to the ground while he scolded her. Bella listened to him. She needed his firm hand. This was the right place for her. I chatted with the farmer and shared information about Bella while the sons drooped around beside us. I told them how Bella loved to go for car rides and her favorite snack was raw carrots. When it came time for me to leave, I asked the farmer to take Bella into the house because I didn't want her to see me leave. I cried as I drove away.

For years after, the farmer generously sent me pictures of Bella. Bella in the spring fields sitting amongst newly sprouted crocuses. Bella riding in the truck. Bella eating carrots. Bella sitting beside the tree at Christmas. And best of all, Bella with his sons, who glowed with happiness while Bella sat on their laps with her eyes shining with fulfillment. Bella got what she needed. She got a farm. She lost all her excess weight. She got a home with people who adored her. She got a job. Bella healed those sad men with her energy and joy. The farmer told me she changed their lives. That was a wondrous thing.

Rio and I knew we had done the right thing for Bella. It was the hardest choice we ever made. It was a good choice. We both cried at the loss of Bella from our lives. I don't think Rio ever got over her leaving us. There are so many people who are dog owners who will completely understand this story I tell. There is a love shared with a family pet who is not just a pet but a cherished family member. Losing that family member is no different than losing a person who is deeply loved.

Some say a dog doesn't feel love. Others say a dog absolutely does love. Still others say the love of a dog is a vibrational response to the love of its owner. Isn't that what love is for all of us anyway—never mind bolts of lightning—a vibration in the body and heart to a powerful connection with another, be it a dog or a person?

Beautiful Bella. We still miss her.

Our response to the loss of love always seems to be pain. Is there some other way the loss of love can be experienced? Could there be gratitude instead of grief? It reminded me of my sister. It reminded me of my ending with Giorgio. That had been a deeply painful thing for me, like a part of my body had been stripped away from me. What if I could have chosen gratitude instead? Even in the days after I left Giorgio, I knew I should have been grateful instead of miserable, but I wasn't grateful. What is it that makes us choose pain over gratitude? When you think about it, it seemed a pretty foolish choice.

Chapter 26

Calgary: A Perfect Storm

After Bella went to her new home, Rio wrapped up the property settlement of the townhouse that his ex-wife and children lived in. Somehow, the lawyers had never completed the settlement at the time of the divorce. Rio's lawyer couldn't understand how it had been missed. For eight years, Rio had been paying the mortgage and bills on the home. Now, in the settlement, he was entitled to half its equity.

Rio knew his ex-wife would be hard-pressed to take on the remaining mortgage. It would be completely impossible for her to pay out his 50 percent of the equity. It meant the home would have to be sold in a settlement. Rio worried about what to do. He said he could not leave his children in the street. In the end, he gave up his share of the equity as a gesture of goodwill. Things had been difficult with his children over the years. He thought that might ease the strain in their relationship. He was wrong. Once the settlement was finalized, to Rio's shock, his kids stopped returning his calls at all.

In the fall, Rio had surgery to correct bulging veins in one of his legs that had been causing frequent pain and swelling in the past year. The leg had been damaged during the war when Rio was 20 years old. He had been severely beaten by six Serbian officers and left in a ditch to die. Now, the veins had become swollen from his knee to his foot and required surgery.

Rio's injury from the war was corrected. He took time off to recuperate. He passed the Canadian Citizenship exam and was slated for the swearing-in ceremony in the spring. He went back to work when his leg was healed, but after a few weeks, his employer laid off a bunch of employees, including Rio. In the months before Christmas, Rio had no work, no replies to his calls to his children, no dog. He had nothing to do but think. He began sinking into a depression. When he had painful thoughts about his children, he numbed them with alcohol. The depression only got worse.

At Christmas, Rio and I went to visit Dad on the farm. Dad was not doing well. He had lost a lot of weight and was now walking with the cane that his grandfather had carved from wood a hundred years earlier. He had a lot of pain. His doctor said it was arthritis and recommended painkillers, but Dad would have none of it. He was a man and would rather tough it out than take medication.

Dad had changed a lot in the year since his 90th birthday. The Vancouver Sister and the Youngest Sister never called him since the drama of the snowy drive from Saskatoon. I tried to call my Youngest Sister, but she never returned my calls or Christmas greetings. I knew she had fallen in with the Vancouver Sister. Access helped me a lot, but I'd be lying if I said I was completely past the entire business. Even with clarity from Access, I still had distress coming up. It seemed everyone around me was on the brink of a crisis that always came back to me. I began having intermittent pain in my own body.

By January, Rio was in a deep depression. Rio said he just wanted to die. His doctor prescribed anti-depressants. Rio was told it could take eight weeks for the medication to work. Without my knowledge, Rio used alcohol to suppress his pain despite alcohol being prohibited with antidepressants. January and February were a nightmare. Rio made multiple trips to the doctor, three trips to the ER when things reached a crisis point, and then a trip to a detox program to help him get off the alcohol crutch. The first night he was in detox, he had a brain seizure in the middle of the night and was rushed to the hospital in critical condition.

Rio was in the ICU for three days. Doctors were not certain he would make it. After the most intense danger had passed, Rio was moved to a unit. For two weeks, he was kept in a profoundly sedated state to keep his brain calm, prevent another seizure, and allow him the chance to recover. Most days, he barely ever woke. He could hardly communicate. He never moved from his bed.

I took my laptop to the hospital and worked in Rio's room all day, every day. When he finally was brought out of the sedation, he couldn't walk. He couldn't even sit up in bed. He looked stunned, as if he had been somewhere else for too long. He had no idea how he got to the hospital, why he was there, or how long he had been there.

Rio was put through a battery of tests to see what damage the seizure had done. His doctor's orders were that he was to begin walking every day with a walker and two nurses supporting him. He was told that he would need physiotherapy. He was told that he would need to be put into a program of rehabilitation before he could ever consider going back to work. He was told he would be put into an alcohol addiction program. He could never touch a drop of alcohol again, or it could set off another seizure. Only time would tell what damage had been done to his brain. The hospital was busy and short of staff. The nurses were spread too thin and barely had time to take him for even one walk each day. Rio lay inert in his bed day after day. Things were going nowhere. I arrived at Rio's bedside one day and said, "Rio, can you maneuver your body around so your head is at the foot of the bed? I'm going to run your Bars."

He maneuvered himself as I asked. I sat with my hands on his head for over an hour, moving them from position to position. The next day, I ran his Bars again. The third day when I arrived at the hospital and stopped at the desk on his unit to sign in, the nurse said to me, "Look," and motioned with her eyes. There was Rio walking up and down the halls by himself with his walker, no supporting nurses.

Rio walked non-stop for the next two days like a man on a mission. He had enough of the hospital and wanted to get out. He was released three days later. He had been in the hospital for almost a month.

No one said anything about Rio's unexpected rapid recovery. The hospital was too busy dealing with a high patient load and concerns about a virus that was spreading through the world. Rio was told to go home, get a walker, and wait to be contacted to set up physiotherapy, rehabilitation, and an alcohol addiction program. As we were leaving the hospital, we passed staff stationed at the front entrance, masked and dressed in green hospital gowns. They stopped people to check their reasons for coming into the hospital and made them sanitize their hands. COVID was on.

When Rio got home, I brought out the walker I had rented. He said, "I don't need that." He was a little unsteady going up the stairs to the bedroom on his first attempt. After that, it was no problem. With the pandemic declared, no one called Rio to set up any programs. It was all forgotten. That was just fine. Rio was foggy for the first while at home. I continued to run his Bars and filled him in about his time in the hospital. He remembered none of it. He may have been in a fog about all of that, but about one thing, he was very clear. With full comprehension of what had happened to him, he looked at me with wide-eyed clarity and said, "How could I have done that to myself?"

Despite the prognosis he had been given and no follow-up programs, Rio fully returned to normal. I saw what had happened to him. It was a perfect storm of events or what some might call a dark night of the soul. With the loss of his dog, his children, and his job, he had lost himself. On the other side of the dark night was a new light of day. Rio would tell you he is better now than he was before. He has not touched a drop of alcohol since the seizure. In his joking way, he says that he didn't quit alcohol. Alcohol quit him. Yes, he makes light. But he is committed. In all the time he was in the hospital, his children never reached out. Not once. That angered me a lot, but for Rio, that was something that mattered the least. He calmly told me, "If my kids don't want to see me, I will not kill myself over them."

Chapter 27

Saskatoon: A Game of Chess

As Rio got stronger, Dad's health deteriorated rapidly. He was now thin as a rail and could barely walk. He couldn't cook his meals and wasn't eating properly. He couldn't keep his house in order as he had done so fastidiously over the 30 years since Mom died. Over all those years, he never entertained the notion of finding another partner. Now, he was there on the farm, completely alone in his misery. Dad had constant and often acute pain, yet he refused to go back to his doctor or consider moving from his home. If anyone was unwise enough to broach the topic of moving, the door was essentially slammed in their face. Dad was not willing to consider it. He said to me, "This house is not a palace, but it's my home."

The situation was becoming critical. I planned a trip to visit Dad to see if I could possibly open a conversation with him about his situation. Dad once said I stood in my mother's shoes. Maybe I could find a small opening. I thought of the Access perspective that a person's choices were their own to make, no matter if you liked their choices or not. Was that true in a situation like this? How could anyone possibly watch another person they loved suffer? I thought I'd drive out to the farm and give a talk with Dad a shot. If it worked, great. If it didn't, I tried.

Before I left, I asked Rio, "Do you have any advice for me?"

He immediately said, "Yes. When you talk to your Dad, think of it as a chess game. You make a move, and you sit back and wait for him to make his move. You don't try to move all your pieces at once."

"Oh my God, that's exactly what I do. I try to hit him with all my reasoning and rationale at once."

"Try one piece at a time."

I took Rio's advice to heart and tried to talk with Dad about the possibility of him leaving the farm and making a new start in the city. What's the use of moving your chess piece and waiting for the other player to move theirs when they simply refused to make a move? My talk with Dad went nowhere. My Younger Brother, who was at the farm during that visit, said, "You made a great attempt to talk with Dad. It was really good."

But Dad would not accept any support, whether through convincing, cajoling, manipulation, or even love.

During my visit with Dad, I noticed he began talking about his life, almost as if he was doing a review. He and my mom had lived in Regina when they were first married. They loved it there and had lots of friends. I was born there. One of the male friends and Dad planned to start a business together. Then, Dad got a call from his father, who had retired from the farm and left it to be run by Dad's older brother. Unfortunately, the brother and his wife were unable to have children. For my grandfather, it was imperative the farm be passed on in the family. So, Dad was called and was told to come back to the farm. It was not an option. It was an order.

As Dad reminisced, he wondered what his life would have been like if he and Mom had stayed in Regina. Would he have run a successful business? Would he and Mom have had as many kids as they did—not that he didn't want any of the ones he had? No, he was happy having the children he had. Would Mom still be alive? I just listened and gave him space to talk.

My Saskatoon Sister, the middle one of my three sisters, called a Seniors Counselling Service for advice about what we could do for Dad. She was told there was nothing they could do to help in the situation other than offer support for the family. There is nothing anyone can do to convince an elderly person to move if they are not willing because the elderly person still has a choice. I had to keep reminding myself of that, too. Wouldn't I be furious if people started treating me like I was old and feeble and couldn't make choices for myself?

Dad was making a choice whether anyone in the family liked it or not. I had to admire him for his fortitude and unwillingness to let anyone sway him, even though the rest of us thought he was daft. He probably knew what we thought and dug in even more. Dad was beyond stubborn. He willfully refused to accept love and support from anyone. Dad was a tough nut to crack. It's painful to watch someone in a situation like the one he was in. More pain of love.

Before I left the farm after that weekend visit, I went into the living room where Dad was lying flat on his back on the couch. I leaned over him to give him a hug and looked into his eyes. He looked back at me, his eyes pleading, pleading. Ah, this was a man who knew he needed help but could not, would not allow himself to receive it. That wasn't strength. It was weakness. And it was still his choice. It was no use trying to talk to him. He wouldn't hear of it.

I talked with my Saskatoon Sister about what to do for Dad. His arthritis was severe, and he was becoming frighteningly thin. One day in the fall, Dad called her. He was in a crisis. She raced to the farm to find him completely unable to move or walk. She drove her car up the lawn to the front door of the house and somehow navigated him into her car. She drove him to the small hospital in the town nearby where he was admitted.

Dad went back and forth between lucidity and delirium. Tests were run. Nothing dire was discovered. It was just arthritis and a poor diet. After a couple of weeks, Dad got notice that a place had opened for him in a seniors residence in Saskatoon. With his physical condition and admission to the hospital, the doctors said they could now make a professional decision about what was necessary for his care. Things were out of his hands. Dad was moved from the hospital to Columbian Manor, a senior's residence, shortly after. We all breathed a sigh of relief. The only difficulty was the COVID pandemic was going on in full force. Hospitals and residences were in full lockdown, and no one could visit Dad except my Saskatoon Sister, who was designated as his caregiver and had the heavy responsibility of managing all of his care. Dad spent Christmas in the senior's residence in a wheelchair. My two brothers, my Saskatoon Sister, and I had a Zoom visit with him at Christmas. The other two sisters were still MIA.

* * *

There had been too much stress for me over recent years. I began gaining weight and had occasional flairs of arthritis myself. I had not forgotten about the tumor a few years earlier. I knew I needed to take better care of myself and put a higher priority on my own life, not just other people's problems. But other people's crises always seemed more urgent than my personal needs and my Access facilitator goals. To top things off, now there was the COVID pandemic.

Everything seemed to weigh heavier and heavier on me, despite all the great tools at my disposal from Access Consciousness. I used those tools and got a lot of amazing benefits. It seemed there was still a lot that I had to learn and could learn from Access, but with the onslaught of trauma and drama in my life, it seemed the wonderful wisdom I got from Access was outstripped as fast as I could learn it. There was only one option. Just keep going.

Chapter 28

Saskatoon: Nice Day for a Drive

My daughter and her husband were expecting their second child, due to arrive shortly after Dad went into the senior's residence. Darling Poppy would have a brother. My daughter's pregnancy began easily enough, but by her third trimester, she began having difficulties and needed my help. I was back to babysitting Poppy, and my personal targets around work and health went out the window. Again.

At the same time, Dad was taken from the senior's residence to the Saskatoon hospital in a delirium. Tests were being run. Rehabilitation was being planned to address his loss of mobility. With the COVID pandemic happening, the hospital was in lockdown. I hadn't seen Dad since I left him the summer before as he lay on his couch with pleading eyes.

My Saskatoon Sister planned a Facetime for me with Dad while she visited him in the hospital. Rio and I were in a restaurant having pizza with Poppy when the call came in. When I saw Dad's face on the screen and registered his almost skeletal face and wild white hair, I knew in an instant he was dying. Rio and I exchanged glances. Rio saw it, too. I gave Dad my most radiant smile and talked warmly with him. He looked at me like he was seeing someone from a distant past. He didn't really want to talk. He only wanted to look at me.

I said nothing to anyone other than Rio about the realization Dad was dying. I thought about my Vancouver Sister, who had not spoken a word to him for more than two years. She would be devastated if he died and they had not had a chance to reconcile. I was thinking about her one morning as I pulled my car in front of my daughter's house to babysit. I decided to call. I was brief.

"Hi. How are you?" I opened.

"I'm fine." She sounded calm.

"I've just arrived to babysit Poppy and thought I'd give you a quick call. I'm running late and only have a minute. I wanted to let you know that Dad is really not doing well in the hospital. I wonder if you might call him?"

"I don't know." Her voice trailed away. "Nobody in the family has been calling me," she added resentfully.

"I know how things have been between you and Dad. We all know what he's like. He will not call you. That's how he is. You might have to be the one who breaks the ice. Look, it's totally up to you. I'm just calling to let you know he is really not well. Sorry to cut the call short, but Poppy is waiting for me. Talk to you soon."

The call was easy. My sister was calm. We ended the call without any drama. I had done the best I could. The next day I got an angry, nasty text back from her. A few days after that, she called Dad. A few weeks later, Dad was diagnosed with bone cancer and given only a couple of months to live. He asked the doctor who delivered the news, "Are there any other possible outcomes?"

"No, there are not."

Dad's time was very short. He was still not allowed visitors in the hospital because of COVID. It was so fundamentally unacceptable to me that a dying man could not have his children visit him. I thought of going to Saskatoon to show up for a visit, but my Saskatoon Sister told me that she heard of people traveling a long distance to visit someone in the hospital only to be turned away. The situation was unacceptable.

One morning a week later, I was sitting at my desk, beginning my day with my journal and a cup of coffee as usual. I was in a peaceful place as I wrote and organized the things on my desk. Unexpectedly, I heard a voice speak to me, a voice that I heard in my head but it was not in my head, a voice that was faint and yet crystal clear. The voice simply said, "It's a nice day for a drive."

I sat up straight and looked around the room. I knew I heard the voice plain as day. I paused, then looked out my window. It was a beautiful, sunny, almost spring morning. I replayed what the voice had said to me, then got up from my desk and started putting clothes in an overnight travel bag. I know what the voice meant to tell me. "It's a nice day for a drive." I would drive to Saskatoon to go to see Dad.

I got in the car and started driving. I made a quick call to Rio to tell him where I was going. I made another call to my Saskatoon Sister to tell her I was on my way. I settled in behind the wheel and began my seven-hour trip. It really was a lovely day. Every time I started to think about what would happen when I reached Saskatoon, I stopped myself, relaxed in my seat, looked out the window at the passing landscape, and reminded myself that I was just out because it was a nice day for a drive. The countryside was at the point of coming out of winter dormancy. Things had not yet begun to turn green, but I noticed the sense of new life in the land and sky as I drove.

I reached Saskatoon in the late afternoon and drove to my sister's house. She had finished her day working from home due to COVID and was getting ready to go for her daily visit with Dad. She told me she wouldn't tell Dad I had come to town. She didn't want him to be disappointed that he would not see me. *We'll see*, I thought.

My Saskatoon Sister was a lovely blond woman who was a single mom and who had a busy, successful career in human resources. She was a powerhouse of organization, smarts, and self-determination. Yet, I wondered, *Who supported her while she worked and raised two kids? And who supported her now that so much of her energy was required to look after Dad's needs? Who gave her caring or congratulated her for a job well done when she put so much of herself into doing everything to the highest standard?* We were seven years apart in age and had not been close as children. We were adult women now. Wouldn't it be wonderful to have a relationship with a sister that included mutual support and kindness? I realized with surprise that in the fishbowl of the family that I grew up in, true kindness was rarely expressed.

While my sister was gone to visit Dad, I went to the grocery store and bought things for dinner. I bought a bouquet of flowers for her table. Her kids and I talked happily while I cooked. When my sister walked in the door, she said it was wonderful to smell dinner cooking and know a meal was ready. We enjoyed our dinner and talked a lot. We are a family of non-stop talkers.

The next day, my sister was working from home again.

"I'm going to get out of your house so I don't bother you." I said. "I thought I'd drive out to the farm and check that everything is okay there."

"While you are there, maybe you can take pictures," she said. "We'll have to put the farm on the market once Dad is gone. It would be nice to have pictures."

"I will," I said. "I'll see you later in the afternoon when you are finished work."

No one had been in Dad's house since he left in the fall. I would check on things and take photos for the real estate listing that would be placed. But that was not my first order of business. I left my sister's house and drove straight to the hospital.

Saskatoon's Royal University Hospital was a complex of century-old buildings set at the edge of the university campus overlooking the wide, calm Saskatchewan River in the expansive valley below. The entrance to the hospital grounds was a roadway through two lovely stone arches that led into a central circular drive surrounded by historic buildings. From what I recalled from previous visits, the main entrance and emergency access had been two of the buildings in that circular drive. Now, the whole hospital was being renovated. Everything had changed. There were no signs anywhere to indicate an entrance of any kind. There were no people around. I had no idea where to go.

I remembered the facilitator in the Bars class in Pigeon Lake telling me to ask my car to take me home when I thought I was too dizzy to drive. I'd try it again. I said, "Car, take me," and relaxed my grip to hold the steering wheel lightly in my hands. I lifted my foot from the brake and let the car begin to roll forward. There was a small gravel roadway to the left going out of the circular drive. That seemed to be where my car was headed, so I followed the road as it passed under the cement pillars of a parkade, then wound up the side and to the top of the parkade. I let the car travel between the rows of cars until I saw an open spot and turned the steering wheel to pull in. When I put the car in park, I looked up out of my windshield and saw the sign on the building directly in front of me: Main Entrance. I stared for a moment at the surprise of seeing the entrance right there. I got out of my car and went inside.

There were three checkpoints for COVID. One was a desk with a sign requesting that all visitors sanitize their hands. A second checkpoint was a table with two seated women who asked me the purpose of my visit, gave me a mask, and directed me to the third checkpoint, a wicket window where a man sat inside a small room, looking at his computer screen. He asked me my business. I simply stated, "I'm here to see my dad."

The man asked for Dad's name and my name and then consulted his computer screen.

"Your name is not on the visitors' list."

"I know. But I'm here to see my Dad."

I looked at him and smiled. I felt the smile on my face. It was a knowing smile. A sweet you-can't-say-no-to-me smile. I thought of Mona Lisa's mysterious knowing smile. The man looked very confused. He shuffled the papers on his desk and looked at his computer screen as if it would tell him something he didn't know. He looked at me again, and I smiled back. I was certain I would not be turned away. Something sent me there that day. Something had my back. He would not be able to say no.

Finally, he got an idea. He called up to the unit Dad was on and asked them if I could go up. The call was very quick. When he put down the phone, he turned to look at me and said, "You can go up. Third floor. Room 301."

I ran like a child off to the playground. I found the elevator and pushed the button. When I got off and turned down the hall toward the unit my father was on, a woman in scrubs came toward me. She stopped to step aside for me, gave me a small bow and graceful sweeping gesture with her hand in the direction of the unit just ahead. It seemed so surreal.

I found Dad's room and went inside. He had one of the two beds in the room, the one closest to the window that looked out to the dreary grey concrete and glass building across the complex. I walked around the curtain divider and saw him lying somberly in his bed. He caught sight of me, and I said, "Surprise!"

His mouth dropped open.

I walked to his bedside and said, "Hi, Dad. How are you?' and gave him a light kiss on the cheek.

He stared at me as if he hadn't seen me for years, the same way he stared at me on Facetime in the pizza restaurant a month earlier. At that moment, a nurse came in to change his bedding and asked me to step outside his room for a moment. At that instant, my phone rang. It was my sister wondering if I was near the farm yet. I said, "I'm here with Dad."

"Oh my God! I'm so happy you are there!" she exclaimed.

Back in Dad's room, I took in the change in him over the last eight months. He had been a tall, sturdy, powerful man, handsome with thick dark hair and hazel-brown eyes. Now, he was nothing but bone. Cancerous bone. The hospital gown that he wore seemed too large for him and sagged down from his chest, exposing his thin neck and collar bones. His face was hollow and gaunt, his hair shocking white. His hazel eyes stood out from his face and looked startlingly luminous, almost a washed-out blue.

Dad was not someone who generally looked people in the eye. He had been labeled as shy when he was a kid. I don't believe shyness told the whole story. There had been other stories of him being flogged with the buckle end of the belt. Now, he looked me directly in the eyes, taking me in without a word. I noted Dad wore his prized watch, one of the small luxuries he indulged in. The watch dangled on his arm like a bangle. He was so thin. I smiled and drew up a chair to visit. All I wanted was to give him some comfort.

Not long after, lunch was brought in. Dad was too weak to lift his arms to reach his tray or lift his spoon to his mouth to eat his soup, so I fed him. He ate his entire lunch. He had always had a great appetite. That obviously hadn't changed. He looked at his tray to see what else he had been given.

"What's for dessert?"

"Applesauce."

He wrinkled his nose and shook his head when I offered it. He always loved a bit of something sweet to end his meal.

"Dad, there's a coffee shop downstairs on the main floor. Would you like me to get you something for dessert?"

"Yes."

"Okay, I'll be right back."

The coffee shop was a cafeteria-style café. I walked past the case of sandwiches, salads, and fruit and found the dessert shelf. There, sitting by itself in the middle of the otherwise empty shelf like it was waiting for me, was a glistening piece of lemon meringue pie. One of my Dad's favorites.

I bought the pie and two cups of coffee and went back to Dad's room. When he saw the lightly toasted meringue and bright yellow custard, his eyes widened. I fed him the pie hoping it wouldn't clog up his system but had another thought. If you are dying, eat the pie! Dad ate the entire piece. I handed him his coffee cup, which he took in his hands and rested on his chest, bowing his head for small sips. I saw the pleasure he got from something so simple as holding his own cup and drinking his own coffee.

"Oh, that's good coffee," he said.

We talked lightly and drank our coffee together. The sun from the south side of the hospital bounced off the windows of the building across from his north-facing window and reflected warm light back into his barren room with its stark white walls. I had a sudden memory of us as we used to sit on so many mornings at the farm in his tired old kitchen on the worn vinyl-covered chairs that he and my mother had reupholstered decades before. We had breakfast of toast and eggs on summer mornings while golden light streamed in from the east. In his hospital room now, we could have been sitting and having breakfast at the farm. Light and peace flooded into his room. Dad was more himself than I had seen him in years.

After we chatted for a while, Dad asked me to rub his neck and the back of his head where the cancer had gone into his skull. Really, he had pain everywhere. He mostly endured it.

After a while, I said, "Dad, I'm going to go now. I'm planning to drive out to the farm to check on things there. You might want to take a nap. I'll be back tomorrow. That is if they let me in again. You know, I was ready to fight somebody if they hadn't let me in today."

Dad rewarded me with the snort of one of his short boyish laughs. It had been a long time since I heard one of those. I didn't know it at the time, but that was the last meaningful visit between my father and me. It was full of magic.

I left the hospital and drove out to the farm. Dad had said that it was not a palace, but it was his home. It truly was not a palace, but somehow it looked pretty that day with the sun shining in, as though the house knew I was there to take pictures and wanted to look its best. There was a sense of peace inside as I walked from room to room and took photos. There was no sense of the house having been vacant for months. It had a presence. The photos turned out great. Glowing with happiness, I drove back to the city to my sister's house, where she was wrapping up her day's work.

I went back to visit Dad the next day. Instead of the man of the previous day, there was a woman at the wicket window.

I said, "I'm here to see my Dad."

I gave his name and my name, only to be told again that I was not on the list.

"Yes, I know. But I was here yesterday."

She looked at her screen.

"There is no record of you having been here."

"I know. But I was," I said mysteriously.

She looked confused and very, very angry but abruptly waved me in.

I hurried up to Dad's room and found him speaking with the nurse. She was telling him that he was being transferred the next day to a hospice called Glengarda. He looked like he wasn't sure what she was talking about, and when she left, he asked, "What did the nurse mean about transferring me? Where am I going?"

"Dad, there's nothing more this hospital can give you. The hospice you are going to will be able to give you so much more. You don't have to stay in this room any longer. I've heard Glengarda is a beautiful place, and they are amazing at taking care of everything you might need. The nice thing is that the family will be able to come and visit you. Glengarda doesn't have the same COVID restrictions as the hospital."

He looked unsure like he had no idea what lay ahead. He didn't. Do any of us? He was a see-it-to-believe-it kind of guy anyway. We had another nice visit. I massaged his neck and shoulders for him again. Nurses were constantly coming in and out of the room to get things ready for his departure the next day. We didn't have the sweet peaceful visit we had the day before, but that was okay. I'm so grateful I had that one special day with him. It was truly a gift.

When it was time for me to leave, I said, "Dad, I'm going back to Calgary this afternoon. My daughter is having her baby. She is being induced in the morning. Poppy is coming to stay with us for a couple of days, so I have to go back. But I'll see you again once you are in Glengarda." Something melancholy hummed in my mind. "See you again in Glengarda." It almost sounded like a farewell song.

I told Dad I loved him as I had done many times before. As usual, he never said "I love you" back. Once, he replied "Likewise" to my "I love you." Most of the time, he just nodded. That was okay for me. He was who he was.

Dad was transferred to Glengarda Hospice the day after my visit, the same day my new grandson, Scotty, was born. At Glengarda, Dad had a large room with a TV, fireplace, comfortable bed, and big sunny south-facing windows. He wasn't quite sure if he hadn't been taken to some kind of hotel. The nursing care was cheerful and beyond excellent.

Dad rediscovered his sense of humor in his short time at Glengarda. He played a few pranks on the nurses, especially one young nurse who came to check on him in the middle of the night. She had leaned in close to make sure he was still breathing. Dad had his eyes closed but was not asleep. He said, "Boo!" and almost scared her out of her skin. Another nurse asked him if she could read him a short passage from the bible. He said yes and when the reading went on for much longer than he expected, he said dryly, "Give them an inch; they'll take a mile." The nurses were so good to Dad. There are not enough words to express the gratitude they deserve.

There was a young woman who played guitar and went from room to room singing for patients. She sat outside the door of Dad's room and played for him because he wasn't comfortable with her coming in. During my visit, I asked him if he would like me to invite her in. He agreed. The young woman sang Johnny Cash's *Folsom Prison Blues* at Dad's request while he relaxed his head back on his pillow and listened, lost in her singing. He told a story of going to a country music festival with Mom where they saw Johnny Cash perform live. A train went by and blew its horn just as Cash was singing *Folsom Prison Blues*. As the young woman sang and played her guitar, I could see Dad reliving that time again.

My Younger Brother brought Dad's big black Labrador mix Benny for a visit. Benny knew the score, I'm sure. He sat at the door and barked at anyone who came into the room. He was not a barker. Family and friends took turns visiting. Dad had a lot of pain, but he still resisted painkillers and suspiciously scrutinized every pill a nurse tried to give him. He would rather endure the pain than take pills. Seven weeks after he arrived at Glengarda, Dad passed away. The Tiffany lamp that sat in the lobby to be turned on when someone died was turned on for my Dad. I loved him very much.

Death is not something I fear. I acquired an awareness from the many life experiences with death and even the beyond-death in my life that there isn't anything to fear. We don't end or disappear into nothingness. I'm certain of that. I even learned to love the Death card in the tarot deck. Death is just a transformation, not something scary. I had transformed many times in my flitting bee life. Death is just a fresh start, a new journey. I was happy Dad was out of pain and had a peaceful ending to life. It was beautiful. There was no need for tears, only rejoicing.

In his last moments, a nurse said she saw Dad lying in his bed with his arms reaching to the sky, arms he could no longer lift to feed himself. He was reaching. She heard him call out his mother's name. When the nurse came back 15 minutes later, he was gone. Well, that made me cry a little bit because it was simply a miracle.

Dad was not an easy man and did not have an easy life. There had been corporal punishment when he was a child. There had been the order from his father to return to live on the farm when he had been happy living in Regina with Mom. He left his dreams behind to do his father's bidding. Is that why he had been such an angry man? He gave up his dreams? I saw a shadow of regret pass over his face one day as he lay dying in Glengarda. It gave me a pang. If any of us think it's okay to give up on our dreams, all I can say is, "Don't do it! Grab all of life you can. One day, it will be over, and the last thing any of us needs is to die with regret for what might have been. Don't do it!"

Dad was who he was and lived how he lived. Whatever life he might have ahead, I wished for him to have greater. I felt peace at his passing. All the time Dad had been in my life, I knew his challenging behaviours had nothing to do with me. It made it easier for me to have a relationship with him that satisfied me. Some members of the family did not have it as easy.

I gave a joint eulogy with my brothers at the funeral. I tried to give an honest, generous view of the man he had been, his challenges, and his strengths. My Vancouver Sister came to me afterward to thank me for my words. My Vancouver Brother's wife, who I hadn't seen for 10 years, was there. She really was a lovely woman, after all. We shared a warm embrace. My Saskatoon Sister handled matters around Dad's illness and passing. She did it with grace and skill.

After Dad's funeral, Rio and I made a trip to the farm to help my Saskatoon Sister and Younger Brother start the presale cleanup. The farm had been in the family for 112 years. None of the siblings wanted to make a life on the farm, so it was sold, contrary to any desires my grandfather might have had. Now there was a century's worth of junk to clear out of the yard. Things in the house hadn't been changed or moved since Mom died 35 years earlier. We spent the weekend cleaning. It was going to take a lot more work than that.

Rio and I went back again in the fall before the new owners took possession. Rio is like a train engine and a great catalyst for getting things done. Once he starts, he doesn't stop and draws everyone else around him along in his wake. Rio and my brother cleared out the old falling-down barn that contained Dad's plumbing and farming supplies while my sister and I worked in the house. At the end of the massive job, all four of us felt a sense of gratification, as if all our efforts were a way of saying goodbye to the family farm that had been in the family for generations. The farm was sold to a nice young couple who had big plans to have a family and make a life there. That was a cause for joy.

Time and space yawned before me after the farm was sold. Rio and I sold our house in Discovery and moved to a townhouse. Our plan was to reduce household expenses and responsibilities to be able to start traveling. I didn't have any idea of exactly what the future would look like. I just knew that things had been cleared from my life so I could do the things I had been longing to do for years. Traveling and living life with a different perspective was the thing I wanted most from life now. The new space in my life felt delicious. It felt like the space of a time that had finally come.

I made a trip to Puerto Vallarta, Mexico, in June for an Access Body Class, which is all about hands-on processes to deliver beneficial energy to the body. My body needed more than a little attention. I returned through bustling Mexican and U.S. airports to arrive in the barren Calgary airport just before COVID quarantine requirements ended in Canada.

COVID had been lousy. Family events for years had been extremely difficult. Yet, there was a space opening before me, a beautiful beckoning space. Goodbye, Dad. Goodbye, farm. Hello Future.

I wondered, "Now! What would I truly like for my life? Truly. What could I transform into? What do I have to offer?"

Chapter 29

Rome: Committing

The next spring, Putin invaded Ukraine. My certification with Access had lapsed in the past year, and I wasn't sure I was going to renew it. Was I flaking out again? I had space and time open before me with no idea what to do with it. I was bored with Calgary, bored with Rio, bored with Access, bored with babysitting and bored with my life. Just plain bored. The boredom took me into a funk. I was feeling a bit sick, I had no appetite, and my motivation for even the smallest things was very low. I was in a quasi-depression. I told Rio I was bored. He said I was bitchy. How true!

And I will not lie. Getting older and looking older did not please me. Occasionally, subliminal thoughts surfaced in my mind that my window of productive time was shrinking. I knew that was just bullshit. I was eternally young at heart, sometimes childishly so. I could start fresh whenever I wanted to. Old yearnings for Italy and returning whispers of Frankincense and Roses began pressing on me. Finally, I said, "Enough! Time to choose a direction for my life once and for all."

I decided I would take time away from all the things I was doing. I would call this time "My Sabbatical." I would take a time-out from involvement in Access and my intentions around being a facilitator. Maybe that had been the same thing as my desire for a retreat in Springbank which turned out to be only a retreat for me. Maybe Access had only been about a facilitation for me.

But what should I do? I considered another painting trip. Maybe in southern Spain or Sicily. I have always wanted to go to those places. Travel was always the thing that lit me up the most. Maybe, as well as being an exploring Marco Polo, I should have been a nomad, just me and a suitcase, no house. That lifestyle would have suited me best.

A painting trip just didn't excite me. I had not been painting the last few years. It seemed like a stretch to pick it up again. Suddenly, an idea popped. What about a writing trip? I thought about writing for years. The open space I sensed stretched open even wider.

Going away to write had been on my bucket list all the way back to the days when I told Rio of my idea to go to Sicily to write while he fished during the day. I had a list of titles of books on my laptop that were never written. I wrote every day in a journal template I created on my desktop, which gave me the flexibility to write faster than by hand, add glowing photos, and explore all the things I was curious about. I once thought of converting my journal to a blog but never did. Now, I thought of all the things I could write. I knew I could write well, and my skills had grown through my daily journal practice. I could write anything I put my mind to. Travel, romance, fiction, non-fiction, even erotica. Why didn't I finally commit to writing?

There was some confidence lacking. Maybe a lack of confidence was the reason I flaked out on the many things I started. No, I knew some part of that was not true. There was something I gained from each pursuit I jumped into. All the years of flitting might very well have been required learning to arrive at the choice to write. Maybe it was time to bring it all together and create something that would give me a full sense of accomplishment.

I found a writers' retreat in Greece that wowed me. It started in a few weeks in June. When I tried to book it, I found the retreat was full. Disappointed, I searched for another one and found one in Tuscany in three weeks that still had a space available. I booked it.

At the time, I was reading a series of workbooks written by Access founder Gary Douglas on *How to Become Money*. I was looking to solve my tendency to worry about money. The Access perspective on money was very unorthodox, but Gary's advice was also very practical. In one of the books, Gary wrote about how everyone has something they are good at and love doing. It's where you can make money, but there is the necessity of closing your back door. The back door was your escape hatch, your excuses, your sneaky unconscious weasel ways for wiggling out of creating what you know you can create and are good at but are ultimately afraid to choose. The back door includes all the things that come up in your life, like problems with other people—yes, problems that include family—and how in some weird and wonderful way, you use those problems as an excuse for not committing to your life and having money. The back door is about not being willing to commit. In order to truly commit to something, you have to close all your back doors and then let nothing stop you from doing what you say you wish to do. Do it. No matter what.

My god! I realized somehow I had confused commitment with a straight jacket and work as the kind of thing my mother and father did, which was not far from being slaves rowing a galley ship. That was not me, but somewhere on the road of life, I had decided I was expected to live as they did. I had been ultra-responsible in many ways, but when it came to committing to work on the things I love, I subconsciously rejected work as being akin to slavery, and I resisted it all my life. I told myself I just wanted to be free.

Had I lived as a truly free person? I could look back at the events of my life, my successes and failures, and honestly say I did my best at any given time. I could also see that some part of me had never been truly free. What was that? Being free was me allowing myself to be true to myself and claiming ownership of what I made of my own life. No matter what.

What if commitment was not about a straight jacket but the wide-open and expansive space of my future? Something shifted. I would go. I would commit to writing the book that had been pushing into my awareness, the book I had been putting off for years, the book that even had a title that came to me one day. Finally, I would commit to this new direction in my life. No matter what.

Another thought. I would write my story, and I would hold nothing back. Was I willing to write things that people might not like? Was I really willing to come out of hiding and open myself to tell the private details of my life, my virtues, and my sins as if I were back in the confessional of my Catholic childhood? The thought gave me a shiver of fear. And even a little rush of excitement. Damn it! Was I going to commit or not?

I committed.

In the middle of June, I left for Italy in the midst of post-COVID airline cancellations, delays, and luggage mayhem. I flew from Calgary to Vancouver to Frankfurt to Rome, where I landed and immediately caught a train to Florence. The travel was made up of mad races through airports to reach departure gates on the slim chance of making my connecting flights. By some strange magic, I managed to make all my connections and checked into my Florence hotel a day later.

I spent two days in Florence, which was in the middle of an unusual June heat wave. Temperatures reached 40 degrees each day. After two days of exhausting walking and sightseeing, I met the members of the writing group I was joining at the Santa Maria Novella train station for our trip to the town of Poppi—no kidding, Poppi. It reminded me of my little fearless granddaughter, my inspiration.

Poppi was a small quiet village an hour from Florence in the Tuscan hills. It was situated on a high point in the land overlooking a lovely green village-dotted valley. Our writing retreat was held in a large stone house down from the town where it had a view of the soft, rolling hills of the valley. There were ten astonishingly brilliant women participating in the retreat, women from varying places in the world and diverse backgrounds—dedicated writers, a lawyer, a Greenpeace executive, a teacher, an academic, a social activist, a lingerie designer, a screenwriter, and me. What fun! Each woman was there for her own reasons, something that drew her to writing. What about me? I had booked the trip on an impulse and with the idea of the long-delayed writing I wished to do. How that would show up, I had no idea. I had nothing concrete.

We had lovely meals served for us each day, met for writing sessions and discussions and had lots of free time to write. In the evenings, we had a sharing time where we sat in the setting sun of the day while women took turns reading from their work. The women produced brilliant writing. Even the women who came from professions other than writing created wonderful essays that received accolades from the generous group. It was glorious. I had nothing. I had a title of a book and an idea but it was too big and too unformed for me to share.

I diddled on getting down to writing for the first couple of days until my internal pressure to produce something to share forced me to sit down and write. There had been an assigned writing exercise we had been asked to complete for the retreat. It was a piece of writing on travel. I signed up for the retreat at the last moment and hadn't gotten to the exercise. I sat in my room on the third day of the retreat and started to write.

There is magic in sitting down with intention, even if you have no sense of direction, and letting the words simply spill onto the page. I began writing about a short shopping experience I had a couple of days before my flight. It became a small piece that flourished in the serenity and wonder of the place I was writing in. It captured the hopeful innocence of me, my romantic spirit, and my past loves. It was the first heartbeat of this story I write. It flowed to me and embraced me like a loving friend. I read my piece to the group that evening. The women's overflowing enthusiasm was like a lovely affirmation. I could do this.

By the end of a joy-filled week of connecting and sharing with those women and all the generosity each one lavished on the others, the group returned to Florence. I caught a train to Rome in the evening with a plan to have a few days of sightseeing. I vibrated with excitement about my retreat and the over-the-moon thrill of going to Rome.

Rome was packed with tourists. Now that the COVID pandemic was winding up, people launched into travel with a vengeance. The streets were packed, and temperatures soared above 40 degrees each day. It was just too, too hot to sightsee. I went out to walk each day, hugging the shady side of the streets to stay out of the baking sun, past the throngs of people at the Trevi Fountain, down the crowded streets toward the *Piazza del Popolo*, ducking every now and then into a shop or restaurant to get a reprieve from the heat.

By the second day, I had heat exhaustion, and all my sightseeing plans evaporated. No *Parco Borghese*, my most beloved spot in Rome. I stayed in bed with chills and began having muddled, intense dreams. It was as if past and present were morphing into a confused reality. I began dreaming of Giorgio. It had been ten years since I had seen him, but now suddenly, everything we had shared came back to me with a powerful longing. Was it my proximity to him in Rome, heat exhaustion, or something uncanny in Rome that had me dreaming? I wound my blankets tight around me and shivered.

In the evening, I forced myself out of bed to go out for something to eat. It was a little cooler now that the heat of the day was passing. I wandered down the street from my little hotel near the Trevi fountain and found a restaurant with a promising-looking patio. *Trattoria Tritone.* With no reservation, I was seated in a stuffy back room, not the patio as I had hoped. There was a couple sitting to the right of me and a large group of people to the left. An older man who was my waiter brought me a menu. He may have been in his fifties. Older man? Who was I kidding? He was probably younger than me. He reminded me of Giorgio.

I placed my order. *Pollo alla romana.* I didn't really care what I ate. As I sat back to wait for my meal, my waiter served the couple to my right. The waiter was light of spirit and youthfully quick of body for his age. He was gracious to the couple. They treated him with cold superiority and disdain. I felt my blood start to boil. I recalled an exercise from Access that involved expanding your energy to fill a room and imagining your energy encompassing everything and everyone in it. The Access lesson was that you can then change the energy of the room with the energy you put out. That's what I did. Feeling sick or not, I imagined my energy pushing out and up against every wall until I had a sense of being as big as the room, like an Alice in Wonderland.

My chicken arrived, and after I had a few bites, the waiter stopped to ask how my meal was. I gave a dazzling smile, my energy swelled, and I said warmly, "It's wonderful!" The waiter almost bounced and shimmied with pleasure as he moved on from my table. The bus girl who picked up my empty plate glanced keenly at me from the corners of her eyes. The waiter returned to my table with a shot of limoncello. With a small respectful bow, he said, "For you." I smiled radiantly at him and gave an exuberant thank you. He literally skipped away. He came back with an order of panna cotta, which I said was my favorite Italian dessert. Between mouthfuls, I noticed people from the group to the left of me turning to look at me curiously. When our eyes met, I motioned to my dessert.

"Try the panna cotta," I said, waving my spoon at my bowl. "It's delicious."

The waiter seemed to dance as he returned to my table with the gift of a second glass of limoncello. No, it was time for me to go. As I got up, I noticed the oh-so-superior couple to my right. They didn't look so superior anymore. They were sitting very still, their heads tipped toward their plates. They looked almost chastened. I smiled to myself. It's easy to make magic when you choose to try it. I wasn't feeling as sick as I had before dinner. I went back to my room and slept peacefully.

The next morning as I prepared to go to the airport for my flight home, I checked my email and messages. Somehow, I had received a LinkedIn notice. It was about Giorgio's son, that sweet teenage boy I met years ago, who was now listed as the owner of the hotel. He was marketing it as a wedding destination. There was a picture of the boy I met when he was 15 years old, now a young man. He looked like a younger version of his dad, the man I had loved so passionately. An uplifting surge of utter joy filled me. How wonderful for Giorgio's son. How absolutely wonderful for Giorgio. He was free of the trap of hotel responsibilities to live life for himself. I was never so happy for anyone in my life. I was so happy, I cried. I hoped he found everything he was looking for.

Chapter 30

Croatia: Traveling Writer

I flew back to Canada to arrive in Montreal for a stop-over and found my flight to Calgary canceled. There was a plane waiting on the tarmac, but no pilot to fly it. I stood in line at the airline's customer service counter from midnight to 6 a.m. with hundreds of other passengers whose flights had also been canceled in the post-COVID airline mayhem. The buzz from people in the line around me was that flights were being rebooked for one or two days later. I was still not feeling entirely well and said in my head, "Universe, I need a miracle, please."

When I finally got my turn at the counter, I asked the man who served me if I could please have the earliest possible flight. He searched his screen and said in surprise,

"I think I found one. It leaves in a little over an hour."

He called his superior to come and verify the seat. She said yes, he could book the seat for me. It would be standby. She looked at me reassuringly and said, "Don't worry. You will get on this flight."

Do you ever get the sense that things are just magical? I've learned that creating magic takes only a little bit of practice. It starts with being willing to just ask for it.

I got home to a scorching heat wave in Calgary. The city was a furnace. My luggage with all my summer clothing had been lost by the airline, and my fridge resentfully stopped working in the hottest July on record. My Saskatoon Sister and her kids were coming for a two-day visit. They arrived in the middle of me trying to use camping coolers to store the least perishable things from my fridge while I threw out the rest.

The airline found my luggage a day later. When I went to the airport to pick it up, it was sitting right in front of the sea of lost luggage, sitting out as if it wanted to make sure I could find it easily, as if it were patiently waiting for me to pick it up. I picked it up, grinning with delight.

I had no fridge for a month. A repairman made multiple warranty calls until he finally declared it unrepairable. While a new fridge was on the way, my clothes dryer broke down. Was my house trying to kick me out? I created a string clothesline on the deck outside my master bedroom and hung my wash by hand. It reminded me of my childhood on the farm where my mother hung laundry on a pulley clothesline to flap in the breeze and dry in the sun. The sweet smell of fresh laundry wafted through my house every day from my gently drying clothes.

I was trying to lose weight. I had been for a few years. With COVID and all the family stress, I had gained weight that no diet or exercise plan I tried ever changed. I tried intermittent fasting, the Mount Athos diet, a gut biome diet, and a step-tracking app to increase my daily exercise. Nothing was changing. I remember losing 25 pounds without even trying over two visits to Italy with Giorgio. Why was this so hard now? I felt bound and tied and unable to move my life forward. That feeling overtook me every time I returned to my home in Calgary. Was Calgary trying to kick me out?

I could sense myself going into a gloomy place. It was too easy for thoughts about the past to resurface. I reminded myself of the unexpected gifts that come out of crisis. I kept reminding myself to choose gratitude for everything that had occurred and let go. I used Access tools. No, No, No!! I would not go into another dark hole of boredom and problems that took me away from what I truly wanted in life. I had closed my back door to all of that. I had committed to writing. Committed! I could commit and still be the bee. I booked a trip to Croatia in the fall. I would go away and continue to write.

Rio and I went to Croatia in November. He went to visit his family in Pristina for three weeks while I rented an apartment in Split for a month. I spent three glorious weeks alone with undisturbed time to myself to write, shop for light fresh food in the outdoor Pazar market down the street, take sightseeing mind-clearing walks around the old city, and dream. I experienced the pleasure of being immersed in my writing. It was joy.

Now that I was writing, my book started talking to me. I gave my book a pet name. Bella. I would wake in the morning with Bella's story running in my head. I would settle down in the evening to watch a Netflix movie and find that whatever I watched somehow miraculously contributed something to my work. In a movie called *Luckiest Girl Alive*, a journalist played by Mila Kunis who had a difficult story to write was told by her editor to write the story as if no one would read it but her. I could do that, too. Write as though no one would read it but me. That set me free.

Unexpectedly, I received an email about a Zoom planned with the women of the Poppi writing group. I told the women where I was and how wonderful it was to have that space in Croatia to immerse in my writing. One of the women said, "Oh, I know what you should do. You should become a traveling writer."

"Yes, that's exactly what I'd like."

I worked every day at a leisurely pace. There was so much ease in living in that little apartment in Split. My writing started to flow. By the time I returned to Canada, my book was more than half-written.

After three weeks, Rio joined me from Pristina. We had a week together to enjoy the city. Our week started in sunshine. We strolled through the old city and dined out, finding an Italian restaurant we liked best. Croatian is one of the six languages Rio speaks. I could see the connection he had with people and places based on language. It brought out something in him I did not see at home in Calgary. There was a sense of peace around him, a sense of feeling himself to be the great man he was. I loved seeing him like that.

Rio bought me an onyx and diamond ring from a jewelry store on Split's shop-and-restaurant-lined promenade along the sea. The same idea about the ring popped into both of our heads at the same time as we walked the promenade. An engagement ring. Rio had long wanted to marry me but I always said no. No more marriage for me. But now I told him I wouldn't mind being engaged and wear a ring to signify that. We were engaged in a long-term relationship, after all. I'd be happy to agree to an engagement ring that would not lead to the exchange of vows but was an acknowledgment of our relationship. I didn't want to get married again. I would make no promises for a future where life changes, and promises made may not be ones that could be kept. My thought was, *Why promise in the first place?*

Rio once asked me to promise him that if he died before me, I would not find someone new. I said I could not promise that. I didn't know what it would be like for me if he was gone. I wasn't going to promise to stay single. What if I was miserable and lonely? Would he want me to live my life that way? He accepted my point. Engagement in the terms we were discussing now was something I could happily do. Rio was very pleased, and I was pleased that he was pleased.

World Cup soccer began the week we were in Split. The city of Split has been very quiet prior to that. In the fall, tourists leave, many restaurants and shops close for the season, and tour operators to Croatia's famous natural sites shut down. The early December weather turned to rain, warm Croatian rain that felt nourishing. Soccer changed the tone of the city. Amazingly, the Croatian team did very well and made it into the semi-finals. The night Croatia beat Brazil to take the bronze medal, the city became electric. Fireworks exploded, people thronged to the streets, cars honked, and cruise ships in the harbor blew their baritone horns long and loud. It was our last night in Split. Croatia had been good to us.

Chapter 31

Calgary: Isabella Rossellini

As the new year started, I continued writing, but the necessity of continuing to make greater changes in my life became imperative. The spaces between joyful trips and times at home in Calgary were dead spaces where I tended to drift into apathy despite my attempts to be happy and enthusiastic. I had enough. My future was calling.

Where will I live? For a long time, I had wanted to live in Europe, not Canada.

How will I complete my book? How will I make sure I dedicate my time and elude the constant demands of other people's needs and catastrophes? I set up office hours to write. I learned to politely say no, even when I heard the need or the disappointment in the voices of others. I was committed. No weaseling out for babysitting jobs, no matter how much I loved my grandchildren.

There were less concrete things I was looking for in my life, too. How could I use more curiosity to create a wonderful life for myself? How could I be more present? How could I be a less judgmental person? How could I have more gratitude, more joy and actualize my dreams? So many questions, really, and no real answers. That's the thing about life. There are so few definitive answers despite our efforts to create absolutes and predictability. You have to just keep trying. Keep choosing. Don't stop.

I was dreaming a lot. I dreamed of what it would be like to claim and authentically live as the something free and out-of-the-norm in me. What would it take to fly again? For all the years I lived as a mother and family member, there was an adventurer and explorer in me eager to sail the seas to find new lands and adventures. I dreamed of stepping out and actually achieving something, not just living my life as a wonderful, flitting little bee.

What would my true calling be? What could success be for me, a woman now in her 60s? Would writing, the thing I always just did, did easily, and loved, give me the sense of achievement I had never had? I could sense a future stretching out with that.

I dreamed of going to Croatia to live, maybe Zadar, with its lovely proximity to the hundreds of lush islands offshore in the Adriatic, the same Adriatic I've seen from other places and other times. I dreamed of Spain. I dreamed of Greek islands.

I remember the writing retreat in Greece that I was so eager to attend the year before, only to find it was full. This time, I'd not miss my chance. I would finish the book I started in Tuscany in Greece. I signed up for the retreat and continued to work on my book.

In the spring, Rio got a new job as a foreman for a construction company. He hired Ukrainian refugees who spoke no English to work on his crew. That was okay for Rio, who spoke to them in a hodgepodge of words from Bulgarian, Moldovan, Bosnian, and whatever other Eastern European languages he had picked up somewhere along the road in life. Rio spoke six languages fluently, and after a few months of working with the Ukrainian, he could add a seventh. Ukrainian.

The Ukrainians he hired were powerful workers like Rio. They form a hard-working, invincible team with Rio as their unstoppable foreman. Rio's latent leadership skills began to shine. He and his crew became a roaring success. In a few months, they were one of the most reputable crews in the city. I was so happy for him.

* * *

I wrote sporadically in my days. I was productive but kept stalling out on the ending of Bella Book. Then, there were the difficult passages on family. I didn't want to offend anyone, but I needed to write about those experiences. They were part of me growing and finding myself, growing through the pain. I was so distracted, so frustrated, and couldn't understand why. Something whispered to me, "You are not living in the place where your heart is."

Calgary had never been the place in my heart. Never in the more than 30 years I lived there. There were dozens of places I would rather have been than Calgary. The city made me feel stagnant. For those who loved Calgary, I'm happy for you. For those who say, "Grow where you are planted," I ask, "Can a tropical flower grow on the Arctic tundra?" Sometimes saying grow where you are planted is nonsense.

One day, Rio and I watched a Netflix movie called *Faraway* about a woman who inherits a house in Croatia from her late mother. She leaves her ungrateful husband and boring life in London and moves in an instant. There is a scene where she steps into the view of the camera and looks out at the Croatian vista of the mountains and sea before her. I knew that view. My body knew Croatia. I felt the longing rising from my body and soul.

I booked my flights to Greece. I had an inexplicable sense that the ending of Bella Book that was eluding me was waiting for me in Greece. I needed to go to Greece. Something told me that I would find what I was looking for there.

I hired a personal trainer to help me lose the extra COVID weight, then hurt my back and had to quit. I continued with Access programs that always gave me a lift and confidence to tackle any issue in my life. I used Access energetic programs to work with my writing. Dain from Access recommended starting a Miracle List and record all miracles, large and seemingly small. My list began to grow.

A woman who was canvassing for an upcoming provincial election came to my door to campaign one day. After a chat in my front entrance, she turned to go, then turned back and asked me, "Has anyone ever told you that you look like Isabella Rossellini?"

I laughed, "For anyone to see that, I may need to dye my blonde hair black."

I Googled Isabella Rossellini and found a blurb on a book she wrote about her life from her birth in Rome—oh, to have been born in Rome

—through years as a model and actress to now being a mature woman who wrote on aging gracefully. I was inspired. I'll have that! And yes, with dark hair, I could look like Isabella Rossellini, the woman I saw looking back at me from the picture on her book.

Isabella somehow led me to Audrey Hepburn, who inspired me with her choice to live her life by her plan, not Hollywood's, and travel as a goodwill ambassador for UNICEF. I'll have that, too, travel and live by my own plan! Audrey led me to buy a gorgeous pair of Tiffany sunglasses for my writing trip to Greece. Shall I find my purpose at last like those women?

Only the Future Me knows for sure. All I have to do is go.

Chapter 32

Greece: Where Icarus Fell

June arrived, and I made my way to Greece. I flew from Calgary to London to Athens to the city of Mytilene on the island of Lesvos, where my retreat was being held. With three legs of flying from Calgary, it took me three days to arrive. I spent a day in Athens, then another in Mytilene to acclimatize. The following day, I met the group of writers who would be attending the retreat. We traveled by van to a little resort town on the southwest side of the island.

We arrived in an idyllic Greek village paradise along the deep azure Aegean Sea. It felt untouched by the greater world. It was like we had stepped back into a simpler time. I had a small room in a crisp white hotel with cobalt-blue trim and a breakfast terrace that overlooked the sea. The part of town we were in was known as the summer town. It ran along the beach and was down from the main part of town farther up in the hills. There was a quiet sidewalk I walked each day that wound from my hotel, past shops and restaurants painted in Mediterranean whites, blues, and greens, wending its way to where the writers met through the day for daily instruction and writing time.

The instruction we received from our coaches was like a writing course condensed into the space of a week. It was astoundingly good. The work I had done so far began to come to life. We writers sat at our laptops for most of the day in small café terraces while the Aegean sea played on the beach below us. We spent luxurious hours in writing talks or engrossed in individual work with occasional breaks for lunch of simple fresh Greek food. It was heavenly!

The myth of Icarus had appeared and reappeared in my thoughts since the day I left Giorgio in Italy. It had popped into my mind in that terrible flight after leaving him where I wanted to jump from the plane, where I thought I had flown too close to the sun or had been too prideful in my lust for him and for the dazzling taste of life I shared with him. The myth whispered to me softly through the writing of my story.

It seemed my time with Giorgio was followed by so much disappointment. It was as though I had fallen from a very high place. Now here I was on Lesvos, where I could look south toward Ikaria, the island where Icarus' body is said to have washed ashore. Something had called me to come here. Okay. Whatever thing you are, show me!

One evening as the group of writers sat together over dinner and ouzo on ice, I chatted with one of the women in the group. She began to talk about love.

"Sometimes, there is one great love who appears in your life but is never permanent in your life. He seems to appear and reappear, time after time, no matter how you try to move on. I've experienced that."

She looked at me meaningfully and asked, "How will *you* find the thrill in your life to replace your great love who's gone?"

How was she asking me that? I didn't recall saying anything about a great love or a lost love. I felt the smallest of tremors in my core. How do you find something that will light you up the way a rapturous love once had? I thought about rapture. It has the sense of being overtaken, being swept away by overwhelming beauty or love, being so overcome that you temporarily leave your body. You tremble. You shudder with its orgasmic bliss.

You fly.

After a few moments of silence, I told the woman, "I have the sense that some of the thrill I'm asking for will come from other things in life and perhaps grow out of what I am doing now. Writing." My answer sounded a little hollow. Still, I had hope.

How she had begun talking to me about love made me wonder. And what did I know about what future my writing would bring? Yet I sensed it was calling me. I just couldn't explain it. I could only stay committed and ask for it to answer my dreams.

* * *

As the week of the retreat was drawing to a close, I still had no ending for my book. On the second last day, I reread my writing for the umpteenth time for edits, starting from the beginning. I reread my story of Giorgio and remembered. I remembered deeply. The story seemed to swell, surge, and come vividly alive in the humid Greek air. I was flooded with an old, long-silenced longing, an aching yearning burning for him, and those glorious days in Italy where I flew on the path around the lake behind his hotel. My memories came back so powerfully I could almost taste him, almost feel him. It seemed it was only a moment ago that I had seen him, loved him, and he loved me. The feeling was so intense that when I went to bed that night in my little room in the hotel along the sea, I sat on the edge of my bed, my heart throbbing, and I cried out to the gods in anguish, "Please! Dear gods in heaven! I BEG YOU! Please, let me see him just one more time."

There was nothing more that I could do than ask. And wasn't this all just a silly obsession anyway?

My room was too hot to sleep in pajamas that night despite the cooling draft from the air-conditioning unit on the wall, so I stripped my pajamas off. I crawled naked between the sheets, turned off the light, and tossed for at least an hour, my body miserable and unable to settle. I finally drifted into a fitful sleep.

When I woke in the morning, even before I opened my eyes, the first thing I noticed was the sweet sensation of the nakedness of my body. With my eyes still closed, I registered how silky my skin felt in the sheets, how alive my body was, how the smallest hairs on my body stood on end, how my body was electric as if it were picking up on a presence near me. I basked in the sensation, not daring to open my eyes.

I knew that sensation. My body memory exploded fully to life. Trembling, my body remembered, and I remembered that first morning with Giorgio, the two of us completely intertwined, skin on skin, our faces pressed together, his breath sweet and soft on my cheek. He had opened his blue, blue eyes and looked smiling into mine.

I slowly opened my eyes now but he was not there. Had he been there? I savored the sensation of him. The sensation did not dissipate in the waking as most dreams do but lingered past the sweet dawn hours. As I left my room for the day, a sense of his presence stayed with me, calm and sweet. It was as if I had been granted some small part of my plea to the gods.

The day turned sultry and hot with humidity that seemed to coat the skin. Late in the afternoon, I put on my swimsuit and went down to the beach to swim, but I couldn't even get into the water because my eyes began to overflow with tears like a sudden downpour of rain on a sunny day. I sat on the beach and let the tears flow until they abated of their own accord. More tears. How long had I been holding in those tears?

I looked toward the sea that was tossed by wind-blown waves that softly crashed diagonally on the beach in front of me. The air was cooler here. Still, I was eager to enter the clear salty water and let it wash the heat and my tears away. I was sitting on a rock ledge at the edge of the beach, putting on my aqua shoes, when I heard a man's voice speaking in Italian.

Then I saw him.

He was halfway between me and the sea with his back to me, sitting on a towel on the sand. He got up awkwardly and stood with feet apart to steady himself, looking straight ahead out to sea. His hair was very white. His body was well-tanned, but the skin on his back was slack and sagged down around his waist with love handles of age. His legs were thin and had lost their muscle. The sight of him startled me. He was old.

Of course. More than ten years had passed since I knew him. He had been 59 then. Now he was in his 70s. I looked at him, registered his aging with time, and watched as he slowly, unsteadily began to shamble to the edge of the water. It was the gait of an old man. I saw him stop before he stepped into the sea and turned his head to the right to gaze down the beach. I caught my breath. My heart stopped.

It was not him!

My heart began beating again, pounding-pounding in my chest with a vigor, a lust for life, a desire for new life, not old obsessions. Suddenly, somehow, it did not matter if it was Giorgio or not. A realization came home to me. It did not matter whether I ever saw him again. It had been a long time since I kissed him goodbye at Fiumicino, a long time since we had been together and shared that brief wondrous love. I don't know if he ever thought of me. I had thought about him a lot. He had been a gift that vehemently, profoundly shook my world, and losing him had seemed like it might destroy me.

But it didn't.

I was older, too, now. That didn't matter. I wanted my life to speed up, not slow down. I realized I didn't want a quiet life with an older man. I didn't want to be haunted by the echoes of a dream lover from a faraway past, a lover who seemed to have become a tangled, unbreakable thread in my life. Maybe I had been gifted the sight of someone I thought was Giorgio so the Universe could show me he wasn't what I truly wanted, to tell me he and I had always been meant to go in different directions in life and have different purposes, to tell me that the love of our affair was not what Giorgio had been about at all. It was not about a lightning strike of eternal true love and living *la dolce vita* together. It was about Giorgio showing me to me! About Giorgio hearing my voice in those Italian love letters long ago so I could begin to hear my own voice for myself.

My perspective shifted. Suddenly I saw the whole picture of my love story with him differently. Finally, I could tease apart the last filaments of the threads. At last, I was ready to accept it all. I didn't need to let old memories haunt me ever again, but I could be boundlessly, endlessly grateful for the beauty of my experience with him.

Giorgio had been the first one who heard my voice. It was the voice I brought to write my story in this lovely village in Greece. Giorgio had been part of the impetus of the story and an essential part of my story, a story that wove its way through more than ten years of my life. Ah, he had been right when he said he was my springboard. What a beautiful springboard he had been. How lucky I was to have known him. Finally, I could have heart-and-soul gratitude for him in a new way and let him go here by the sea. My heart swelled with love.

I watched the old man wade into the water and begin to swim out from the land, then disappear from my sight. I knew that 200 kilometers beyond where he was swimming was the island of Ikaria, where Icarus is said to have plunged into the sea when the wax of his wings melted as he flew too near the sun. Icarus may have died in the sea when he lost his wings, but I did not die. I did not lose my wings. My wings are more powerful now than they were before.

A knowing filled me. There is no such thing as flying too close to the sun or too much desire or lust in life when you come from your heart and soul, when you come from the love and gratitude for the wonder of it all, and, most importantly, when you come from love and gratitude for the truth of who you are with all your beauty and all your flaws.

I suddenly saw there is always more of my story ahead, no matter how old I get. That is one of the wonders of the endlessly dreaming, endlessly loving, endlessly seeking, unstoppable *Amante* me.

The wings of my joy unfurled and snapped to fullness in the crisp Aegean breeze. The water rippled and sparkled as it stretched out before me with the promise of the future. The breath of the tender wind was soft and sweet on my cheek. The glowing sun smiled down on me with love from the blue, blue sky.

Yes! I would fly again. I began to cry. Soft, awe-filled tears. This time, there were no dark glasses. There was only gratitude. Only joy for the wonder of life.

Acknowledgments

So many wonderful people have come and gone through the years of my life, more than I can count. I am boundlessly grateful for all those who have graced me with their presence and time. In ways large and small, they are all part of my story.

I am grateful for my parents and siblings. They have taught me so much and have been essential to me becoming who I've become.

I am grateful for the literary coaches from Write Away Europe in Tuscany and The Writing Room, Queen of Retreats in Greece who supported and guided me when my book was in its infancy. I am grateful for the amazing people of Access Consciousness who showed me to how see with clearer eyes when times were rocky.

Most of all, I am grateful for my beautiful, wise and wondrous son and daughter, for my magical grandchildren who inspire me with their innocence and joy and for my life partner Rio who stands by me always.

About the Author

This is Cynthia's first book. She is an artist, a dreamer and a lover who searches for the extraordinary in life. She pursues many and varied interests with the heart of a Renaissance woman. She seeks to experience the fullest of life and turn her life into a work of art. She puts her faith in a wider, greater generous world. She lives in Calgary, Canada. For now.

www.ingramcontent.com/pod-product-compliance
Lightning Source LLC
Chambersburg PA
CBHW052135070526
44585CB00017B/1835